EXPERIMENTAL FILM AND ANTHROPOLOGY

EXPERIMENTAL FILM AND ANTHROPOLOGY

Edited by Arnd Schneider and
Caterina Pasqualino

BLOOMSBURY
LONDON • NEW DELHI • NEW YORK • SYDNEY

Bloomsbury Academic
An imprint of Bloomsbury Publishing Plc

50 Bedford Square	1385 Broadway
London	New York
WC1B 3DP	NY 10018
UK	USA

www.bloomsbury.com

Bloomsbury is a registered trade mark of Bloomsbury Publishing Plc

First published 2014

© Arnd Schneider and Caterina Pasqualino, 2014

Arnd Schneider and Caterina Pasqualino have asserted their rights under the Copyright, Designs and Patents Act, 1988, to be identified as Editors of this work.

All rights reserved. No part of this publication may be reproduced or transmitted in any form or by any means, electronic or mechanical, including photocopying, recording, or any information storage or retrieval system, without prior permission in writing from the publishers.

No responsibility for loss caused to any individual or organization acting on or refraining from action as a result of the material in this publication can be accepted by Bloomsbury or the authors.

British Library Cataloguing in Publication Data
A catalogue record for this book is available from the British Library.

ISBN: HB: 978-0-85785-442-1
PB: 978-0-85785-443-8
ePDF: 978-0-85785-822-1
ePub: 978-0-85785-821-4

Library of Congress Cataloging-in-Publication Data
A catalog record for this book is available from the Library of Congress.

Typeset by Fakenham Prepress Solutions, Fakenham, Norfolk NR21 8NN

CONTENTS

List of Figures		vii
Acknowledgments		xi
Contributors		xiii
1.	Experimental Film and Anthropology *Caterina Pasqualino and Arnd Schneider*	1
2.	Stills that Move: Photofilm and Anthropology *Arnd Schneider*	25
3.	Experimental Film, Trance and Near-death Experiences *Caterina Pasqualino*	45
4.	Contemporary Experimental Documentary and the Premises of Anthropology: The Work of Robert Fenz *Nicole Brenez*	63
5.	Our Favorite Film Shocks *Rane Willerslev and Christian Suhr*	79
6.	Do No Harm—the Cameraless Animation of Anthropologist Robert Ascher *Kathryn Ramey*	97
7.	Asynchronicity: Rethinking the Relation of Ear and Eye in Ethnographic Practice *Jennifer L. Heuson and Kevin T. Allen*	113
8.	Memory Objects, Memory Dialogues: Common-sense Experiments in Visual Anthropology *Alyssa Grossman*	131
9.	Beyond the Frames of Film and Aboriginal Fieldwork *Barbara Glowczewski*	147

10. Visual Media Primitivism: Toward a Poetic Ethnography 165
    Martino Nicoletti

11. From the Grain to the Pixel, Aesthetic and Political Choices 183
    Nadine Wanono

Index of Names *199*

LIST OF FIGURES

Figure 1.1	Hostess Soho Uyeda (Sowa Kai Omote Senke School of Tea), framing a shot during the shooting of *The Path*, Donald Rundstrom, Ronald Rundstrom, Clintum Bergum, USA, color, sound, 16 mm, 1971. Courtesy of Ronald Rundstrom.	3
Figure 1.2	Still image from *The Path*, Donald Rundstrom, Ronald Rundstrom, Clintum Bergum, USA, color, sound, 16 mm, 1971. By kind permission of Ronald Rundstrom, digital screen grab courtesy of Jieh Hsiang, National Taiwan University.	4
Figure 1.3	Ben Russell. Ruth. Still frame from *Trypps #7* (Badlands). Courtesy of Ben Russell.	8
Figure 1.4	Raymonde Carasco. Pintos's drummer and dancers, Easter 1995, at Nararachic (Mexico). Courtesy of Régis Hébraud.	9
Figure 1.5	Janet Cardiff and George Bures Miller, *The Paradise Institute*, 2001. Wood, theater seats, video projection, headphones, and mixed media. 118 × 698 × 210 inches (299.72 × 1772.92 × 533.4 cm). Courtesy of Luhring Augustine, New York.	11
Figure 1.6	Margarida Paiva: Still frame from *Who Lives In My Head?*, 2009 (Lowave, 2013). Courtesy of Margarida Paiva.	12
Figure 1.7	Film still, *Lyrical Nitrate*, Peter Delpeut, Netherlands, Ariel Film, 1990, 35 mm, b/w and color, sound. Courtesy of Peter Delpeut.	14
Figure 1.8	Still image from *The Visible and the Invisible of a Body under Tension*, Emmanuel Lefrant, France, 2009. Courtesy of Emmanuel Lefrant.	16
Figure 1.9	"Death/Fast Stairway Frame Fragment Still," Still image from *Death/Fast* (2013) by Brian Karl and Özge Serin. Courtesy of Brian Karl and Özge Serin.	18
Figure 2.1	Family photographs of Gino Nicastro and Gina Mantione, Sutera, Sicily, 2011 (photo: Arnd Schneider).	26
Figure 2.2	Leonore Mau/Hubert Fichte, *Der Tag eines unständigen Hafenarbeiters* (storyboard), 1966. By kind permission and courtesy of Stiftung F. C. Gundlach and S. Fischer Stiftung.	31
Figure 2.3	Leonore Mau and Hubert Fichte, *Der Fischmarkt und die Fische* (source still), 1968. By kind permission and courtesy of Stiftung F. C. Gundlach and S. Fischer Stiftung.	33

Figure 2.4	Leonore Mau and Hubert Fichte, *Zwei mal 45 Bilder/Sätze aus Agadir* (source still), 1971. By kind permission and courtesy of Stiftung F. C. Gundlach and S. Fischer Stiftung.	34
Figure 2.5	Leonore Mau and Hubert Fichte, *Zwei mal 45 Bilder/Sätze aus Agadir* (source still), 1971. By kind permission of Stiftung F. C. Gundlach and S. Fischer Stiftung. Image courtesy of Katja Pratschke.	35
Figure 2.6	Still image from *Making gambarr*, John Haviland, USA, 2009. Courtesy of John Haviland.	37
Figure 2.7	Still image from *A Polish Easter in Chicago*, Dick Blau, USA, 2011. Courtesy of Dick Blau.	39
Figure 3.1	A sacrifice *palo* (photo: Caterina Pasqualino).	47
Figure 3.2	Clusters of *palo* objects (photo: Caterina Pasqualino).	48
Figure 3.3	The *palero* Enrique in front of his altar (photo: Caterina Pasqualino).	49
Figure 3.4	Hieronymus Bosch, *The Ascent of the Blessed* (Due scene dal paradiso/L'ascesa delle anime) (1450–1516), Venice, Museo Palazzo Grimani. By kind permission of the Ministero dei beni e delle attività culturali e del turismo.	50
Figure 3.5	Stan Brakhage: still frames from *Dog Star Man: Part 2*, 1963. Courtesy of Marilyn Brakhage.	54
Figure 3.6	Triny Prada, "Je connais ma vérité (I know my truth)." Still frame from *Genius and Madness*, Lowave, 2013. Courtesy of Triny Prada.	56
Figure 4.1	Robert Fenz, *Meditations on Revolution, Part IV: Greenville, MS*, 2001. Courtesy of Robert Fenz.	67
Figure 4.2	Robert Fenz, *Sole of the Foot*, 2011 (shot 1). Courtesy of Robert Fenz.	69
Figure 4.3	Robert Fenz, *Sole of the Foot*, 2011 (shot 2). Courtesy of Robert Fenz.	70
Figure 4.4	Robert Fenz, *Sole of the Foot*, 2011 (shot 3). Courtesy of Robert Fenz.	71
Figure 4.5	Robert Fenz, *Sole of the Foot*, 2011 (shot 4). Courtesy of Robert Fenz.	72
Figure 5.1	Dziga Vertov, *The Man with the Movie Camera* (Kiev: VUFKU, 1929), 68 mins.	81
Figure 5.2	Timothy Asch and Napoleon Chagnon, *The Ax Fight*, 30 mins, 1975, Watertown, CT: Documentary Educational Resources.	85
Figure 5.3	Gary Kildea and Andrea Simon, *Koriam's Law and the Dead Who Govern*, 110 mins., 2005, Canberra: ANU RSPAS Film Unit and Ronin Films. Courtesy of Gary Kildea.	88
Figure 5.4	Sasha Rubel, *Vertigo, Vodoun, Vérité*, 25 mins., Paris: NIMBY Films. Courtesy of Sasha Rubel.	91

Figure 6.1	Robert Ascher at work. Courtesy of Robert Ascher.	101
Figure 6.2	A still from the film CYCLE, a lotus turns into the evening star. Courtesy of Robert Ascher.	103
Figure 6.3	A photo of pilgrims to the tomb of Shimon Bar Yohai on Mt. Meron, outside Safed, Israel. Ascher used this and other stills from his pilgrimage at the end of his film *Bar Yohai*. Courtesy of Robert Ascher.	104
Figure 6.4	A still from the film *Bar Yohai* of the pomegranate tree and nine people. The viewer is meant to become the tenth and thus form a minyan, or a quorum of ten adults necessary for religious services. Courtesy of Robert Ascher.	105
Figure 6.5	A still from the film *Blue: A Tlingit Odyssey*. The four brothers encounter a sea monster. Courtesy of Robert Ascher.	106
Figure 7.1	Film strip of three frames from *Still Life with Ho Chi Minh*, 2008, by Kevin T. Allen, 3 mins, Super 8mm film, © Small Gauge, Ltd.	118
Figure 7.2	Film still from *Luthier*, 2010, by Kevin T. Allen, 6 mins, Super 8mm film, © Small Gauge, Ltd.	119
Figure 7.3	Production still from *Sonic Geologic*, 2011, by Kevin T. Allen, handmade contact microphones secured with vises, © Small Gauge, Ltd.	122
Figure 7.4	Film still from *Bridge*, 2012, by Kevin T. Allen, 11 mins, Super 8mm film, © Small Gauge, Ltd.	122
Figure 7.5	Film still from *Immokalee, My Home*, 2009, by Kevin T. Allen and Jennifer Heuson, 16 mins, Super 8mm film, © Small Gauge, Ltd.	125
Figure 8.1	Manual typewriter. Digital film still by Alyssa Grossman.	136
Figure 8.2	Ice cube tray. Digital film still by Alyssa Grossman.	136
Figure 8.3	Seltzer bottle. Digital film still by Alyssa Grossman.	136
Figure 8.4	Porcelain bibelot in front of the Palace of the Parliament in Bucharest (formerly known as Ceaușescu's Palace of the People). Photograph by Alyssa Grossman.	139
Figure 8.5	Dual-screen installation of *Memory Objects, Memory Dialogues* (2011). Photograph by Rachel Topham for *Ethnographic Terminalia* 2011: Field, Studio, Lab.	140
Figure 9.1	Film still, *Miradwie*, 16mm, 1976. Courtesy of Barbara Glowczewski.	149
Figure 9.2	Film still, *Miradwie*, 16mm, 1976. Courtesy of Barbara Glowczewski.	152
Figure 9.3	Lex Wotton and his wife Cecilia, Palm Island, 2007: in front of a photo of the debutante ball they won when aged 16. Courtesy of Barbara Glowczewski.	160
Figure 9.4	*Sand Story* by Barbara Gibson Nakamarra (Glowczewski and Vale, 1994) exhibited at *Mémoires Vives. Une histoire de l'Art*	

	aborigène, Musée d'Aquitaine, 2013. Courtesy of Barbara Glowczewski.	161
Figure 9.5	Still from *Kajirri Warlpiri Ceremonies Restricted to Women*, Lajamanu, Central Australia, 1979, 16mm: yawulyu healing ritual, the ochre painting on Pampa Napangardi is feeding her body and her spirit. Courtesy of Barbara Glowczewski.	161
Figure 10.1	Huai Suea Tao village: entrance ticket.	170
Figure 10.2	Frame from the short: *I Must not Look you in the Eyes: The Zoo of the Giraffe Women*. Directed by Martino Nicoletti. UK-Italy. Stenopeica. 6 mins., 2011.	171
Figure 10.3	Frame from the short: *I Must not Look you in the Eyes: The Zoo of the Giraffe Women*. Directed by Martino Nicoletti. UK-Italy. Stenopeica. 6 mins., 2011.	172
Figure 10.4	Frame from the short: *I Must not Look you in the Eyes: The Zoo of the Giraffe Women*. Directed by Martino Nicoletti. UK-Italy. Stenopeica. 6 mins., 2011.	173
Figure 10.5	Frame from the short: *I Must not Look you in the Eyes: The Zoo of the Giraffe Women*. Directed by Martino Nicoletti. UK-Italy. Stenopeica. 6 mins., 2011.	177
Figure 11.1	Interactive Composition conceived by Andi Sojamo from *Ibani or the Blue Scarf*, film of Nadine Wanono, © N. Wanono.	187
Figure 11.2	Rhythm. From the film *Jazz Dance*, © Canarybananafilms.	190
Figure 11.3	*The Crawler*, © Mapping the Web Infome by Lisa Jevbratt.	193
Figure 11.4	*Data Beautiful* by Lev Manovich, © Mapping the Web Infome by Lisa Jevbratt.	193
Figure 11.5	Urban folktale in Pixels. *Phone Tapping*, © Hee Won Lee and Le Fresnoy—Studio national.	194

ACKNOWLEDGMENTS

We would like to thank all our contributors, and we are really delighted and excited by the novel approaches with which they engaged with the themes of this volume. We also thank the anonymous reviewers for their helpful and constructive suggestions. Particular thanks go to Louise Butler and Sophie Hodgson, our editors at Bloomsbury, for seeing this book through to final publication. We also thank Torill Sørsandmo for compiling the index.

We are extremely grateful to all the institutions and individuals who have helped us with our research and made visual and written materials available to us, often waiving or reducing fees for copyright permission. In particular, we thank Karthik Pandian for having made available to us his fascinating artwork *Unearth* (2010) for our cover image, and Martin Rasmussen (Vilma Gold, London) for image materials and facilitating contact.

We would also like to thank colleagues, hosts, and audiences with whom we have discussed our ideas over the last few years: Astrid Anderson (University Library, Oslo), Tobias Becker and Florian Walter (Free University Berlin), Nicole Brenez (Université Sorbonne Nouvelle, Paris 3), Thierry Dufrêne (Université Paris Ouest Nanterre la Défense, Paris), Tim Ingold (University of Aberdeen), Susanne Hammacher (Royal Anthropological Institute, London), Farhad Kalantary (Atopia, Oslo), George E. Marcus (University of California, Irvine), Richard Schechner (New York University), Cecilie Øien (Akershus Museum, Oslo), Luc Régis (Ecole d'Architecture de Versailles), the participants of the Ethnographic Film Seminar at the University of Oslo, and the participants of the Anthropology of Performance Seminar at the EHESS of Paris.

A special thanks goes to Anne-Christine Taylor at the Musée du quai Branly, Paris, for having invited us first to host a specialist seminar (in 2011), and then a major international conference (New Visions: Experimental Film, Art and Anthropology, 2012) which eventually resulted in this book.

A Note on Illustrations and Copyrighted Material

Every reasonable effort has been made to trace and acknowledge the ownership of copyrighted material (including illustrations) included in this book. Any errors that may have occurred are inadvertent and will be corrected in subsequent editions, provided notification is sent to the editors.

CONTRIBUTORS

Kevin T. Allen is a film-maker, sound artist, and independent radio producer whose practice ranges from the ethnographic to the experimental. His films screen at venues such as the Museum of Modern Art, Margaret Mead Film Festival, Berlin International Directors Lounge, Ann Arbor Film Festival, Flaherty NYC, and Ethnographic Terminalia. His sound work is featured on public radio, and exhibited at places such as the Canadian Centre for Architecture, Studio-X NYC, Third Coast International Audio Festival, Deep Wireless Festival of Radio Art. His recent film *Bridge* won first prize at the 2013 Black Maria Film Festival. He is currently working on an ethnographic film about ghost towns in South Dakota. His work is funded by the Jerome Foundation.

Nicole Brenez teaches Cinema Studies at the University of Paris 3-Sorbonne nouvelle. Graduate of the Ecole Normale Supérieure, agrégée of Modern Litterature, she is a Senior Member of the Institut Universitaire de France. She is the author of several books and is the curator of the Cinémathèque française's avant-garde film series.

Among her publications: *De la Figure en général et du Corps en particulier. L'invention figurative au cinéma* (De Boeck Université, 1998), *Abel Ferrara* (University of Illinois Press, 2007), *Cinémas d'avant-garde* (Cahiers du cinéma, 2008), *Cinéma d'avant-garde mode d'emploi* (Gendaishicho-shinsha, 2012). Editor of: *Jeune, dure et pure. Une histoire du cinéma d'avant-garde et expérimental en France* (2001), *Jean-Luc Godard: Documents* (2006), *Jean Epstein. Bonjour Cinéma und andere Schriften zum Kino* (2008), and *Le cinéma critique. De l'argentique au numérique, voies et formes de l'objection visuelle* (2009).

She has organized many film events and retrospectives, notably "Jeune, dure et pure, A History of Avant-garde Cinema in France" for the French Cinémathèque in 2000, and curated series in Buenos Aires, Rio de Janeiro, New York, Tokyo, Vienna, London, Madrid, and Belo Horizonte.

Barbara Glowczewski has a professorial research tenure in anthropology (Directeur de recherche) at the CNRS (Centre National de la Recherche Scientifique) in Paris. She works at the Laboratoire d'Anthropologie Sociale where she coordinates the team "Anthropology of Perception." She teaches at EHESS (Ecole des Hautes Etudes en Sciences Sociales) and coordinates the International Associated Laboratory "TransOceanik: Interactive Research, Mapping, and Creative Agency in the Pacific, the Indian Ocean and the Atlantic," a partnership between the CNRS and JCU. Involved with Aboriginal people since 1979, she has done fieldwork in Central Australia, the Kimberley, and Palm Island. Author of many publications, such as *The Challenge of Indigenous Peoples* (Bardwell Press, 2011) and *Rêves en colère* (Poche, 2004), she also produced various multimedia works, including experimental films she shot in the 1970s and an ongoing digital collaborative archive for Warlpiri people from Lajamanu in Central Australia (http://www.odsas.fr).

Alyssa Grossman is a post-doctoral fellow in Heritage Studies at the University of Gothenburg, Sweden. She holds a Ph.D. in Social Anthropology with Visual Media from the University of Manchester. Her research incorporates film-making and other experimental, sensory, and collaborative practices to explore everyday sites and practices of memory work in post-socialist Romania. She is co-director (with Selena Kimball) of the video installation *Memory Objects, Memory Dialogues* (2011), and director of the award-winning films *In the Light of Memory* (2010) and *Into the Field* (2005).

Jennifer Heuson is a scholar and film-maker whose work critically engages the mediated experience of culture and identity during travel. Her works use *asynchronous ethno-graphy* to reveal the layers of sentiment, memory, and imagination that generate sensory encounters between peoples, places, and things. Her award-winning films have screened internationally at venues as diverse as FLEX Fest, Big Muddy, Black Maria, and the Margaret Mead Film & Video Festival. She has also produced sound ethnographies of the Peruvian Amazon, New York City, and South Dakota's Black Hills. Jen is currently pursuing her Ph.D. in the Department of Media, Culture, and Communication at New York University. Her dissertation, "Sounding Western," explores the role of sound in producing national sensory heritage in the Black Hills. Jen holds an MA in Film and Television Studies and an MA in Philosophy and Cultural Analysis, both from the University of Amsterdam, and a BA in philosophy from the University of Northern Colorado.

Martino Nicoletti, ethnologist, multimedia artist, and writer, has for over 20 years been engaged in visual anthropology, ethnography, and anthropology of art in southern and southeast Asia.

Senior Lecturer in Fine Art Photography at the School of Art and Design of the University of Derby (UK), he is the author of numerous scientific ethnographic essays, multimedia works, photographic and artist's books, and video shorts.

As an artist he has displayed his works at numerous solo and collective exhibitions in Europe, Asia and the US. As art curator, in the past few years, he has curated international events in Thailand, the UK, and Italy, mainly devoted to the relationship between ethnography and contemporary art.

Forthcoming: his fiction *Anime di sabbia* (*Souls of Sand*), a novel directly inspired by the life of Arthur Bernard Deacon, the young British anthropologist who died tragically during his fieldwork on the Island of Malekula (New Hebrides) in 1927.

Caterina Pasqualino (editor) is an anthropologist and documentary film-maker (Research Fellow at CNRS (IIAC/LAIOS Paris. Bronze medal, 2000), and teaches the Anthropology of Performance at EHESS. She first conducted research in Sicily (*Milena. Un paese siciliano vent'anni dopo*, Edizioni Scientifiche italiane, 1990), then on Andalusian flamenco, a musical genre usually perceived in folkloric terms, from a purely anthropological perspective (*Dire le Chant. Les Gitans flamencos d'Andalousie*, EHESS-CNRS, 1998, republished as pocket edition: *Flamenco gitan*, CNRS editions, 2008, and film *Bastian and Lorie, Notes on Gypsy Flamenco* (CNRS, 2009). She is currently researching *palo monte* possession rituals in Cuba. Along with her intention to develop new issues, she has turned toward contemporary and performance art and initiated encounters between ethnographic material and artworks.

Kathryn Ramey has a Ph.D. in Anthropology and an MFA in film, and her work draws on the experimental processes of both disciplines. Her award-winning and strongly personal films are characterized by manipulation of the celluloid, including hand-processing, optical printing, and various direct animation techniques. Her scholarly interest is focused on the social history of the avant garde film community, the anthropology of visual communication and the intersection between avant garde and ethnographic film and art practices. She has been the recipient of numerous awards and fellowships including the Social Science Research Council on the Arts fellowship, the LEF New England Moving Image Grant, the Pennsylvania Council on the Arts Fellowship and the Massachusetts Cultural Council Artist Grant. She has published articles in *Visual Anthropology Review* and *The Independent* as well as the anthologies *Women's Experimental Cinema* and *Made to be Seen*. She has screened films at multiple film festivals and other venues including the Toronto Film Festival, the Tribeca Film Festival, 25fps Experimental Film Festival in Zagreb, Croatia, and the National Museum of Women in the Arts in Washington, DC. She is an associate professor at Emerson College in Boston, MA.

Arnd Schneider (editor) is Professor of Social Anthropology at the University of Oslo. He writes on contemporary art and anthropology, migration, and film. His main publications include *Futures Lost* (Peter Lang, 2000), and *Appropriation as Practice: Art and Identity in Argentina* (Palgrave, 2006). He co-edited (with Chris Wright) *Contemporary Art and Anthropology* (Berg, 2006), *Between Art and Anthropology* (Berg, 2010), and *Anthropology and Art Practice* (Bloomsbury, 2013). He was a co-organizer of the international conference *Fieldworks: Dialogues between Art and Anthropology* (Tate Modern, 2003).

Christian Suhr is a film-maker and a post-doctoral research fellow at the Department of Culture and Society, Aarhus University. He is the director of the award-winning films *Unity through Culture* (with Ton Otto, 2011), *Ngat is Dead* (with Ton Otto and Steffen Dalsgaard, 2009), as well as *Want a Camel, Yes?* (with Mette Bahnsen, 2005). He is author of the forthcoming ethnographic film monograph *Descending with Angels* about Islamic exorcism and Danish psychiatry and the article "Can Film Show the Invisible?: The Work of Montage in Ethnographic Filmmaking (with

Rane Willerslev, *Current Anthropology*, 2012). With Rane Willerslev he has edited the volume *Transcultural Montage* (Berghahn, 2013).

Nadine Wanono has a research tenure position at the CNRS: Centre d'Etudes des Mondes africains, CNRS-Paris 1. She conducted her fieldwork among the Dogon people in Mali, where she produced several films which were selected in numerous ethnographic film festivals and broadcast on Arte. As Visiting Associate Professor at University of California, Santa Barbara (UCSB), she started research on the role and impact of digital technologies in visual anthropology. In 2005–7, she conducted a seminar on the subject Singularités et Technologie. From 2011, in collaboration with Le Cube, digital art centre, she initiated an encounter to promote new forms of expression in social sciences and to encourage creation as a method and means of investigating reality. She is co-editor of the special journal issue *Création et transmission en anthropologie visuelle, Journal des anthropologues* (2013).

Rane Willerslev has his Ph.D. from the University of Cambridge (2003) and is Professor of Anthropology at Aarhus University. He is the author of *Soul Hunters: Hunting, Animism, and Personhood among the Siberian Yukaghirs* (University of California Press, 2007) and *On the Run in Siberia* (University of Minnesota Press, 2012). He is the editor of *Taming Time, Timing Death: Social Technologies and Ritual* (with Dorthe Refslund Christensen, Ashgate Publishing, 2013) and of *Value as Theory* (with Ton Otto, HAU: *Journal of Ethnographic Theory* special issue, 2013), and of *Transcultural Montage* (with Christian Suhr, Berghahn, 2013).

EXPERIMENTAL FILM AND ANTHROPOLOGY

Caterina Pasqualino and Arnd Schneider

In this book, we seek to challenge and overcome a broad realist–narrative paradigm that—with few exceptions—has dominated visual anthropology so far. While, on the whole, visual anthropology had several important innovators (notably, Jean Rouch, Robert Gardner, and David MacDougall),[1] and, at certain points in its history is influenced by innovative movements in film-making (including documentary film-making), such as Italian Neo-Realism, cinéma vérité, and direct cinema, none of these innovators engaged with what were (and are) film's own *experimental* avant-gardes. By this we mean the genealogy of experiments with film's form and material in several pre- and post-avant-garde movements (such as in abstract, futurist, surrealist, absolute, and structuralist film).[2]

We should stress that our approach is deliberately impure and eclectic. We use "film," rather unapologetically, to signify moving image products in the broadest sense, including all post-analog formats. On occasion, for specific theoretical reasons, our arguments are indeed linked to analog films, but not exclusively. Also, we focus principally on moving image products or artefacts—which is the reason why we prefer the term "film" over "cinema." However, a broader argument could perhaps be constructed for the relation between anthropology and experimental cinema, including audience reception, and several contributors point to that direction (for instance Caterina Pasqualino, Christian Suhr, and Rane Willerslev). Experiment, of course, has been used also in another, more literal sense of an orderly arranged test, trial, or procedure, in anthropological film-making. Thus experiments with film have also been used in anthropology of what on the surface seems to be a more positivist understanding of science and the camera as a research tool, but what in fact reflected an eclectic mix of influences from natural and life sciences, psychology, psychiatry, behaviorism, and kinesics (for instance, the films of Ray Birdwhistell).[3] Here the camera was introduced as an investigative agent in the experimental design and arrangement of the film-work, in order to elicit responses among the filmed subjects.[4] Stemming from a long line of precedents, including Margaret Mead and Gregory Bateson's famous work on the Balinese "character," the broader agenda was to study visual communication (often non-verbal) cross-culturally. However, these approaches were heterogenic and cannot be subsumed under one paradigm, even for the work of one film-maker or film-making team. For instance, in the case of the Mead–Bateson collaboration, these included different emphases in film-making: for Mead the camera was primarily an objective, disengaged research tool, whereas for Bateson the hand-held camera allowed close visual engagement in social action. In their films, influences of both approaches are present which also characterize differently the entire oeuvre. Some films (focusing often on childhood behavior) suppose a more disengaged, objective scientific documentation, whereas in others a more interpretive and creative style dominates (such as *Trance and Dance in Bali*, 1952, and *Learning to Dance in Bali*, 1978).[5] The principal idea that the camera is a research tool for observation was reflexively applied and developed through the famous experiment by Sol Worth and John Adair of letting the Navajo film themselves.[6] Donald and Ronald Rundstrom's carefully arranged experimental design of sequences in their film (with film-maker Clintum Bergum) *The Path* (1971)—and detailed study guide—on the Japanese tea ceremony is based on and incorporates the philosophy and point of view of the practitioners. The hostess of the ceremony helped to frame shots (Figure 1.1), and significantly, the last sequence of *The Path* is also a proper experiment in film-making worthy of avant-garde traditions with subtle superimpositions of the implements and gestures in the tea ceremony, both arranged *and* observed (Figure 1.2).[7]

To take on the notion of experiment is important for visual anthropology, and anthropology at large, for a number of reasons. While the *Writing Culture*[8] critique has led to experimentation with text, the visual side had been largely neglected, and visual anthropology followed principally narrative traditions, omitting thereby from the canon experimental works (for instance by Juan Downey, Trinh T. Minh-ha, and Sharon Lockhart) which problematized closeness and distance to the ethnographic subject and the multiple viewpoints of the participant observer.[9] An examination of experimental film traditions has obvious implications for anthropo-logical film practice which are taken up by several contributors to our volume. For instance, Kathryn Ramey writes about the seminal camera-less animation work of Robert Ascher; Barbara Glowczewski on the reasons that led her to abandon experimental film practice with Australian Aborigines; and Jennifer Heuson and Kevin T. Allen explore the asynchronicities of sound and image in their experimental film practice. However, as Arnd Schneider has recently argued, beyond its practical value experimental film is also good to think with for anthropologists, since it questions fundamentally the material processes of visual perception.[10] Experimental film, especially in its 1960s and 1970s incarnations of so-called "structuralist" or "materialist" film (which referenced earlier twentieth-century traditions of abstract and absolute film) interrogated fundamental issues, such as film time (the length of a film) vs. experienced time, narration, the apparatus (e.g. camera, and projection

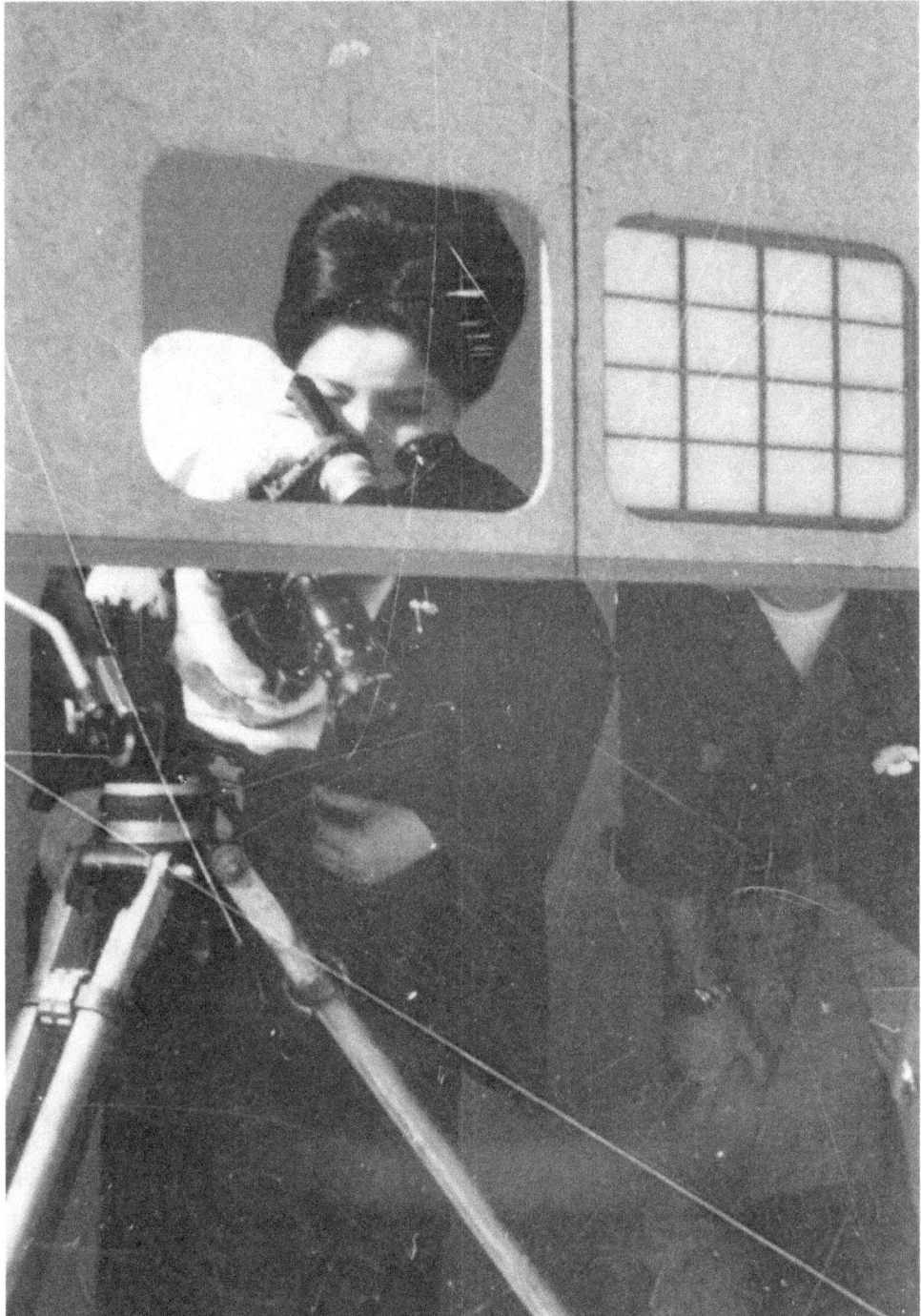

Figure 1.1 Hostess Soho Uyeda (Sowa Kai Omote Senke School of Tea), framing a shot during the shooting of *The Path*, Donald Rundstrom, Ronald Rundstrom, Clintum Bergum, USA, color, sound, 16 mm, 1971. Courtesy of Ronald Rundstrom.

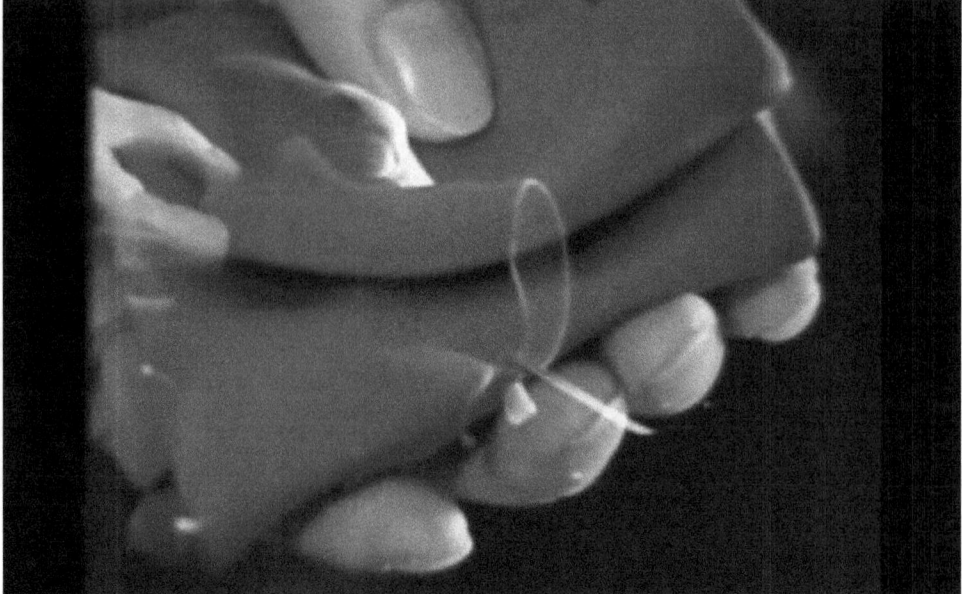

Figure 1.2 Still image from *The Path*, Donald Rundstrom, Ronald Rundstrom, Clintum Bergum, USA, color, sound, 16 mm, 1971. By kind permission of Ronald Rundstrom, digital screen grab courtesy of Jieh Hsiang, National Taiwan University.

devices), and the materiality of film itself. These essential tenets of experimental film suggest a number of implications, and pose some questions for anthropology, such as film as a material object rather than experienced time,[11] or in the words of Nicky Hamlyn the differences between what films *are* (about their narration's subject in mainstream film), or what they *do* (in experimental film).[12] Film (especially analog) is literally a medium that comes between us and the perceived world (i.e. our senses, perception, and representation).[13] Unlike "classical" cinema, the intentions of which are based on narrative, experimental film does not entertain the viewer with a story. In contrast, it invites the spectator to undergo a visual and auditory experience we might describe as a performance.

Experimental film is to a certain degree about what goes on during projection inside the viewer's head[14]—an interesting link to the notions of the virtuality of ritual, or the compositional dimensions—dimensions that condition particular intentionalities in ritual and performance.[15]

However, we should make it clear from the outset that our use of "experiment," and (and hence "experimental film") is somewhat broader than that used by film historians, and no attempt is made here to engage with the history of experimental film in a comprehensive or systematic way.[16] Rather, in the context of this book, we take experiment to mean more narrowly experiments with form (which, of course, in an important conceptual twist, becomes "content" for some experimental filmmakers), and, in a broader sense, any subversion of genre conventions.

With such a subversive agenda, we make deliberate and selective choices which are set against the foil of visual anthropology, and anthropology at large. Therefore, our use of examples with reference to experimental film history is admittedly eclectic and partial. This is not to say that our arguments are irrelevant to experimental film-makers, but the vantage point inevitably remains anthropology. Indeed one would be curious what the reception of an anthropological take on experimental film would be among experimental film-makers and their critics. On the few occasions when the two fields did overlap, in criticism and scholarship (one thinks of Catherine Russell)[17] and in practice (famously Maya Deren), this interdisciplinary impetus came from *within* filmic tradition, not anthropology. Significantly, Maya Deren's writing of *Divine Horsemen*, set up as a more formal ethnography, was kept separate from her experimental film practice, while with hindsight the two endeavors did influence each other, testified through not only the artistic sensibility in the writing of *Divine Horsemen* but also Deren's footage shot in Haiti (and only posthumously edited by her husband Teiji Ito).[18]

Acknowledging these important precedents, but set at a different contemporary juncture, our book is an open invitation to experimental film-makers to come into dialogue with anthropology. In fact, to some degree, this is already happening with the work of Karen Mirza and Brad Butler, Laurent van Lancker, and others.[19]

Disrupting Realist-observational Narrative

Of late, there has also been a renewed engagement with film theory beyond realist paradigms by anthropologists. Dziga Vertov famously claimed that the cine camera, and all techniques involved in film, that is what he called the "Kino Eye," can reveal things not normally visible to the naked human eye—a postulate which has informed many strands of experimental film-making.[20] "Can film show the invisible?" is the main title of a recent article by anthropologists and film-makers Rane Willerslev and Christian Suhr, where they argue, coming from a broadly phenomenological perspective, that beyond observational film genres in ethnographic film-making, montage film (especially in the traditions of Dziga Vertov and Sergei Eistenstein) can evoke hidden dimensions of ethnographic reality.[21] It follows from this that ethnographic film indeed is in need of a "radical shock therapy," the term Suhr and Willerslev apply to montage work disrupting realist–observational narrative,[22] and also use as the leitmotif for their animated discussion of montage in the contribution to our book.

However, in one sense, experimental film in its narrower "form as content" version had already given a very specific answer to the question of the "invisible," by focusing on the invisible aspects of film itself, i.e. frame, surface, and print stock. The "mistakes" made in analog film-making become deliberate tools to probe perception in the hands of the experimental film-maker.[23] They transform the film with sudden zooms, abrupt shifts in the image, unexpected cropping, flashes, or double exposures; while the film is being developed, they sometimes add images to the negative, intensify its color, chemically alter it, smear it with ink, scratch it or scrape it. Others intervene in the editing process, adding layers to the film, creating inversions or mirror images, slowing it down or making stills. Some become involved during screening using an oscilloscope. These methods can elicit malaise but can also arouse feelings of intoxication or elation, or create the impression of déjà vu, a flashback or daydreaming.

Beyond breaking the codes of cinema, experimental film ceaselessly questions perception, observation, and description, and, in this way, challenges anthropocentrism. As noted by Nicole Brenez in her contribution to this book, in Robert Fenz's filmic oeuvre which she characterizes as "solo-forms," portraits of the body in pain, abstract shapes produced by random camera movements offer as much descriptive information as realistic images and propose a broader notion of reality. Distancing himself from the traditional cinematic syntax, Fenz embraces an approach that is tactile and optical through uninterrupted editing.

Experimental Film and Ritual Trance

Maya Deren, one of the most radical members of the experimental film genre, was fascinated by ritual performance. Her interest in performance arose during the Surrealist epoch, which collapsed the boundaries between real and imaginary and situated itself on the edge of consciousness. She was one of the first directors to perceive film-makers as shamans, and considered viewers as participants in a kind of ritual trance; for Deren, the purpose of a film was to plunge spectators into a second state and reveal to them an unfamiliar world.

Like all rituals, "film-performance" is characterized on the one hand by fictive space and time, and, on the other, by recomposing the participants' personalities. In *Experimental Ethnography*, Catherine Russell analyses filmic essays—by Maya Deren, Jean Rouch, or Bill Viola—that approach the idea of possession by way of a romantic vision. In particular, Russell criticizes the fact that Maya Deren would have sought to stage experiences interpreting possession rituals as a utopian form while concealing the historical and political side of voodoo in Haiti.[24] These are valid criticisms; however, Maya Deren's idea of possession is interesting for another reason: it is a *mise en abîme* of subjectivity, and refers back to a kind of "degree zero" of performance phenomena that, by means other than political, returns us to the core of possession.

The rapprochement of experimental cinema and trance therefore deserves special attention. Surrealist writer and ethnographer Michel Leiris, in his research among the Gondar of Ethiopia, provides a remarkable description of a possessed person's behavior in performances that are halfway between life and theater.[25] In theater, the performers' involvement can range from simple identification with a role to an utter transformation; in the most extreme situations—such as a trance—the subjects merge so greatly with their character that they are entirely metamorphosed, surrendering their identity to put on a new skin. This observation can lead anthropologists to suggest new interpretations of trance, principally analysing fluctuations in the participants' emotions.[26]

But trance and possession are complex subjects to tackle. In general, anthropologists are primarily interested in their central phase, a symbolic climax in which the public identifies the possessed as embodying a spirit or death. The beginning and end of the ritual, which are more elusive, receive less attention. Disconcerted by so much confusion, Roberte Hamayon even advised "to put an end to the use of trance," considering these "disorders of the consciousness" as too subjective and obscure.[27] In contrast, Caterina Pasqualino in her contribution to this volume pays particular attention to the first and last phases of the trances she observed in Cuba. Often violent and uninhibited, these ritual sequences have a great emotional intensity, to the point where individuals are said to "lose themselves."

The Disturbance of Consciousness

In his analysis of the possession ceremonies filmed by Jean Rouch in *Les Maîtres fous* (*The Mad Masters*), Michael Taussig underlined how the editing elicits a zone of emptiness capable of altering the protagonists' identity.[28] Certainly, Rouch believed film-makers should not be satisfied with being mere observers and that they should be deeply engaged in the scenes they are shooting. For him, the camera, much more than a simple device, should provoke encounters and experiences. Rouch also spoke of the *"ciné-transe"*: he compared the possessive state with a film-maker, transported to a second state by strong emotion. For Paul Henley, while the cinéma vérité of Vertov transforms facts from everyday life into fiction, Rouch's *ciné-transe* leads us to see film images as comparable to the visions of the possessed. Henley invites us to consider the concept of the *ciné-transe* as a metaphor.[29]

However, we propose to reconsider the concept of *ciné-transe* beyond its metaphorical status, by taking performance into account. According to film-maker Ben Russell, a director's heightened creativity, like the phenomena of possession, involves moments of rupture. Since 2005, Russell has been working on *Trypps*, a series of films evoking ideas of travel, trance, hallucination, and movement. In them, he undertakes a psychophysical exploration of trances induced by music, ritual, dance, or hallucinogens. In *Trypps #7*, for example, the camera, mounted on a tripod facing a canyon, focuses on a woman who has just taken LSD. At one point, the woman disappears, giving way to her inner visions. To create an atmosphere of transcendence, Russell creates sensory devices. According to Geneviève Yue, this work borrows, on the one hand, from experimental ethnography—best represented by Trinh T. Minh-ha, Maya Deren, and Jean Rouch—and, on the other hand, from the avant-garde, playing on ideas of altered perception, as in the work of Stan Brakhage or Paul Sharits (see Figure 1.3).[30]

Figure 1.3 Ben Russell. Ruth. Still frame from *Trypps #7* (Badlands). Courtesy of Ben Russell.

Cinema and Theater

In general, avant-gardists easily cross the boundaries between genres. The anthropologist and theater director Richard Schechner suggests a relationship between screening a film and sequencing in ritual. The emotional impact on the participant is based primarily on the repetition of images. Thus, when a scene is rehearsed, it is enhanced with deeper meaning. As with rituals based on the repetition of gestures, the repetition of images in experimental film would disrupt perception and make viewers dizzy in order to bring them into a fantasy world. The process of altering the participants' consciousness and then reconstructing it is common not only to experimental film and ritual trance, but also to theater.

Schechner comments that theatrical performances are never fully realized the first time, only as of the second or even the umpteenth presentation.[31] The performative act consists of inventing "strips of behavior" allowing individuals, at times on the verge of trance, to experience the sensation of possession. Schechner compares this to a film-maker who has mounted or edited film with the sequences in the wrong order, thus troubling the audience's perception.

One can also compare experimental film to the avant-garde theater of Jerzy Grotowski (active in Poland until 1968, and later a professor of theater anthropology at the College de France) or to Antonin Artaud's theater of cruelty.[32] These artists worked with dramaturgical techniques aimed at deploying as much energy as possible to achieve catharsis. Exploring new approaches to having control over breathing and the body, they sought to overcome the separation between actor and spectator, and between ritual and theatrical performance. Experimental filmmaker Raymonde Carasco was similarly inspired by the work of Artaud and his travels among the indigenous Tarahumara in Mexico.[33] In order to reconstruct the emotional relationship of the Tarahumara to the underworld and the afterlife, she recorded film sequences relative to the materiality of context in which the scenes take place, to dance steps seen in close-up, and to mandatory gestures (for example, in *Tarahumaras 78*) (Figure 1.4).

The Role of the Audience and Expanded Vision Practice

Cinematic spaces and the practices taking place within and around it have been important to experimental film-makers who continuously tried to challenge illusionist viewing assumptions of audiences.

Through video performance (using camera and monitor), Dan Graham invites active participation by the audience, clearly presenting performance as the equivalent of a ritual. Inspired by Brecht's concepts on theater, he seeks to make the audience uncomfortable, forcing them into extreme self-awareness, and has used mirrors and videos to create situations in which the actor would also observe his own acts. In *Two Consciousness Projection(s)* (1972), Graham asked two people to verbalize their perceptions: seated in front of a video screen, a woman would see her own image while a man watched her through a monitor. The man and woman, at once active and passive, were both actors in the performance and its subject.

Figure 1.4 Raymonde Carasco. Pinto's drummer and dancers, Easter 1995, at Nararachic (Mexico). Courtesy of Régis Hébraud.

In *Present Continuous Past* (1974), Graham interrogates the role of the spectator while making use of temporal and spatial data. He uses a mirror, reflection of time present, and video, reflection of time past. The video shows the actions of the actor/spectator either in real time or in the past: in this way, the present and past, transcribed in the mirror and then in the video, were presented as part of the same temporal and spatial whole. Dan Graham's video performances become rituals, by focusing on the connections between the artist, the actor/spectator and the public.

Janet Cardiff and George Bures Miller's installation *The Paradise Institute* (originally shown at the Venice Biennale, 2001) unsettles familiar assumptions by audiences about architectural spaces dedicated to the perception of visual and aural illusions, in other words—cinemas. This is how they describe their work:

> Viewers approach a simple plywood pavilion, mount a set of stairs, and enter a lush, dimly lit interior, complete with red carpet and two rows of velvet-covered seats. Once seated, they peer over the balcony onto a miniature replica of a grand old movie theatre created with hyper-perspective. ... Viewers then put on the headphones provided and the projection begins. ... There is the 'visual film' and its accompanying soundtrack that unfolds before the viewers; layered over this is the 'aural action' of a supposed audience. The film is a mix of genres ... What is more particular about the installation is the personal binaural 'surround sound' that every individual in the audience experiences through the headphones. The sense of isolation each might feel is broken by intrusions seemingly coming from inside the theatre. A cellphone belonging to a member of the audience rings. A close 'female friend' whispers intimately in your ear 'did you check the stove before we left?'[34] (See Figure 1.5.)

Arguably, a wider notion of experimental film would conceive of it as being part of experimental cinema—an expanded understanding which would include the cinematic spaces for screening (not only "cinemas"), audiences, and the reception of cinematic works; as well as the curating and programming practices which realize and fill cinematic spaces in the first place.[35]

New Temporalities

To lead viewers to abandon their temporal point of reference, experimental film-makers, as we have said, also use various techniques to create the scrolling of images. Some have obsessively employed repetition, or have discarded the notion of time by images in acceleration or slow motion that inspire a sense of immediacy or, on the contrary, of distancing.[36] Caterina Pasqualino's anthropological observations here overlap with work on experimental cinema: her hypothesis is, indeed, that experimental film, seen in a new light, is related to ancestral possession techniques that enable an altered state of consciousness. She has observed, for instance, that in *Human Frames* (2012), Lowave productions proposed that the

Figure 1.5 Janet Cardiff and George Bures Miller, *The Paradise Institute*, 2001. Wood, theater seats, video projection, headphones, and mixed media. 118 × 698 × 210 inches (299.72 × 1772.92 × 533.4 cm). Courtesy of Luhring Augustine, New York.

film-makers stage joy, madness, desire, fanaticism, hatred, isolation, and melancholy—passions regularly evoked by shamans.[37] When the experiment succeeds, the audience tumbles into a derealized world. The spectator's dominant feeling is one of merging with the environment while at the same time being outside space and time. Disturbing the rhythm and image sequencing can produce a powerful impression of condensation or expansion of space-time. Reality thus transfigured, one's consciousness of the world is transformed. The viewer can have the sensation of being split or of simultaneously living several spatialities and temporalities. Experimental film therefore shares sensations of contemporaneity or co-presence with trance.

Time

The confrontation between trance and experimental film in anthropological terms reveals another question: how can one reconcile objective time, coming from mechanical design, with subjective time, based on a series of compressions, dilatations and superimpositions? While anthropology seeks to distinguish a perception of time based on "layers of subjectivity," experimental cinema plays with an uninhibited perception of time, capable of intermingling opposites, such as slow motion and acceleration, flashbacks and visions of the future.

How can one account for the complex mechanisms linking reality to the visionary worlds summoned in possession rituals with visions of mediums or of traditional healers, or even hallucinations of subjects under the influence of drugs? In other words, how can one account for situations in which the ego is split? According to a widely shared definition, "madness," which psychiatrists decline in terms of psychosis, schizophrenia, and paranoia, is characterized by varying degrees of mental impairment and by a temporary or lasting split personality. But are those who are "mad" a class of permanently marginalized beings? The answer is quite complex. Michel Foucault argues that their treatment has been likened to that of those who are excluded, locked up, confined, and that the madness is primarily a form of deviance from societal norms.[38] From a clinical perspective, neuroscientists have noted that the "mentally ill" have recurring hallucinatory dreams. For instance, they might be troubled by geometric shapes transformed into emotionally meaningful objects, or have visions of whirlpools.[39] In this way, they are similar to someone in a trance or under hypnosis. For Antonin Artaud, madness was comparable to the second state an artist might experience during an act of heightened creativity.[40] The visions offered in experimental film might also suggest that madness could refer to a state of super- or hyper-normality—epitomized, for instance, in Margarida Paiva's film *Who Lives In My Head?* (2012).[41]

Figure 1.6 Margarida Paiva: Still frame from *Who Lives In My Head?*, 2009 (Lowave, 2012). Courtesy of Margarida Paiva.

Performance in experimental film shares with possession rituals the fact that they are not exactly, to borrow Leonardo da Vinci's famous expression, *cosa mentale* (a mental occupation), but *sensus* (feeling).[42] Neither the former nor the latter can be described as simple representations: they are events in which one participates, and the collective emotion they evoke relates to the arrival of a "force." In rituals, this force was long ago identified by anthropologists, in particular in Marcel Mauss's studies on the Polynesian notion of *mana*.[43] Its presence in ritual is, without a doubt, universal. Caterina Pasqualino identified this in Andalusian Gypsies in the form of the *duende*, or in the Cuban Palo Monte cult, where it is referred to as *ache*.[44]

We are still lacking, however, detailed observations about the precise moment when the force occurs and the performance literally shifts. This usually occurs at the moment when the ritual reaches a peak, marked by a state of communion in the group and magnified by strong collective emotion. Everything starts with an individual "touched by grace" who experiences a release of energy that spreads, triggering a sense of closeness in the community. At this specific moment, shivering and even crying, the participants become one. Caterina Pasqualino, believing they have been misidentified from a theoretical point of view, proposes here to broaden the term *punctum*, which was used by Barthes regarding photography, to include ritual.[45]

Memory

Some interesting problems are also posed by film, especially experimental film's relation to memory. On the one hand, film (together with photography) is a time-based medium par excellence, and always conserves a record, even if manipulated, of time elapsed during shooting—in the case of the products of analog media it also provides a material proof or evidence of that passed time. The hybrid genre of "photofilm" is particularly instructive in this respect, as Arnd Schneider shows in his contribution to this volume. Film-makers of narrative historical documentaries dealt with this manipulated time preserved in the filmic archive in a variety of ways; for instance, by simply using sequences of archival film, or with compilation films made entirely from historical material. Another way is to manipulate the found footage in such a way that its artificial status is clearly shown and it loses its reference as memory storage of the historical record. For example, Peter Delpeut's *Lyrical Nitrate* is a famous compilation film made entirely from found footage material of early, nitrate Dutch film. However, rather than focusing on the historical context, the sense of loss, absence, passing of time, and natural decay of the film material move to the fore. In the words of film scholar André Habib, "[w]hat overwhelms the present of the film is its ruin, which adds itself anachronistically to the image"[46] (Figure 1.7).

Figure 1.7 Film still, *Lyrical Nitrate*, Peter Delpeut, Netherlands, Ariel Film, 1990, 35 mm, b/w and color, sound. Courtesy of Peter Delpeut.

In fact, the found footage then becomes detached from the historical record, signifying the loss of historical memory, the amnesia of historical time—eventually, in the final minutes of film, the self-degrading and decomposing nitrate material bears only witness to itself. In her contribution to this volume, Alyssa Grossman chose yet another way to explore memory by introducing stop-motion animation into an otherwise narrative ethnographic documentary (including portraits of her interview partners) in order to elicit people's memories with particular objects from socialist times in Romania. Her film is a solid reflection on objecthood, as well as things as actors upon people's memories, and surely invites further theoretical comparison—for instance, with Bruno Latour's actor-network theory, and theorizing about agency, things, and artefacts in anthropology (for instance, by Alfred Gell).[47]

One also thinks here of the constant reworking of memory by Jonas Mekas, a pivotal figure in the underground and experimental film avant-garde in New York, through his film diaries with us of different film stocks, the allusion to the genre of home-movies, inspired not least by a wide array of poetic influences, and using his camera like a pen (camera-stylo). A way of working that Mekas described as on the edge, between causality and memory: "Some things that fall in strike some notes maybe with their color, with what they represent, and I begin to look at them, I begin to respond to this or that detail. Of course, the mind is not a computer. But still, it works something like a computer, and everything that falls in, is measured, correspond to the memories, to the realities that have been registered in the brain, or wherever, and it's all very real."[48]

Experimental film-maker and anthropologist Kathryn Ramey (contributing to our book an essay on the seminal animation work of Robert Ascher), in her own film *Yanqui Walker and the Optical Revolution* uses Guy Debord's concept of détournement to work with found footage of instructional films from the 1920s through to the 1980s.[49] These are montaged with her own footage taken on a fieldtrip to Nicaragua, where she explored the history of William Walker, an obscure nineteenth-century American expansionist in Costa Rica and Nicaragua, to create a work which constantly challenges the viewer's assumptions about time, place, language, and received notions of what the film and images *are* about and what they *do*. This is precisely one of the main epistemological points experimental film-makers are making, as Nicky Hamlyn suggests.[50]

Materials

A particularly important area of experimental film concerns materiality or rather the material conditions of film-making. Here, the film-maker turns into an investigator of the conditioning process for the fabrication of new optical realities, a quest shared with epistemologically interested anthropologists, and this has important implications for anthropological research. Film thus materially intervenes in the world (and is itself intervened upon) and is not just an optical illusion (the charge experimental film-makers level against narrative cinema). Ultimately, as Laura Marks argued, film is also haptically and sensuously perceived and experienced.[51]

Material intervention can be taken to its literal "extremes," such as in the work of Emmanuel Lefrant, *The Visible and the Invisible of a Body under Tension*, in which he combined film stock he had buried, and let partially erode, in African soil, with other shots of the same location. Lefrant explains:

> I shot the image of a landscape and buried simultaneously a film strip in the same place where the sequence was shot: the emulsion, the victim of erosion is thus subjected to biochemical degradation. The result of these natural processes of decay are then conserved in the state of their dissolution. Those two images, and their negative versions, are then entangled together thanks to double exposure and bi-packing techniques.
>
> These landscapes in fusion, it's the logic of a world that reveals itself. A bipolar world, where invisible takes shape with the visible, where the first dissolves itself into the second and vice versa.[52]

The viewer seems occasionally to sense the contours of a landscape (which Lefrant saw from his window), but can never be quite sure, as the trained vision habits—trained on and by narrative-realist cinema conventions—are continually disturbed through the flickering rhythm and quickly changing forms and colors.

In a similar vein, *Unearth* by Karthik Pandian (2009), the artwork which we chose for the cover of this book, strikingly epitomizes many issues at the intersection between experimental film and anthropology: the film strip (recording material) is exposed, partly buried, but also unearthed or extracted from the earth (in this case an ancient site of indigenous Americans near St. Louis); just as anthropology (and by extension archaeology) also extracts (its) evidence, and eventually constructs knowledge from the burrowed fields of "other" societies, their environments and peoples.[53]

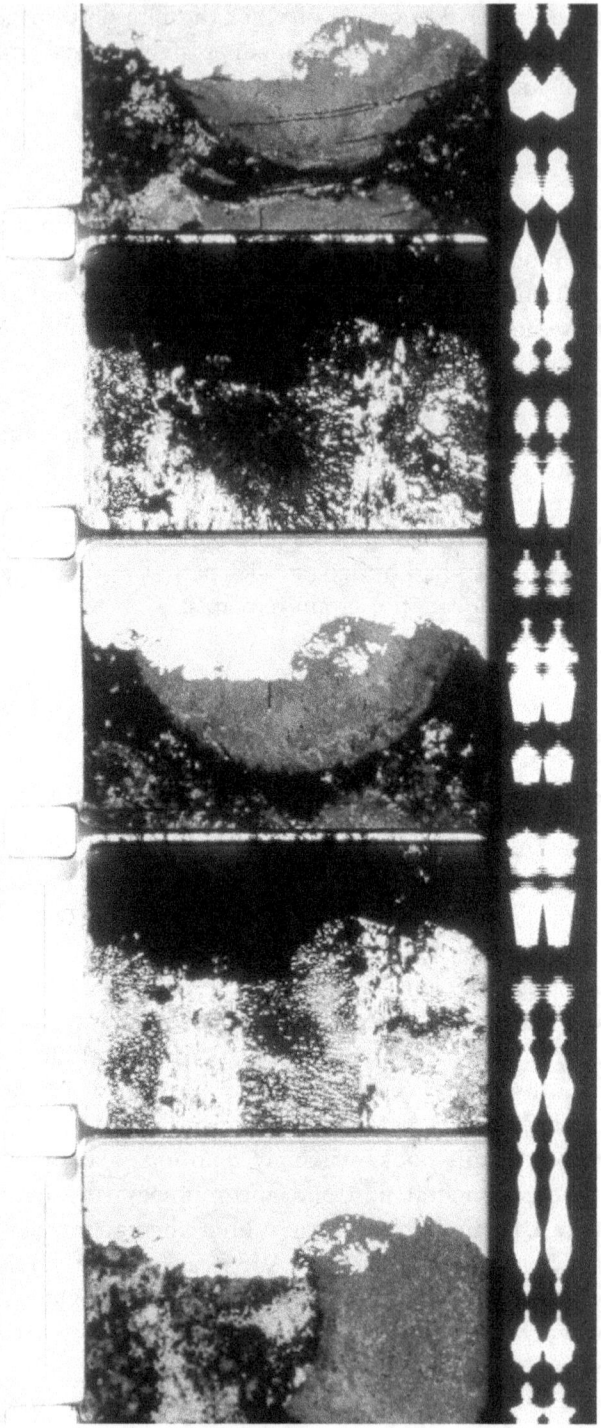

Figure 1.8 Still image from *The Visible and the Invisible of a Body under Tension*, Emmanuel Lefrant, France, 2009. Courtesy of Emmanuel Lefrant.

Formal choices in experimental film are never just aesthetical choices, a kind of *"l'art put l'art"* attitude which would set it apart from politically committed narrative film (and a charge sometimes brought against experimental film-makers). Form is not only understood as content, but also is used to express strong political content—while at the same time challenging the viewer's perceptual training and viewing assumptions. One might by comparison recall the observations of Jacques Rancière on early modern design, where he refutes the idea that there is "autonomous" art on the one hand and "heteronomous" art on the other, rather the two functions are simultaneous.[54] A good example for a film where a strong political message is carried through the formal rhetoric of experimental film language is Brian Karl and Özge Serin's *Death/Fast* (in progress, 2014). The film[55] is about the Death Fast Movement in Turkey, which was started in 2000 by outlawed left-wing organizations as a reaction to the transfer of political prisoners into isolation wards of high security prisons. As the directors wrote:

> *Death/Fast* represents personalized aspects of the extraordinarily long duration of the movement (7 years) and individual self-starvation period before death (up to 558 days) by providing viewpoints of multiple individuals marginalized by mainstream society in a secularist republic haunted by a founding contradiction between explicit democratic ideals simultaneous with de facto authoritarianism and military violence. *Death/Fast* provides compelling portraits of some willing to question existing political order with the ultimate sacrifice: their own lives.[56]

The film uses a number of formal devices to lend weight to its main themes—but their use is never gratuitous or propagandistic. The film opens with a completely black screen with an interview, subtitled text, and the slow voice of a prisoner. This radical withholding of visual information is, at another instance in the film, achieved more gradually through overexposure/whitening of the screen to the point where the face of the person talking is hardly any longer recognizable (this is used when prisoners speak of extreme physical and psychological deprivation resulting from forced isolation, and then fasting). Other devices include a repeat reverse movement of people ascending on a subway staircase, and a flicker-like series of flashes of images of the outside world, suggesting views (perhaps also memories) of a world not available to the prisoners any longer (Figure 1.9).

In fact, practices of experimental film-making, especially when they are voiced in an expressly material, analog medium, are a form of resistance (and often tied to the specific political agendas of topics covered in the film): for Martino Nicoletti (writing also in this present volume) to use vintage visual media becomes a mode and model of critical distancing from the ubiquitous exploitation through the—now largely digital— tourist gaze towards the Kayan women in Thailand[57]; for Kathryn Ramey the use of hand-processing, optical printing, and found footage in her film *Yanqui Walker and the Optical Revolution* is a way of disrupting the narrative of hemispheric hegemony by

Figure 1.9 "Death/Fast Stairway Frame Fragment Still." Still image from *Death/Fast* (2013) by Brian Karl and Özge Serin. Courtesy of Brian Karl and Özge Serin.

the US (and our ways of seeing); for Karen Mirza and Brad Butler (who work with analog media in the cooperative no.w.here they founded) is a way to criticize the understandings of place, time, and participation in a post-colonial context. The use of analog media in the digital age by these film-makers is not a nostalgic longing for a past technological era—although images taken, by their surface appearance, might produce a nostalgic effect—but a deliberate working through, and resisting (against the *grain*) of a dominant and hegemonic digital culture. This culture, of course, is itself subverted by the work of digital artists, as shown by Nadine Wanono in this volume.

This book is also a call to engage with practice, as it is through the practice of experimental film-makers, and by extension the practical and sensuous experience of their works, that theoretical concerns are expressed. In other words, we contend that it is through practice, beyond words, that theoretical arguments are brought forward which are of genuine interest to anthropology.[58]

Filmography

Death /Fast, dirs. Brian Karl and Özge Serin (USA, in progress 2014).
Divine Horsemen, the Living Gods of Haiti, dir. Maya Deren (edited by Teiji and Cherel Ito), 1977/1985; USA, 52 mins.

Human Frames (curators: Silke Schmickl, Masayo Kajimura, Stéphane Gérard, and Victric Thng, edited by Lowave), France, 2012, 96 films, 15 hours.
Learning to Dance in Bali, dirs Gregory Bateson and Margaret Mead, USA, 1978, 10 mins.
Les maîtres fous, dir. Jean Rouch, France, 1955, 36 mins.
Lyrical Nitrate, dir. Peter Delpeut, Netherlands, 1990, 51 mins.
Tarahumaras 98, Raymonde Carasco (produced by Raymonde Carasco Hébraud), France, 1979, 30 mins.
The Path, dirs. Donald Rundstrom, Ronald Rundstrom, and Clintum Bergum, USA, 1971, 34 mins.
The Visible and the Invisible of a Body under Tension, dir. Emmanuel Lefrant, France, 2009, 7 mins.
Trance and Dance in Bali, dirs Gregory Bateson and Margaret Mead, USA, 1952, 22 mins.
Trypps #7, dir. Ben Russell, USA, 2010, American Avant-garde, 9 mins.
Yanqui Walker and the Optical Revolution, dir. Kathryn Ramey, USA, 2009, 33 mins.

Video Installations/Performances

Present Continuous Past, dir. Dan Graham, USA, 1974.
Two Consciousness Projection(s), dir. Dan Graham, USA, 1973.

Notes

1. For us these are the ones who have been most daring in challenging canons of documentation, observation, and representation from within visual anthropology. However, our short-list is by no means exhaustive; for a fuller treatment, see also Peter Loizos, *Innovation in Ethnographic Film: From Innocence to Self-consciousness* (Manchester: Manchester University Press, 1993).
2. For an introduction, see A. L. Rees, *A History of Experimental Film and Video* (2nd edn) (London: BFI and Basingstoke: Palgrave Macmillan, 2011).
3. Catherine Russell, *Experimental Ethnography: The Work of Film in the Age of Video* (Durham, NC: Duke University Press, 1999), 135–40.
4. Emilie De Brigard, "The History of Ethnographic Film," in Paul Hockings (ed.), *Principles of Visual Anthropology* (2nd edn) (Berlin: Mouton de Gruyter, 1995 [1975]).
5. For the most comprehensive recent treatment see Paul Henley, "From Documentation to Representation: Recovering the Films of Margaret Mead and Gregory Bateson," *Visual Anthropology*, 26, 75–108, 2013, and the extensive bibliography contained therein.
6. Sol Worth and John Adair, *Through Navajo Eyes: An Exploration in Film Communication and Anthropology* (Bloomington, IN: Indiana University Press, 1972). For the film series *Navajo Film Themselves* (1966), see http://www.penn.museum/sites/navajofilmthemselves/ (accessed July 11, 2013).
7. Donald Rundstrom, Ronald Rundstrom, Clintum Bergum, *Japanese Tea: The Ritual, the Aesthetics, the Way: An Ethnographic Companion to 'The Path'* (Andover, MA: Warner Modular Publication,

1973); Donald Rundstrom, "Imaging Anthropology," in Jack Rollwagen (ed.), *Anthropological Filmmaking: Anthropological Perspectives on the Production of Film and Video for General Public Audiences* (Chur: Harwood Academic Publishers, 1988). We are grateful to David Blundell, for having made us aware of *The Path*, and providing contact with Ronald Rundstrom and Jieh Hsiang who generously helped with the two still images. Blundell was trained by the Rundstroms, and continues to make films on Buddhist monks and religious culture.
8. James Clifford and George Marcus, *Writing Cultures: The Poetics and Politics of Ethnography*. (Berkeley, CA: University of California Press, 1986).
9. Arnd Schneider, "Three Modes of Experimentation with Art and Ethnography," *Journal of the Royal Anthropological Institute*, 14 (1), 2008, 171–94.
10. Arnd Schneider, "Expanded Visions: Rethinking Anthropological Research and Representation Through Experimental Film," in Tim Ingold (ed.), *Redrawing Anthropology: Materials, Movements, Lines* (Aldgate: Ashgate, 2011), 172.
11. *Ibid.*, 180.
12. Nicky Hamlyn, *Film Art Phenomena* (London: BFI Publications, 2003), 60.
13. Schneider, "Expanded Visions," p. 178. Cf. Maya Deren, "La cinématographie ou l'usage créatif de la réalité," in *Ecrits sur le cinéma* (Paris: Paris Expérimental, 2004), 93.
14. Hamlyn, *Film Art Phenomena*, 59.
15. Bruce Kapferer and Angela Hobart, "Introduction: The Aesthetics of Symbolic Construction of Experience," in Bruce Kapferer and Angela Hobart (eds), *Aesthetics in Performance: Formations of Symbolic Construction and Experience* (New York and Oxford: Berghahn, 2005), 5. Caterina Pasqualino, "Habilitation à diriger les recherches (H.D.R.)," *Une anthropologie de la performance*, sous le tutorat de Anne Christine Taylor, Université de Nanterre, Paris, 2013, 55.
16. For a good overview and introduction see: Rees, *A History of Experimental Film and Video*, and the extensive notes and bibliography therein. Some histories have more focus on specific tradions, i.e. US, UK, French, continental Europe, etc. P. Adams Sitney, *Visionary Film—The American Avantgarde* (3rd edn) (New York: Oxford University Press, 2002); David Curtis, *A History of Artists' Film and Video in Britain* (London: BFI, 2007); Dominique Noguez, *Éloge du cinéma expérimental* (3rd edn) (Paris: Paris Expérimental/Centre Pompidou, 2010); Hans Scheugl and Ernst Schmidt Jr., *Eine Subgeschichte des Films: Lexikon des Avantgarde-, Experimental- und Undergroundfilms*, 2 vols (Frankfurt: Suhrkamp, 1974).
17. Russell, *Experimental Ethnography*.
18. Maya Deren, *Divine Horsemen* (London: Thames & Hudson, 1953); there is a substantial scholarly literature now on Maya Deren's ethnographic and film work; Catrina Neimann, "An Introduction to the Notebook of Maya Deren, 1947," *October*, 14 (Autumn), 1980, 3–15; Russell, *Experimental Ethnography*, 206–18; Moira Sullivan, "Maya Deren's Ethnographic Representation of Ritual and Magic in Haiti," in Bill Nichols (ed.), *Maya Deren and the American Avantgarde* (Berkeley, CA: University of California Press, 2001); in relation to anthropology and art, also, Arnd Schneider, "Unfinished Dialogues: Notes Toward a History of Art and Anthropology," in Marcus Banks and Jay Ruby (eds), *Made to be Seen: Perspectives on the History of Visual Anthropology* (Chicago, IL: University of Chicago Press, 2011).
19. See Brad Butler and Karen Mirza, "On Collections and Collectivity: A Conversation between Brad Butler, Karen Mirza and Chris Wright," in Arnd Schneider and Christopher Wright (eds), *Anthropology and Art Practice* (London: Bloomsbury, 2013); Brad Butler, *How Can Structural Film Expand the Language of Ethnography*, unpublished Ph.D. thesis (London: University of the Arts, 2011); Laurent van Lancker, "With(in) Each Other: Sensorial Practices in Recent Audiovisual Works," in A. Schneider and C. Wright (eds), *Anthropology and Art Practice*; Laurent van

Lancker, *Experiencing Cultures: Sensory, Narrative and Collaborative Strategies in Documentary Cinema*, unpublished Ph.D. thesis (Ghent: University of Ghent, 2012).
20. Dziga Vertov, *Kino-Eye: The Writings of Dziga Vertov*. Edited and with an introduction by Annette Michelson (Berkeley, CA: University of California Press, 1984).
21. Christian Suhr and Rane Willerslev, "Can Film Show the Invisible? The Work of Montage in Ethnographic Filmmaking," *Current Anthropology*, 53 (3), 2012, 282–301, 282, 284; see also their recently edited volume *Transcultural Montage* (Berghahn, 2013) – published after this volume went to press.
22. *Ibid*. 285.
23. Rees, *A History of Experimental Film and Video*, 87.
24. Catherine Russell, *Experimental Ethnography*, 193–238. On Deren's notions of film's effects for spectators, see Maya Deren, *Ecrits sur l'art et le cinéma* (Paris: Paris Expérimental, 2004), 21. Also, Alain Alcide Sudre wrote that Deren's film ritual is characterized by the *depersonalization* of the individual. See *Dialogues théoriques avec Maya Deren. Du cinèma expérimental au film ethnographique* (Paris: L'Harmattan, 1996), 377–8.
25. Michel Leiris, *La possession et ses aspects théâtraux chez les Ethiopiens de Gondar* (Paris: Le Sycomore, 1980 [1958]), 26. More generally, on the relationship between trance and technical, especially "new" media, see the forthcoming volume *Trance Mediums and New Media: Spirit Possession in the Age of Technical Reproduction*, edited by Heike Behrend, Anja Dreschke and Martin Zillinger (New York: Fordham University Press, 2014).
26. In music and trance, Gilbert Rouget proposed that we see possession essentially as a way of identification. Through her research in neuroscience and biology, Judith Becker showed that identification and mimetism of the gods are essentially emotional phenomena. Gilbert Rouget, *La musique et la transe. Esquisse d'une théorie générale des relations de la musique et de la possession*. Préface de Michel Leiris (Paris: Gallimard, 1990 [1980]); Judith Becker, *Deep Listeners. Music, Emotion and Trancing* (Bloomington and Indianapolis, IN: Indiana University Press, 2004).
27. Roberte Hamayon, "Pour en finir avec la 'transe' et l'extase dans l'étude du chamanisme," *Etudes mongoles et sibériennes*, No. 26 (1995), "Variations chamaniques 2," 155–90, 175, 180.
28. Michael Taussig, *Mimesis and Alterity: A Particular History of the Senses* (London: Routledge 1993), 242–3; Michael Taussig, *Shamanism, Colonialism, and the Wild Man: A Study in Terror and Healing* (Chicago, IL: University of Chicago Press, 1986), 441–3.
29. Paul Henley, *The Adventure of the Real: Jean Rouch and the Craft of Ethnographic Cinema* (Chicago, IL and London: University of Chicago Press, 2009), 275.
30. Genevieve Yue, *Magnetic Disorientation: Navigating Ben Russell's Trypps*, talk presented at the Society for Cinema and Media Studies conference, Chicago, March 2013.
31. Richard Schechner, "Restoration of Behavior," Chapter 2 of *Between Theater and Anthropology* (Philadephia, PA: University of Pennsylvania Press, 1985). One should note that this observation has significance from an anthropological point of view: the faithfulness of a performance could allow its transmission for generations; faced with people's difficulty to remember exactly what information to communicate, the repetition of the performative act would in fact be a mnemotechnical process. The past would thus be reconstructed from fragments of lived experiences mixed with fantastical elements.
32. Cf. Jerzy Grotowski, *La Lignée organique au théâtre et dans le rituel*: Conférence et cours, 2 CD MP3 (Paris: Livre Qui Parle, Collection Collège de France, 2008). Antonin Artaud, *The Peyote Dance* (orig. *Les Tarahumara*) (New York: Farrar, Straus and Giroux, 1975). By pushing, modifying, and intensifying the voice's range, breathing plays an important role in Antonin Artaud's "theater of cruelty." See Antonin Artaud, "Le théatre de la cruauté (premier manifeste)" in *Le théatre et son double* (Paris: Gallimard, 1938), 7.

33. Following in the footsteps first of Eisenstein, then of Artaud in Mexico, Raymonde Carasco made a series of ethnographic films, her partner Régis Hébraud, being the cameraman and editor, including: *Tarahumaras 78* (1979), *Tutuguri* (1980), *Los Pintos* (1982), *Los Pascoleros* (1996), *Artaud et les Tarahumaras* (1996), *Ciguri 98—La Danse du Peyotl* (1998), *Ciguri 99—Le dernier Chaman* (1999), *La Fêlure du temps* (2004); for a full list and production details, see http://raymonde.carasco.online.fr/ (accessed December 20, 2013).
34. From http://www.cardiffmiller.com/artworks/inst/paradise_institute.html (accessed March 20, 2013).
35. Tarek Elhaik, "Anthropology & Images: Pedagogical Notes on Cinematic Boudoirs," *La critica sociologica*, XLII (166), 2008, 49–59; "The Incurable Image: Curation & Repetition on a Tri-continental Scene," in Iain Chambers et al. (eds), *The Post-Colonial Museum: The Arts of Memory & The Pressures of History* (Farnham: Ashgate, 2013).
36. See Caterina Pasqualino, "Le ralenti comme instrument de connaissance. Filmer les chants gitans," in *Ethnomusicologie et anthropologie musicale historique de l'espace français* (Paris: L'Harmattan, 2008); Caterina Pasqualino, "Filming Emotion: The Place of Video in Anthropology," *Visual Anthropology Review*, special issue on European Anthropology, co-editors Peter di Biella and Colette Piault, 23 (1), 2007, 84–91; Caterina Pasqualino, "In Praise of Slow Motion," in Arnd Schneider and Christopher Wright (eds), *Anthropology and Art Practice* (London: Bloomsbury, 2013), pp. 143, 147; Caterina Pasqualino, *Bastian et Lorie. Notes sur le chant et la danse flamencos*, CNRS, 20', Paris, 2009. Selection for the Festival Jean Rouch, "Narrativités singulières" section, Le Cube Paris, November 14, 2011.
37. Caterina Pasqualino, "Madness," in *Human Frames*, curators: Silke Schmickl, Masayo Kajimura, Stéphane Gérard, Victric Thng, Lowave, 96 films, 15 hours, PAL/NTSC, 2012.
38. Michel Foucault, *Histoire de la folie à l'âge classique. Folie et déraison* (Paris: Gallimard, 1972), 583.
39. Silvia Bünning and Olaf Blanke, "The Out-of-Body Experience: Precipitating Factors and Neural Correlates," in Steven Laureys (ed.), *The Boundaries of Consciousness: Neurobiology and Neuropathology* (Amsterdam: Elsevier, 2005).
40. Antonin Artaud, *Nouveaux écrits de Rodez* (Paris: Gallimard, 1977), 100.
41. Margarida Paiva has proposed a singular interpretation of madness. In one long sequence, a series of photograms, scenes in increasing close-up with the help of the camera lens, she invites the viewer to climb a staircase. In a room, a young woman is without strength, almost dying. First sitting, then standing, she takes a few steps and sits again. Editing effects—as in one sequence, where the fluid movement becomes syncopated by a repeated series of slow motion photograms—create a surrealistic atmosphere. One hears in voice-over: "Who lives in my head?" This phrase, obsessively repeated and accompanied by the tick-tock of a watch, interrupts the unsettling silence. Margarida Paiva, *Who Lives In My Head?*, in *Madness, Human Frames*, Lowave, 2012.
42. Leonardo da Vinci, *Treatise on Painting, Codex Urbinas Latinus 1270*, translation Philip McMahon, introduction by Ludwig. H. Heydenreich (Princeton, NJ: Princeton University Press, 1956).
43. *Marcel Mauss*, "Essai sur le don," *Sociologie et anthropologie*, collection of essays, preface by Claude Lévi-Stauss (Paris: PUF, 1950).
44. During her research on the *palo monte* rituals in Santiago de Cuba, Caterina Pasqualino compared the Gypsy notion of *duende* to the idea of *ache*. Like *duende*, *ache* can incite mounting emotion in participants, which manifests itself as chills. Variations on the famous Polynesian concept of *mana* as studied by Mauss, *duende* and *ache* mark a phase of emotional intensification during the ritual. See Caterina Pasqualino, *Flamenco gitan* (Paris: CNRS éditions, 2008) (pocket

re-edition of *Dire le chant. Les Gitans flamencos d'Andalousie*, Paris: EHESS-CNRS, 1998), and subsequent articles ("La voix, le souffle. Une séance de chant flamenco chez les Gitans de Jerez de la Frontera," *Etudes Tsiganes*, special issue directed by Patrick Williams entitled "Jeux, tours et manèges. Une ethnologie des Tsiganes," 1994, 2 (37), 83–104; "La souffrance des chanteurs gitans flamencos (Andalousie, Espagne)," in Michel Demeuldre (ed.), *Sentiments doux-amers dans les musiques du monde* (Paris: l'Harmattan, 2004). See also, regarding the Cuban idea of *ache*: *Performance rituelle et artistique*, HDR, dir. Anne Christine Taylor (Université de Nanterre, October 2013), 44–7, 146. Martin Holbraad analyses the concept of *ache* as both a medicinal power essential to completing rituals, and a spiritual power or grace. See Martin Holbraad, Amiria Henare, Hoolbrad, and Sari Wastell (eds), *Thinking Through Things: Theorising Artefacts Ethnographically* (Abingdon and New York: Routledge, 2007).
45. Roland Barthes, *La Chambre Claire, Note sur la photographie* (Paris: Gallimard, 1980).
46. André Habib, "Ruin, Archive and the Time of Cinema: Peter Delpeut's 'Lyrical Nitrate'," *SubStance*, 35 (2), 110, 2006, 120–39, 134.
47. Bruno Latour, *Reassembling the Social: An Introduction to Actor Network Theory* (Oxford: Oxford University Press, 2005). Alfred Gell, *Art and Agency: An Anthropological Theory* (Oxford: Oxford University Press, 1998).
48. Jonas Mekas, "The Diary Film", in P. Adams Sitney (ed.), *The Avant-Garde Film: A Reader of Theory and Criticism* (New York: Anthology Film), 190–8, 193. Archives, 1978). Jonas Mekas, Museum Ludwig/Serpentine Gallery (catalogue), Cologne and London: 2009.
49. Guy Debord, *Society of the Spectacle* (Detroit, MI: Black & Red Press, 1983). Kathryn Ramey, "A Word is not Always a Word: Musings about the Film YANQUI WALKER AND THE OPTICAL REVOLUTION," in A. Schneider and C. Wright (eds), *Anthropology and Art Practice*.
50. Hamlyn, *Film Art Phenomena*, 60.
51. Laura Marks, *The Skin of the Film: Intercultural Cinema, Embodiment and the Senses* (Durham, NC: Duke University Press, 2000).
52. Emmanuel Lefrant, "The Visible and the Invisible of a Body under Tension" (2009), see http://lightcone.org/en/film-5833-parties-visible-et-invisible-d-un-ensemble-sous-tension (accessed February 2, 2013).
53. For more on his exhibition project "Unearth" see http://whitney.org/Exhibitions/KarthikPandian (accessed August 13, 2013).
54. Jacques Rancière, "The Surface of Design," in Jacques Rancière, *The Future of the Image*, (London: Verso, 2009), 106.
55. Called by the directors an "hour-long experimental video" (directors' statement, courtesy Brian Karl).
56. From *Ibid.* courtesy Brian Karl.
57. Martino Nicoletti, *The Zoo of the Giraffe Women: A Journey among the Kayan of Northern Thailand* (Kathmandu: Vajra Publications, 2013).
58. A similar argument, in the relation of anthropology to contemporary art, has been made by Arnd Schneider and Christopher Wright, "The Challenge of Practice," in Arnd Schneider and Christopher Wright (eds), *Contemporary Art and Anthropology* (Oxford: Berg, 2006).

2

STILLS THAT MOVE: PHOTOFILM AND ANTHROPOLOGY

Arnd Schneider

Film/Photo: Remarks on an Intrinsic Kinship

Received wisdom seems to suggest that film and photo stand in a relationship of opposites to each other: movement here, stillness there; on the one hand, the succession of sequences, even when they are single shots in filmic montage, on the other hand, the singular composition of the individual image.

Of course, such binary opposites only artificially uphold and reify a boundary between film and photography which, upon closer inspection, does not even remotely do justice to the histories and practices of either field. Historically, photography precedes film and cinema, but experiments to put images into sequential form and "animate" them are similarly ancient, if not older. While photos often consist of a singular image representing a moment of arrested movement or life, they are also sequential (and contextual) in the nature of their displays, in that they are preceded and followed, and indeed are surrounded, by other photos. Leaving aside, for a moment, the digital storage and usage of photos, sequential context is most clearly evident in our practical use of photos in books and journals or magazines, when we flick through them establishing an intended or unintended order, or sequence. This is actually true both when we flick forward or backward, a movement which is sequential but preserves the individual integrity of each photo, and as such is structurally different to a "rewind" operation in analog film or video which disrupts, and in fact reverts the order of movement. Such intrinsic sequentiality (and to some degree contemporaneity of photos as singular frames) becomes also apparent from their narrative use and arrangement when we talk about photos—in anthropological fieldwork, for example, with our research subjects. For instance, among a family of returned emigrants in a Sicilian village I interviewed in 2011, the family photographs were laid out on the table (Figure 2. 1).[1] I then re-photographed them individually, partly guided by the narrative of my interview partners. It was clear that these images were not just isolated shots of arrested movement, but were animated through, and perceived in, sequences through the stories connected to them (not always linear, and not necessarily laid out on the table as such). The intrinsic sequential nature of photographic displays, and the fact that photos have to be animated by narrative, and more mechanically—but linked to this—by movement, is exploited by sequential devices such as the photographic flip book, but also revealed through the sequential order in private photo albums, or slide shows (whether analog or digital), where, in the words of Marcus Banks, "… single images become the repository of sequential but self-contained verbal narratives."[2] In turn, the film or video camera might also be used as a stills camera; as Banks highlights, "[a]mateur videographers, especially infrequent users on holiday, may actually produce material to be read in this way by treating their video camera as a stills camera, to take "shots" of the scenes and places they visit, which are then presumably viewed much as a slide show be viewed."[3]

If movement, and not only arrested movement or life, is inherent in photos (in the plural!), then their physical animation is not only a logical possibility, but rather a consequence, and indeed next practical step. Whereas, analog film is a sequence of images on rolling stock, of 24 frames per second (where, during projection, the

Figure 2.1 Family photographs of Gino Nicastro and Gina Mantione, Sutera, Sicily, 2011 (Photo: Arnd Schneider).

single frame remains imperceptible to the eye),[4] classical animation, on the other hand, is the sequence of deliberately individually composed images filmed as single shots (sometimes they are just double frames, 12 per second) with a rostrum camera, or in camera-less animation drawn directly onto single celluloid frames. In connection to anthropology, we might think of the films of Len Lye here, mixing abstraction and indigenous influences from Australia, New Zealand, Polynesia, and later Africa; and of course, more recently, the seminal work of Robert Ascher featured in Kathryn Ramey's contribution to this book.[5] In both cases, filmed and camera-less animation, the single shot or frame, then, is hypothetically equivalent to a single still photo—but *not* so in photofilm.

Photofilm

To "animate," that is to bestow life, and to give movement which is already inherent in the sequential nature of photographs, is the underlying principle of photofilm, a minor genre and a somewhat arcane visual practice, at the crossroads between film and photography, and which reveals shared principles of, and roots in, animation writ large. The animistic core of photos then is extricated, laid bare, and curiously reanimated through photofilm (defined as the filming in sequence of singular still shots, or photographs). The single frame in film, of course, is not equivalent to a single shot in photofilm: even if the basis for it is indeed a single photograph, as the exposure/duration necessarily is longer than the 1/24th of a second frame in film and can include camera movements of all kinds. In this procedure the photos experience a curious effect of dilation, in that their arrested time, that which made them stills originally, gets extended, almost over-determined in time, an effect which gets further enhanced by filmic effects *sui generis* used in photofilm, such as panning, wiping, and zooming. Film scholar Barbara Filser suggested that such filmic effects in photofilm besiege or harass the photographic essence without completely deleting it.[6] The photos used in photofilm are also doubly exposed (but *not* "double-exposed"), opened onto animated inspection once more after their life as photographic prints (obviously, I am referencing analog vs. digital practices here). The time-medium specific qualities of film–photofilm–photo become also clear when we think about a classic prerequisite to film production, the storyboard which, based on the script, is itself an annotated and preconceived sequence of singular key shots (often hand-drawn) standing in for (and thus representing a fragment of) longer camera takes, or entire scenes which eventually get transposed and made into the final film (through shooting and editing). By contrast, shot-analysis (also called shot breakdown and analysis, or shot-by-shot analysis), a device from film studies, in its printed form reconverts a finished film, for the purposes of analysis and interpretation, into frame-like film stills which again represent longer shots or scenes, this time from the finished film; and so does, curiously, slow-motion both as a creative device and as an analytic tool for the dissection of movement, as explored, for example, in the work of Caterina Pasqualino's film *Bastian et Lorie*.

Notes sur le chant et la danse flamencos (2009).[7] One also can think here of the early experiments with chronophotgraphy, for instance, by Eadweard Muybridge, Étienne-Jules Marey, and Felix-Louis Regnault.

The other reference for photofilm is painting, in its finished form itself a kind of arrested and accreted process (read: life or movement) visible eventually in a single "frame," or canvas. Indeed painting, as a subject, is at the core of what are conventionally regarded as the first fully developed photofilms, *Van Gogh* (1948), and *Guernica* (1950) by Alain Resnais. Both works already contain as hallmarks the formal, stylistic devices of later photofilms, such as zooming, wiping, and panning over photos, as well as fading in and out. Certainly, there had been previous usage of still sequences within moving pictures (film), or experimenting both with setting into motion of stills and the freezing of motion, to paraphrase film scholar Thomas Tode, who mentions Sergei Eistenstein's *Strike* (1925), and Dziga Vertov's *Man with a Movie Camera* (1928/9) as examples.[8]

Remarking on another famous film from this period, Susan Sontag captures well the life–death, animate–inanimate, moving–still tensions which power the two, only seemingly separate genres of film and photography, that lie at the heart of these and later experiments:

> Some working-class Berliners in Robert Siodmak's film *Menschen am Sonntag* (1929) are having their pictures taken at the end of a Sunday outing. One by one they step before the itinerant photographer's black box—grin, look anxious, clown, stare. The movie camera lingers in close-up to let us savor the mobility of each face; then we see the face frozen in the last of its expressions, embalmed in a still. The photographs shock, in the flow of the movie—transmuting, in an instant, present into past, life into death. And one of the most disquieting films ever made, Chris Marker's *La Jetée* (1963), is the tale of a man who forsees his own death—narrated entirely with still photographs.[9]

Except, we should add, for one scene in the middle, where a girl's eyes open in the morning, which was shot with a movie camera. *La Jetée* is rightly seen as a seminal achievement in this genre, and perhaps can count as its example par excellence. Chris Marker, of course, had been a collaborator in Alain Resnais's early photofilms (and so had another film-maker, Agnès Varda), and thus he was familiar with the technique. He calls his film a *photo-roman*, or "photo-novel," and the experiments with time and disruption of linear narrative from literature come to mind here (such as in the *noveau roman*, or in Julio Cortázar's *Rayuela* [*Hopscotch*], published first in 1963). Thomas Tode writes: "[the] reference system [for *La Jetée*] is precisely not linearity, chronology, and movement, but ambiguous parallel worlds, the frenzy of different layers of time[s], and the painfully extended duration [of the film] with a contemporaneous formal lack of movement."[10] For Chris Marker, then, time conceived of as the duration of the film, and not movement, is the principal concern.

Photofilm, in sum, does not create or pretend the illusion of movement, but incites temporal and mental movement for the viewer.

Sensibilities of the Ethnographic between Photography and Ethnopoetry: The Photofilms of Leonore Mau and Hubert Fichte

Because of their consecutive lining up of still images, photofilms, even when they *narrate* through image order and voice, always question (and push up against) the illusionary time-creating character of mainstream narrative film. In this, they are implicitly close to the preoccupations of experimental film-makers, interested in making visible and perceptible the conditions of the film-making process itself (for instance, by focusing on the apparatus, i.e. the camera, projector, and film, as material).[11] Exploring the potentials and limits of "pure perception" as offered by photography has also been attributed to the work of writer Hubert Fichte[12] and his partner, the photographer Leonore Mau. Their genre transcending collaborations included literature, photography, photo (film), and radioplay. Fichte was an important writer in Germany from the mid–1960s till his death in 1986, although with an outsider status because of his homosexuality, experimental writing style, and subjects, often anthropological, such as his extensive writings on Afro-American religions, challenging genres of both the scientific study and the novel. Fichte's work has often been described as ethnopoetry, but it really defies genre categorizations.[13] Leonore Mau, a photographer 19 years his senior, had left her married life and family in 1961 to live with Fichte. Both published work in their own right, with Fichte the much better known, public figure on the German literary scene, and Mau experiencing a further reappraisal of her work since his death. Together, Leonore Mau and Hubert Fichte are mainly known for the large-format photo-books resulting from their joint travels in the Americas and Africa.[14] However, preceding their transatlantic explorations into Afro-American religions, Fichte and Mau had already travelled extensively in Europe, and also visited North Africa in the 1960s.

The ethnographic sensibility characteristic for their later transatlantic work is, in fact, already present in a number of photofilms which were commissioned from Mau and Fichte by German television stations,[15] sympathetic to formal experimentation in the latter part of the 1960s. The first of these describes the "day of a casual dock worker" (from the title, i.e. *Der Tag eines unständigen Hafenarbeiters*, 1966) in the Hamburg harbor. We first see close-ups of the unnamed dockworker engaging in a variety of activities, such as washing himself, eating, blowing his nose, and smoking. This is followed by a sequence of photos, which almost have the character of index cards, and point to an absent subject (recounted in Fichte's spoken narrative) who for the most part is visualized through objects assuming an anonymous third-person status and in this is similar to other people, later in the film, such as his work mates, and also foremen and the boss who hired them. These objects—which are shown in close detail—are the personal belongings of the dockworker, the utensils in his humble flat, as well as the special working tools needed in the docks (before the container age) to unload coal, coffee, bananas, sunflower and peanut expeller. Through this procedure the dockworker (though briefly introduced through the close-up at the start of the film) is effectively de-personified, with things standing in for him, and pointing to the alienating nature of the work in the docks (cf. Figure 2.2). In terms of visual effect, this sequence anticipates Sophie Calle's artwork *The Hotel* (1981), resulting from her work as a chambermaid, when she intruded into the private sphere of unknown hotel guests photographing their rooms and personal belongings. Later in the photofilm, however, the flow of still images is interrupted three times by movie sequences: first, a TV clip of a soccer match showing the Hamburg soccer club, HSV, with German national soccer star Uwe Seeler (soccer games being one of the obvious distraction for the dockers), then a short TV clip from an advert showing a joyous and playful middle class couple enjoying beer whilst playing Ping-Pong—a world far removed from the cramped conditions in the dockworker's flat. After that, the film returns to still sequences focusing on the precariousness of work, with working conditions meticulously described, as are the places of cheap entertainment after work, such as the pubs and bars in Hamburg's port and nearby Reeperbahn district, including the famous Star Club (to which another short moving sequence is dedicated). The film ends by showing Heidi, the dockworker's wife, breast-feeding their baby.

The research for the film and photo shoots was done by Leonore Mau over several weeks, whilst Fichte was at home bed-stricken with hepatitis. A curious working relationship developed between the two, where the writer/ethnopoet/ethnographer was confined to bed, and his photographer-companion doubled as ethnographer. In an interview with Gerd Roscher in 2005, Mau mentioned that Fichte had told her: "You need 500 photos for 20 minutes of film. Now you can go out every day [and shoot], and when you come back, you'll cook mashed potatoes for me."[16] Mau immersed herself in the milieu of the dockworkers, and took stills of them every morning when they went to the "auction," to be hired. She could not photograph the auction itself. Only after she had gained the trust of the boss in the hiring office, who accompanied her, was she able to get personal contact with one family—that of the dockworker shown in the film. She continued:

> I also had to go on a ship. As I arrived with a small launch, I had to go up the ship on a rusty ladder; one camera was dangling in front the other in the back. … And I had vertigo, but suddenly I was on the ship, in between sacks of sugar, and I don't know what. Then I really was at work, and I enjoyed that. I don't know how many hours I was on the ship. And I had to come back down again. But I managed without falling into the [river] Elbe.[17]

However, in a way, we might say, Fichte did not need to be there with her; he intimately knew the world of the Hamburg harbor, and especially the places of after-work amusement, such as the Reeperbahn, Hamburg's red light district. He also had very clear ideas about how to make a film, and animation directors of photography at German TV stations were surprised at, and appreciated, the precision of the instructions in his storyboards (cf. Figure 2.2). Fichte's writing

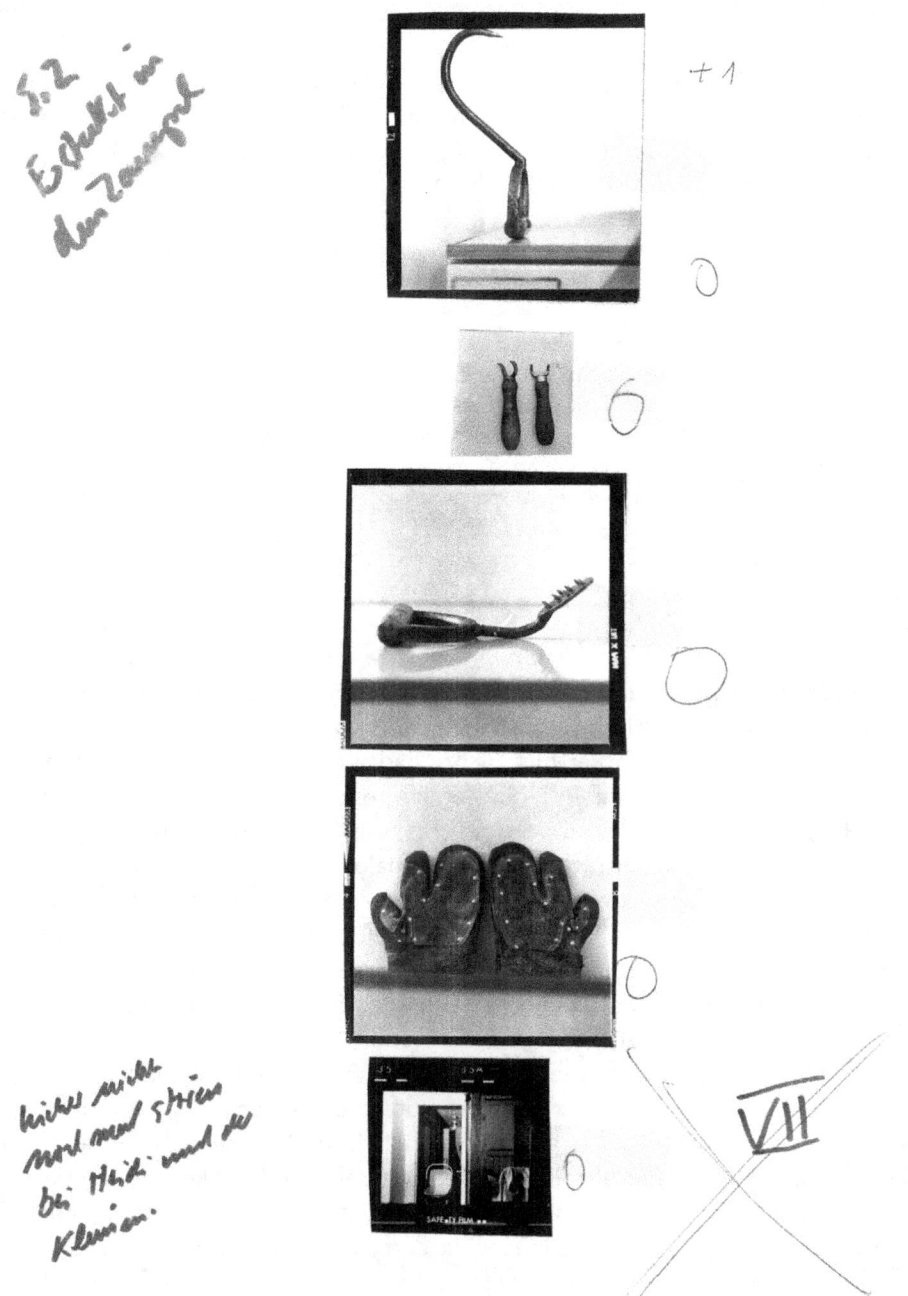

Figure 2.2 Leonore Mau and Hubert Fichte, *Der Tag eines unständigen Hafenarbeiters* (storyboard), 1966. By kind permission and courtesy of Stiftung F. C. Gundlach and S. Fischer Stiftung.

styles have been likened to filmic montage and he acknowledged being influenced by John Dos Passos's narrative mode of "Newsreels," that is the collages of newspaper cuttings and song lyrics, in the *U.S.A. Trilogy* (1938) (another narrative mode for Dos Passos was called the "Camera Eye").[18] Importantly, for the photofilms Mau shot stills different than in her previous photographic work, and also appreciated Fichte's obvious talent at the genre:

> It's completely different when one takes photos one by one as singular images, or when one makes photos for a film. There are photos I would never make, if it wasn't for a film. For instance, the woman in the dockworkers film who stands in a very humble kitchen and makes sandwiches for her husband. (...) One thinks more in sequences, and considers things important, which I wouldn't include in an ordinary photo. Hubert [Fichte] then adjusted the texts to the time of the duration of the film. He wrote on the back of each photo how long it should appear in the film, for example, five seconds. I don't know where he had this knowledge from. People were enthusiastic. In the animation studio of Norddeutscher Rundfunk [cf. note 15] a camera was suspended from above [i.e. an animation camera], and below were the photos, and they released the shutter, so and so many seconds. And that then resulted in the film.[19]

Their next photofilm, *Der Fischmarkt und die Fische* (*The Fish Market and the Fish*, 1968), made two years later, retained Hubert Fichte's strong authorial voice, expressing robust social criticism of living conditions in a Portuguese fishing town. But whereas in the dockworker film Fichte had used almost exclusively the third person to speak about his subject (and only later switched to the second person "you"), he now addressed his subject, a fisherman in the Portuguese fishing town of Sesimbra (Cezimbra), with the seemingly dialogical "you." The film opens with an overhead establishing shot of the fish market, and then describes the living and working conditions of the fishermen. Image and commentary are deliberately out of joint, and create a tension between what is seen (shown) and what is heard (spoken). As the film proceeds, the narrator (i.e. Fichte) becomes more personal and even asks the (fictional) fisherman a question: "Why are you telling me this?" In this latter part of the film, the narrator, a writer of fiction after all, also creates several possibilities or scenarios for his protagonist when commenting on the fisherman's future prospects, in respect of marriage, migration, work, and army draft. The final part of the film is a challenging collage of spoken descriptions on the intricacies of political life, abuse, torture, and being drafted for the colonial war Salazar's regime was then waging in Angola, and close-ups of a large number of fish, superficially showing their great variety and strangeness as animals to the North European viewer, but on a deeper level metaphorically suggesting the bestiality of humans in an authoritarian society (Figure 2.3).

Zwei mal 45 Bilder/Sätze aus Agadir (*Two times 45 images/Sentences from Agadir*) from 1971 is conceptual in the title and also in the structural make-up. Its raw material stems from a visit Mau and Fichte made to the Moroccan seaside town in

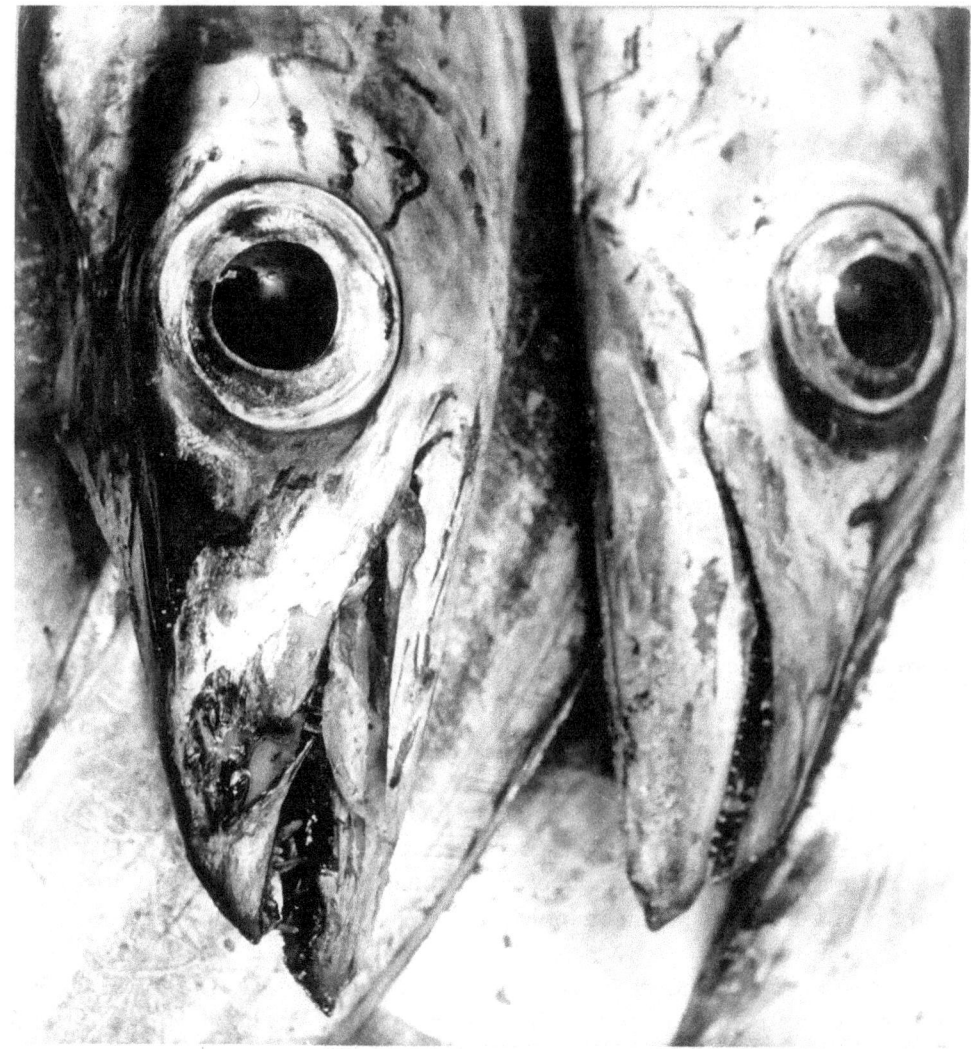

Figure 2.3 Leonore Mau and Hubert Fichte, *Der Fischmarkt und die Fische* (source still), 1968. By kind permission and courtesy of Stiftung F. C. Gundlach and S. Fischer Stiftung.

1968, which had been devastated by a disastrous earthquake in 1960. Their main focus in this photofilm is the reconstructed "modern" city on the one hand, and the continuing precarious living conditions and bleak opportunities of the inhabitants on the other. Commentary is by the narrator's first person, who assumes the position of an inhabitant of Agadir (using material from interviews and conversations), and is spoken exactly over the images of the areas reconstructed in modernist architecture, providing an intended and stark contrast to the images of Agadir residents, over which texts from glossy brochures and propaganda of the public administration

Figure 2.4 Leonore Mau and Hubert Fichte, *Zwei mal 45 Bilder/Sätze aus Agadir* (source still), 1971. By kind permission and courtesy of Stiftung F. C. Gundlach and S. Fischer Stiftung.

glorifying the reconstruction are spoken by a second narrator (Figure 2.4 and Figure 2.5). This simple, but effective device achieves a very contrastive black-and-white effect of image and text, and is, of course, familiar from 1920s and 1930s political montage, in both film and the graphic arts.[20] While the photofilms by Fichte and Mau retain a strong authorial voice, this is not to be confused with the off-screen, "voice of God." The sequences of the images in their films are both set in rhythmic counterpoint to themselves and to the spoken text, propel the films forward, and continuously unsettle a unified authorial voice and photographer's gaze.

Photofilm as Narrated Evidence: John Haviland's Australian Research Films

Whilst stills and moving images are at the center of the discipline of visual anthropology, the hybrid practice of photofilm hardly has received attention, and few have explored the genre practically or theoretically so far.[21] An exception—and there might be more—is *Making Gambarr* (2009) by John Haviland, a distinguished linguistic anthropologist at the University of California at San Diego, which is based on his black-and-white photos from fieldwork in Australia in 1977 and interviews recorded later, in 1983. In contrast to the films by Fichte and Mau, in *Making Gambarr* the voice of his research subjects in conversation with Haviland is used to guide us through the images and their particular subject, that is the fabrication of

Figure 2.5 Leonore Mau and Hubert Fichte, *Zwei mal 45 Bilder/Sätze aus Agadir* (source still), 1971. By kind permission of Stiftung F. C. Gundlach and S. Fischer Stiftung. Image courtesy of Katja Pratschke.

gambarr (a particular tar made from ironbark roots, used as a kind of glue to make spears called *womeras*). This detailed conversation also brings "alive" the persons in the photos (they having passed away by the time of the recording in 1983) and in the recordings (their brothers, having passed away by the time the photofilm was made in 2009).

Haviland explains the process in some detail:

> In about 1977, at their request, I accompanied a couple of old men (one my fictive "father" in the community) to make the "traditional" tar (from the root of the ironbark tree) used as a kind of glue to make spears, wommeras, etc. The old men were among the last still to go out into the bush to make it, and whatever quantities they made were quickly snapped up by younger men who wanted the spears for hunting and fishing. I shot several rolls of film with my old Nikon and promptly put them away and forgot about them. By 1983 or so, both of those old men had died, and one day I printed out some of the photos and sat down with two of their surviving brothers to look at them and talk about them (a process we continued

for several weeks). We had the vague idea that we would make a little booklet for the school, and we recorded several hours of conversation about that idea, as we looked at the pictures. (The conversation was in the peculiar mixture of Guugu Ylmithirr and somewhat archaic and elegant English that men who grew up at the mission in the teens and 1920s used.) In the end, both of those men also died before I could proceed and sometime in the mid 1980s—in fact at Tim Asch's [22] urging, when we were colleagues at ANU, and he wanted to mount some of our ethnographic photos on the walls of the anthropology department—I put together a photo sequence of the gambarr-making process with a text, extracted from the tape recorded conversations, all in (a somewhat artificial) "pure" Guugu Yimithirr for an event in the Anthropology Dept. That, at the time, was that.

In 2009 (...) I traveled to Hopevale with a large amount of old audio visual material which I intended to "repatriate." I had digitized all of my surviving old photographs, and quite a bit of audio and video (originally old sound film) material, too. I decided in preparation for the trip to try combining my old photos of the Gambarr-making process with an edited audiotape drawn from the recorded conversations with the two brothers of the deceased tar makers. The idea was to encourage people—especially my fictive kinsmen whose ancestors the people in both pictures and audio were—to think about the past, about the way old people used to talk, about sharing knowledge (and images), and new ways to do it. I also wanted to try my hand in putting this stuff together in a filmic form. I edited the audio, then edited it together with the photos using Adobe Premiere. At Hopevale I showed the result to my kinsmen, with somewhat mixed and politically ambivalent results. During the three weeks we spent in the community I also decided to try taking old recordings of the tales I had published decades before—but this time in the original Guugu Yimithirr and not in English—and subtitling them over panned photos of the original paintings from that early book.

(Haviland, personal communication, February 29, 2012)

Haviland's extensive testimony is instructive not only about the meticulous ethnographic methods employed, but also about the transfer from analog source material (the original stills photographs) to a digital photofilm format. While photo elicitation, the discussion of photographs with research subjects (which Haviland used in the conversation recorded in 1983), is a standard research method (with many variations) in the social sciences, including specialized sub-disciplines of visual sociology and visual anthropology, photofilms, on the other hand, have hardly been explored as a research tool in the way de Haviland does—although this might change in the future because of the now wide availability of specific software (e.g. Adobe Photoshop), and also the ubiquity of and familiarity with sequential image presentation in digital formats (e.g. PowerPoint).

Movement in this photofilm here is *within* and *without* the photographs, through the precise recording of arrested action, and the formal-stylistic devices Haviland uses to focus on the materials and working processes he and his research subjects are interested in (Figure 2.6). Haviland uses to subtle effect zooming and panning across, or down, the photographs to emphasize details of material or of the particular person(s), addressed or speaking at that moment in the narrative (soundtrack). The so-called "Ken Burns effect", which is actually named after the renowned American documentarian, who made the technique famous in his grand depictions of American history, e.g. *The Civil War* (1990), or of iconic practices, such as *Baseball* (1994), can now easily be achieved with computer programs. Burns, as he himself admitted, was not the first to use the technique now largely associated with his name (he mentions photographer and film-maker Jerome Liebling as his influence)[23], and we have of course seen earlier in this essay how Alain Resnais already had used it in his films on painters, and presumably it has been around as long as stills and freeze frames were used in film, sometimes for entire sequences.

We could perhaps at this point ask what the possible benefits of photofilm are for anthropological research; or, put otherwise, what can such a (photo) film achieve beyond moving film images in visual anthropology film and video production, and where lies the advantage of stills used in moving sequences? More discussion, not least among practitioners, on this is needed, but one advantage is certainly that the eye can rest longer on individual scenes and explore details (similar in this to slow motion) than would have been the case with incessantly moving images.

Figure 2.6 Still image from *Making Gambarr*, John Haviland, USA, 2009. Courtesy of John Haviland.

Visual Poetry and Sonic Collage: Dick Blau's *A Polish Easter in Chicago*

My third example is *A Polish Easter in Chicago* (2011) by Dick Blau, an acclaimed stills photographer, and professor of film at the University of Wisconsin, Milwaukee, as well as a collaborator in a number of books with anthropologist Steven Feld.[24] The stills for *A Polish Easter in Chicago* were taken during a three-day Easter Service among the Polish community in Chicago in 2005. Narrative voiceover, interview, or recorded conversation, on the other hand, are entirely dispensed with, and instead we have a collage of sounds from the Good Friday service in 2005, and the Easter Sunday service in 2011.

We could say that by using photofilm as his genre, rather than film, Blau halts the ceremony for the eye through the stills, only newly to be woven together through the choice of position in sequence, and the soundtrack recorded at the liturgy, recorded at different times, as well as several times overlaid atmospheric or "presence tracks", to convey a "… living breathing coughing world filled with people, bodies, and echoes."[25] Furthermore, his strategy of letting individual photos speak to us, concurrent with movement as sound, allows us to focus more precisely on individuals, their faces, expressions, gestures, the things they wear, than would have been the case with a continuously moving picture (Figure 2.7). Of course, sound here is not an "objective," reified underlying sound (for example, in the form of prerecorded religious music), but the sonic source is the "real" sound recorded at the event, which then gets worked through in a collage of actual liturgy, and atmospheric sound both inside and outside the church (including birdsong, which Blau uses several times). We have to remind ourselves here that sound both creates space and is placed in space, in other words, it creates spatial imagination. In no way thus is the sound recording just an objective, or perhaps not even representative sonic depiction of this mass, but only one possibility, among many (indeed of the many participating members of the congregation), telling us as much about the placement or location of sound recordist and equipment, as about the auditory experience of the religious ceremony. Although sound is concurrent to the flow of photos, we can also say with film scholar Gunnar Iversen that it "emerges" from the photo.[26] Blau uses close-ups, frequent quick fading between pictures, and blurred photographs achieved through longer exposure times. In this photofilm the photos, part of a temporally structured, and forward moving ceremony, themselves instill motion, rather than being threatened by motion,[27] or moving pictures being needed to achieve the impression of movement.

Dick Blau writes on the background:

> The subject itself comes from two sources. After we finished *Polka Happiness*,[28] I did some sporadic shooting in Chicago, something I called Three Polonias, which looked at the performance of identity and culture/class desire in three different parts of the community. That developed for me into an idea for a book that would be called Polonia USA, a study of Polish Chicago. (…) [The project] comes for me out of an interest in theater as much as in ethnography. I grew up in a theater and (…)

I have always been interested in exploring its roots in demotic performance. The idea to make this series as both a set of stills and also as a film was there from the beginning. I've always loved optical printing in 16mm film—see *Tintinnabula*[29]—because it opens up a world (and a time) between the still and the moving image that I find fascinating to explore. In this case, I thought it was a perfect way to both tell and ponder the story—not to speak of creating a new picture between the two that were dissolving—and yet still keep moving the story forward. As for the sound, I loved Steve Feld's sound pieces for *Bright Balkan Morning and Skyros Carnival*, so it just seemed natural to bring someone to record when I went down to Chicago to shoot. I shot using two cameras. For one set I used a 4 megapixel canon with a silent shutter and what I realize now was the world's most discrete focus beam; for the other I used a Canon 20d. The first thing I did was to have a friend photoshop the pictures, then we imported them and the sound into Final Cut Pro.

(Dick Blau, personal communication, February 26, 2012)

Figure 2.7 Still image from *A Polish Easter in Chicago*, Dick Blau, USA, 2011. Courtesy of Dick Blau.

Blau's photofilm is a way of describing, analysing, and understanding religious ritual, not through the continuous filming of action in movement, nor in the segmentation through single photographic shots, but through the reassembly of single frames into subjective, and sound-built and guided sequences. In this, by focusing on the experiential and subjective character of ritual, Blau's approach resonates with some experimental writing on religious festivals; for instance, by

Richard Swiderski, whose superb treatment of the festival of the patron saint of Italo-Americans in Gloucester, Massachusetts, sets the observer into a dialogic relation to the different participants of the festival, switching viewpoints continuously, and contemplating different scenarios of participation and observation and, ultimately, refusing a unitary interpretive voice.[30] It is this kind of dialogical principle which is evolved through Blau's rendering of the Easter Services, in that each image is opened up to inspection, taken out of the flow of movement of both ceremonial sequence (and implicit filmic representation), only to attain a new movement of its own.

Conclusions

Anthropologists make both moving images and still photos—in the digital age often within the same device. Our review of a number of experiments with photofilm has demonstrated the potentials for anthropology, in both practical and theoretical terms, of the still image beyond its singular significance as an index of arrested movements. Through their "renanimation" in photofilm, both visual and sonic, stills attain the status of twice-lived material objects.

This emerges clearly from the ethnopoetic photofilms of Mau and Fichte, but also, and perhaps unexpectedly, from Haviland's research films which provide a detail of inspection for the specific techniques pertaining to the manufacture of an indigenous implement, in a way a "movie" might not have been able, or at least only in different ways, to provide—enhanced also by the detailed recorded conversation. In rather different ways it also applies in terms of poetic evocation to Blau's photofilm of the Polish American Easter services. Moreover, the examples discussed also underscore the great variety of stylistic, methodic, and theoretical potential available to photofilm. For Mau and Fichte photofilms were carefully planned and had to convey a strong political message through an original and poetic combination of text/commentary and image sequences. Haviland's photofilm was made digitally from analog stills initially not intended for this purpose, but which post hoc turned out to be very congenial to this genre, and in fact in this way reveal more than as single images. Blau's photofilm, finally, arrests the seamless unfolding of a religious ceremony, to allow the viewer to come "in-between" and "within" an otherwise unremitting ritual. Concurrently, all these photofilms, as does photofilm in general, arguably point to the common roots of animation—if not animism[31]—for both film and photography: they lay bare the now lifeless "souls" of photographs, and reanimate them through the sound and movement of film.

Filmography

A Polish Easter in Chicago, dir. Dick Blau, USA, 2011, 10 mins.

Baseball (TV series), dir. Ken Burns, USA, 1994, 1140 mins.
Bastian et Lorie. Notes sur le chant et la danse flamencos, dir. Caterina Pasqualino, Paris: CNRS, 2009, 20 mins.
Der Fischmarkt und die Fische, dirs. Leonore Mau and Hubert Fichte, Germany, 1968, 9 mins.
Der Tag eines unständigen Hafenarbeiters, dirs. Leonore Mau and Hubert Fichte, Germany, 1966, 13 mins.
Guernica, dirs. Alain Resnais and Robert Hessens, France, 1950, 13 mins.
La Jetée, dir. Chris Marker, France, 1962, 28 mins.
Making Gambarr, dir. John Haviland, USA, 2009, 13 mins.
Menschen am Sonntag, dirs. Robert Siodmak and Edgar G. Ulmer, Germany, 1930, 74 mins.
Strike, Sergei Eistenstein, Soviet Union, 1925, 82 mins.
The Civil War (TV series), dir. Ken Burns, USA, 1990, 690 mins.
The Man with the Movie Camera, dir. Dziga Vertov, Soviet Union, 1929, 68 mins.
Tintinnabula, dirs. Dick Blau and Dawn Wiedemann, 1986, USA, 8 mins.
Van Gogh, dir. Alain Resnais, France, 1948, 19 mins.
Zwei Mal 45 Bilder/Sätze aus Agadir, dirs. Leonore Mau and Hubert Fichte, Germany, 1971, 13 mins.

Notes

1. I did fieldwork in Sicily in the mid-1980s, and have kept in touch with a number of families since, see my *Emigration und Rückwanderung von "Gastarbeitern" in einem sizilianischen Dorf* [Migration and Return Migration of "Guest Workers" in a Sicilian Village] (Frankfurt, Berne, and New York: Peter Lang Verlag, 1990).
2. Marcus Banks, *Visual Methods in Social Research* (London: Sage, 2001), 23.
3. Ibid.
4. 24 fps is the standard frame rate, other frame rates, of course, also exist(ed).
5. For example in his hand-painted film *Tusalava* (1929); see also Roger Harrocks, *Len Lye: A Biography* (Auckland: Auckland University Press, 2002) and *Art that Moves: The Work of Len Lye* (Auckland: Auckland University Press, 2009).
6. Filser was commenting specifically on Chris Marker's *La Jetée*, 1962, on which more further on; see Barbara Filser, *Chris Marker und die Ungewissheit der Bilder* (Munich: Wilhelm Fink, 2010), 184.
7. See also her "In Praise of Slow Motion," in Arnd Schneider and Christopher Wright (eds), *Anthropology and Art Practice* (London: Bloomsbury, 2013).
8. Thomas Tode, "Kurze Geschichte des Stillbildes im Film," in Gusztáv Hámos, Katja Pratschke, and Thomas Tode (eds), *Viva Fotofilm: Bewegt/unbewegt* (Marburg: Schüren, 2010), 17.
9. Susan Sontag, *On Photography* (London: Penguin, 2008 [1971]), 70–1. Another famous reference to the still sequences in *Menschen am Sonntag* is in Rudolf Arnheim's *Film as Art* (1959 [1932]), section on the use of stills.
10. Tode, Thomas, "Filme aus Fotografien: Plädoyer für eine Bastardisierung," *Viva Fotofilm: Bewegt/unbewegt*, in Gusztáv Hámos, Katja Pratschke, and Thomas Tode (eds) (Marburg: Schüren, 2010), 31; all translations from German in this and subsequent quotes are mine.

11. A. L. Rees, *A History of Experimental Film and Video* (2nd edn), (London: BFI and Basingstoke: Palgrave Macmillan, 2011); Malcolm Le Grice, *Experimental Cinema in the Digital Age* (London: BFI Publications, 2006); Nicky Hamlyn, *Film Art Phenomena* (London: BFI, 2003); in relation to anthropology, Arnd Schneider, "Expanded Visions: Rethinking Anthropological Research and Representation through Experimental Film," in Tim Ingold (ed.), *Redrawing Anthropology: Materials, Movements, Lines* (Aldgate: Ashgate, 2011).
12. See Denise Fragner, *Links davon das Morgenrot Sehen, Subjekt und Sinnlichkeit im Werk des Ethnologen und Schriftstellers Hubert Fichte*, Mag.Phil. thesis, University of Vienna, 2010, from http://othes.univie.ac.at/10142/ (accessed May 13, 2013).
13. Certainly, Fichte was well read in anthropology, publishing, among other things, a very critical appraisal of Claude Lévi-Strauss's *Triste Tropique*, and a critique of anthropology more generally, see, for example, Hubert Fichte, "Das Land des Lächelns: Polemische Anmerkungen zu 'Tristes Tropiques' von Claude Lévi-Strauss," *Literaturmagazin*, 13 (1980), 87–166; and "Heretical Remarks Concerning a New Science of Man" (English version of a lecture first held at the Frobenius Institute, Frankfurt, January 12, 1977), in *Object Atlas: Fieldwork in the Museum*, ed. Clémentine Deliss (Frankfurt am Main: Weltkulturen Museum, 2012). He also maintained loose contact with a number of German anthropology departments, but his work was generally shunned and not considered by a conservative anthropology establishment in the 1970s, despite the fact that Fichte published a few articles in a small-circulation journal of medical anthropology, *Ethnomedizin*.
14. *Xango: Die Afroamerikanischen Religionen. Bahia. Tahiti. Trinidad* (1976), followed by *Petersilie: Die afroamerikanischen Religionen III. Santo Domingo Venezuela Miami Grenada* (1980). *Psyche*, the last photo-book, based on travels in West Africa and research into mental illness and psychiatric institutions, was published only in 2005, Fichtes's text had appeared already in 1990. From the travels Fichte also published separate work in a hybrid style of novel, research report, and travel journal. These publications were integrated into his *opus magnum Die Geschichte der Empfindlichkeit* [The History of Sensibility], a cycle of 19 planned novels (17 published altogether, many of them posthumously). Fichte has had a certain attention in queer literary studies, but, overall, little of his work has been translated into English, and most critical work remains in German. His anthropological work still awaits a full appraisal in any language.
15. Mau and Fichte gained commissions from Norddeutscher Rundfunk (NDR), and Westdeutscher Rundfunk (WDR).
16. Gerd Roscher, "Fotofilm—man denkt in Abfolgen: Ein Gespräch mit Leonore Mau," in Gusztáv Hámos, Katja Pratschke, and Thomas Tode (eds) *Viva Fotofilm: Bewegt/unbewegt* (Marburg: Schüren, 2010), 293.
17. Roscher, "Fotofilm," 292–3.
18. See Denise Fragner, *Links davon das Morgenrot Sehen, Subjekt und Sinnlichkeit im Werk des Ethnologen und Schriftstellers Hubert Fichte*, Mag.Phil. thesis, University of Vienna, 2010, 54, see http://othes.univie.ac.at/10142/ (accessed May 13, 2013).
19. Roscher, Fotofilm, 294.
20. Mau's and Fichte's radical deconstruction of the modernizing impetus motivating the post-earthquake reconstruction of Agadir invites comparison with, and reference to, critical anthropological work on French modernist town planning and architecture in Morocco, see Paul Rabinow, *French Modern: Norms and Forms of the Social Environment* (Chicago, IL: University of Chicago Press, 1989), especially ch. 9, "Techno-Cosmopolitanism: Governing Morocco," 277–319.
21. Of course, a number of visual anthropologists, Peter Biella foremost (but also Jay Ruby, Roderick Coover, and others), have experimented with interactive hypertext, of embedding and linking up

still images, film/video clips and text in hypertext environments for educational purposes. For an example, see P. Biella, N. A. Chagnon, and G. Seaman, *Yanomamo Interactive: The Ax Fight* (Watertown, MA: Eastgate, 1999). For a comparative study of the hypertext projects, see Rulon Matley Wood, *Hypertext and Ethnographic Representation*, Ph.D., University of Utah, Department of Communication, 2011.
22. The reference is to Timothy Asch (1932–94), the famous ethnographic film-maker.
23. See Wikipedia entry "Ken Burns Effect," from https://en.wikipedia.org/wiki/Ken_Burns_effect (accessed May 17, 2013).
24. See Charles Keil, Angeliki V. Keil, and Dick Blau, *Polka Happiness* (Philadelphia, PA: Temple University Press, 1992); Jane Gallopp (photography by Dick Blau), *Living with his Camera* (Durham, NC: Duke University Press, 2003); Dick Blau, Charles Keil, Angeliki Vellou Keil, and Steven Feld, *Bright Balkan Mornings: Romani Lives and the Power of Music in Greek Macedonia* (Middletown, CT: Wesleyan University Press, 2002); Dick Blau, Agapi Amanatidis, Panayotis Panopoulos, and Steven Feld, *Skyros Carnival* (Santa Fe, NM: VoxLox, 2010).
25. Dick Blau, personal communication, March 24, 2013.
26. Gunnar Iversen, "Added Value: The Role of Sound in Documentary Film Theory," in Gunnar Iversen and Jan Ketil Simonsen (eds), *Beyond the Visual: Sound and Image in Ethnographic and Documentary Film* (Højbjerg, Denmark: Intervention Press, 2010). More generally, on the significance of sound in film, see Michel Chion, *Audio Vision—Sound on Screen* (New York: Columbia University Press, 1994), and also the chapter by Kevin T. Allen and Jennifer Heuson in this volume.
27. See Filser's observation, mentioned earlier in this chapter (p. 27), on the harassing or besieging effect of motion on stills in the genre of photofilm (see also note 6).
28. Cf. note 24.
29. *Tintinnabula*, Dick Blau and Dawn Wiedemann, 8 mins, 16mm, color/sound, USA, 1986.
30. See Richard M. Swiderski, *Voices: An Anthropologist's Dialogue with an Italian-American Festival* (London, Ontario/Bowling Green, OH: Centre for Humanistic Studies/University of Western Ontario/Bowling Green University Popular Press, 1986), especially ch. 9, "Consummation."
31. Animism, as belief, practice, and indeed analytic device, has recently had a renaissance both in anthropology (the theories of Philippe Descola, for instance), and in the contemporary arts—for example, an exhibition curated by Anselm Franke. Cf. Philippe Descola, *Beyond Nature and Culture* (Chicago, IL: University of Chicago Press, 2013); *Animism*, Vol. 1, (ed. Anselm Franke). (Berlin and New York: Sternberg Press, 2010).

3

EXPERIMENTAL FILM, TRANCE AND NEAR-DEATH EXPERIENCES

Caterina Pasqualino

Experimental film puts the spectator strongly to the test. By accelerating or slowing down time, intensifying images or sounds, or conjuring hallucinatory figures, it disrupts our visual perception and our understanding of the world. This is particularly interesting in relation to anthropological research. The worlds of experimental film and trance point toward fantasies of the afterlife that share many common points.

Although there had been previous anthropological studies, the first major debates on trance date back to the late 1950s with the publication of three books now considered seminal references: *Le vaudou haïtien* by Alfred Metraux, *Le Candomblé de Bahia* by Roger Bastide, and *La Possession et ses aspects théâtraux* by Michel Leiris.[1] In subsequent decades, one sees a tendency to relegate trance rituals to an instinctive ability, which, according to the authors, is characterized by an innate disposition, automatism, or conditioned reflex. Further research in social anthropology approaches rituals with a touch of functionalism, by evaluating how they can resolve tension between individuals, groups, or social classes. For others, anthropology articulates mythological or symbolic exegeses.[2] In addition, it delineates such categories as possession rituals, shamanic rituals, trance, and mystical ecstasy. The distinction has sometimes been pushed even further, separating them in terms of cultural areas. For example, in African rituals of obedience possession, "overlapping" topics were considered passive because they were tributaries of powers from the afterlife, while in Euro-Asian shamanisms, trances were perceived as active: shamans, even if their visions returned to inner travels, were meant to remain masters of their destiny.[3]

Generally speaking, one flaw in these ideas is that anthropologists have been referred exclusively to the externalized aspects of ritual performance at the expense of an individual's inner life. In particular, researchers have paid little attention to a ritual's beginning and end. Of course, these confused, unpredictable phases are inconsistent with a perfectly ordered protocol, and are therefore difficult to describe. Yet they correspond to moments that are crucial to understanding trance. They mark an individual's shift from shared understanding to "paranormal" perception and, conversely, to his or her return to the common world. My contribution here consists of examining the process that gives a subject access to a vision of the afterlife. Along the way, we will explore a universe that has still been little addressed by anthropologists: the testimony of individuals who have had near-death experiences and who have reported their pre-mortem visions. More importantly, this will lead us to address similarities between the worlds of trance and experimental film which so far have not been explored.

The *palo monte*

In 2009, when I began my research in Cuba on an Afro-Cuban religion called *palo monte*, I noticed that believers, generally black and from the poorest strata of Cuban society, are thought to be giving in to "savage impulses."[4] True, the possessed adopt some surprising attitudes. Their voices can suggest bestiality, and at times one finds them prostrate on the ground in sacrificial blood.[5]

The Cuban population is subject to rules by an authoritarian government that causes *palo monte* followers to suffer so that they want to flee. The most desperate try to leave the island illegally, usually without success. As a last resort, it seems, they escape in their minds, outside socialized time and space. By taking on voices perceived as ancient and distant, *palo monte* followers invest in an afterlife inhabited by chthonic powers, the dead.[6] Forgetting their poverty and their daily lives allows them to change their frame of mind and, at times, to avoid going mad.

Adherents rely on proven techniques to go outside themselves. The preliminary stage is crucial. It takes place in a collective atmosphere charged with intense emotion. Groups can remain for long hours, jammed into the dark, suffocating spaces of someone's house, listening to numerous incantations, and dancing to the haunting sound of tom-toms until one individual is overcome by strange behavior. The outward signs of an imminent possession—which can occur at any time—do not disappoint. The candidate feels shivers that make his or her hair stand on end, then uncontrollable tremors. During this process, he or she passes several times from a state of great lucidity to a state of quasi-unconsciousness, with symptoms slowing down, disappearing, then rising up again. When the subject is next shaken by stronger spasms, it is said the powers of the afterlife are attacking so that one gets "lost". Little by little, the joints stiffen, especially at the shoulders. For some, the process is quicker than for others, but each mentions a threshold point after which they lose total control. At this point, the subject enters into a trance, a moment of unparalleled violence. Followers compare this experience to lightning striking or an unstoppable hurricane.

For those who have not prepared this kind of experience in a spiritual center, first trances are traumatic. Amilka reported that in the midst of a dense crowd on Santa Barbara Feast Day, she felt intoxicated with the frenetic rhythm of the drums

Figure 3.1 A sacrifice *palo* (photo: Caterina Pasqualino).

and her entire body began to tremble. She felt increasingly stiff, then limp, and then, like an epileptic, fell to the ground, seemingly lifeless and unable to protect herself. Michel said he had long desired to be possessed by Sieterayo but without success. Then, on Saint Barbara Feast Day, he had tachycardia, felt a cold draft (*escalofrío*) from his head to his toes and lost control of his limbs. Limonta recalled spending long hours in front of an altar (*prenda*) before feeling a shock, like an electric current (*corriente como una trasmisión*).

These stories of first possession experiences corroborate the testimony of *palo monte* priests who, upon first meeting the dead individual devoted to them, feel a similarly violent electric shock. In this phase, everything happens in sudden outbursts. The subject feels as if an outside energy was forcing its way in and penetrating his body. This energy usually enters through the feet but sometimes by other extremities, then goes through the body at lightning speed. At this stage, called "the dog" (*el perro*), the possessed utters growling and barking sounds. When that energy reaches the head, the possessed person feels as if being rapidly pulled into a vortex leading to the bottom of the sea. The subject feels dizzy, as if having lost footing (*yo me pierdo*).

The Disorder of the Senses

The *palo* ritual is generally characterized by two stages: first, going into the trance, and, second, returning to a normal state, with the subject undergoing sudden flashes.

Figure 3.2 Clusters of *palo* objects (photo: Caterina Pasqualino).

In between, the subject is possessed by a dead person. The public eagerly awaits this moment, as the possessed person utters prophecies. In interviews, the possessed have spoken about feeling both exceptional power and overwhelming fatigue.

In the first phase, strong physical sensations lead the possessed person to lose references to space and time. The intensity is so great that the person falls to the ground in a state of semi-consciousness. This is eventually neutralized by a priest placing a cross on his knuckles in order to immobilize, or rather "congeal" the subject. Insiders recount that the trance subject then becomes *material*, an "inert material." Like a flash, the force that penetrated the subject flows through his or her body, moves to the head and takes control. The body feels terribly heavy and the actions mechanical, like a robot, and slowed down as if the subject was in shackles.[7]

During this time, everything seems slow. The possessed feels as if split in two. Many, during our interviews, said that after feeling they were losing consciousness and then dragged to the bottom of the sea, they felt reborn, as if floating in the air. Vision is disturbed; those nearby appear like faraway, distorted silhouettes. Hearing is muffled; ritual music and the voices of those officiating seem remote, as if emanating from a distant place. At the same time, the voice of the possessed becomes slow, thick, and hoarse, and seems to come from a distant world. Coming to comfort and guide the living, the dead speak to the possessed, informing the

Figure 3.3 The *palero* Enrique in front of his altar (photo: Caterina Pasqualino).

Figure 3.4 Hieronymus Bosch, *The Ascent of the Blessed* (Due scene dal paradiso/L'ascesa delle anime) (1450–1516), Venice, Museo Palazzo Grimani. By kind permission of the Ministero dei beni e delle attività culturali e del turismo.

audience about the past, present, and future. But their words are often incomprehensible, abstruse, as if uttered in an archaic language.

Near-death Experiences

Is there a universal vision beyond the post-mortem hereafter? The passage to the afterlife vividly recalls pre-mortem statements of individuals completely unaware of *palo monte*, who came back to life after being declared clinically dead following an accident or deep coma. This phenomenon lived "between life and death" is called a near-death experience, or NDE. Stories of those who have undergone this strange experience are numerous. They describe the following features. As of the initial shock, the subject sees images from his or her entire life flash before the eyes in rapid succession. The subject then has the sense of being drawn uncontrollably into a tunnel. This image has perhaps been meaningful since time immemorial: a painting by Hieronymus Bosch (1450–1516), *The Ascent of the Blessed*, evokes precisely this scene: the deceased, accompanied by angels, are sucked into a dark tunnel, at the end of which one sees a blinding light (see figure 3.4).

Here is the testimony of one subject experiencing an NDE:

> At the moment, I am moving rapidly inside a tunnel. I had been standing, and now feel as if I were being swept into the tunnel. It is very narrow, and I am soaring. I see a pinpoint of light at the other end of the tunnel. I move rapidly towards that light. It's as if I were on some kind of light beam that propels me forward. I go out. I enter another dimension and then slow down completely. I find myself just in front of the spot of light, which I am now slowly passing through. Everything is green. The contrast of the brightness with the tunnel's darkness is almost blinding. It's a different sensation. And now, it's as if a powerful energy were hugging me. It's an extraordinary feeling. It is energy of a new dimension.[8]

According to Raymond Moody,[9] who conducted research in Europe and the United States but also outside the Western hemisphere in India, a patient coming back from an NDE remembers feelings of distress, seeing a panoramic life review before his eyes, hearing unpleasant noises, and the sensation of being carried away and going through a long, dark tunnel before seeing a bright light. He would then be overcome by feelings of joy, love, and peace. Some witnesses claim they have met with the deceased, either loved ones or celebrities. More importantly, they recount having been disembodied. This, known as an out-of-body experience or OBE,[10] refers to a feeling of leaving the body, most often from the top of the head but also through the feet, navel, or other places. At that moment, the subject has the sensation of floating in the air and recalls being able to move around freely to visit other places. Perception becomes exceedingly acute, and the subjects sees objects simultaneously from all angles, and can even see through matter. The subject also has the ability to "zoom" without limits from the infinitely small to the infinitely large.

No conclusive explanation can rationalize such testimony, which is as astonishing as it is frequent. Leading experts are convinced this shows that brain responses to certain stimuli are universal. As evidence, they cite the fact that the "mentally ill" share recurring hallucinatory dreams. In the first phase, the subject suffering from hallucinations sees geometric shapes: such as dots, zigzags, and grids. The subject then has the sensation of being drawn into a whirlwind or tunnel, and perceives bright lights at the end. In the second phase, monsters or animals appear—fantastical images sometimes compared to a series of three-dimensional scenes or films projected on the walls. At this stage, the subject may feel as if he or she is flying, or metamorphosing into an animal.[11]

P. Dewavrin suggests that an NDE is a mystical experience that occurs even in the least spiritual-minded people, and he proposes a psychodynamic interpretation.[12] If one separates the body from self-consciousness, the unconscious would react by providing a sense of bodily detachment, time dilatation, and distance. This spatiotemporal escape would permit one, in the wake of imminent death, to eliminate an unbearable reality from consciousness and create the illusion of receiving life messages. Others try to explain this phenomenon in strictly biological terms. Based on the known fact that consciousness is altered by both anoxia, problems in delivering oxygen to the body enzymes, and hyperpnea, one might link agony, itself marked by a lack of oxygen, to epileptic-style neuronal discharges in the temporal lobe. For instance, Kenneth Ring assimilates the pre-mortem state to a mechanism in which high-frequency vibrations eliminate notions of space and time.[13] Once these are destroyed, everything would be lived synchronously, which explains the individual's panoramic life review. The rapid movement through the tunnel of death would convey the passage from the three-dimensional world of everyday reality to a holographic universe. High vibrational frequencies would artificially evoke recognizable visual and auditory phenomena: magical light, brilliant colors, wonderful music.

The experiences reported by the *palo monte*, by those who have had an NDE, and by the mentally ill with hallucinations seem to converge. No matter whether these stories are based on true-life experience or on pure imagination, the point of interest here is that all of them describe sensations of altered consciousness that accentuate two types of perception of images and sounds. At first, the overriding feeling is of a world streaming past at high speed. In the second phase, the subject seems, on the contrary, to be in slow motion. All evidence points to an unnatural sense of time, which can be either faster or slower than normal unless everything is perceived simultaneously, at which point time and space lose all meaning.[14]

Experimental film

These "perceived" sensations are unnerving reminders of the "screening-performances" proposed in some types of experimental film: the performance aspect submits the audience to visual and auditory impulses that distort their sensorial perception. On a cognitive level, the public is immersed in an unreal world.

Experimental film-makers have developed a kind of visual and auditory abstraction to satisfy their demand for complete freedom of expression, and to demonstrate their rejection of realistic, overly academic images. By filming the world differently, inventing new ways of presenting films or intervening directly on the celluloid, their work integrates rapid film reviews and slow motion as well as blurring, stills images, looping sequences, visual collage, ruptures, light flashes, sound overload and other features.

Stan Brakhage is undoubtedly one of the masters of this genre. According to Jean-Michel Bouhours, in the 1950s Brakhage provoked a shift in the gaze as radical as the artistic revolution Picasso created with Cubism.[15] Rejecting the foundations of a representing space inherited from the Renaissance, he began working on visual phenomena he called "infra oculist," that is, eidetic imagery of dream visions and phosphenes, or artificial developments of light or stains in the visual field. He conceived each frame as an energetic discharge. Although all his films were of his daily environment and family—his children and wife on their isolated Colorado farm—he transposed them to create a dream world combining three kinds of imagery. The first, filmed with neutrality, refers to his environment. The second relates to biographical events. The third is meant to reflect his inner world using distortions made with optical devices and filters.[16] Brakhage stated he wanted to restore his mental images, which he called his mind's eye's brain, and also spoke of his inner visions as brain movies.

One of his references, which he called closed eye vision or hypnagogic vision, is a retinal game of shapes and colors seen under closed eyelids and sometimes on the eye's surface. When one presses lightly on the eyelids, the brain records reflections and vibrant images that it interprets as flapping butterfly wings. This is how Stan Brakhage described this source of inspiration:

> Closing these eyelids, shutting Pandora's trap for awhile, believing even in the reality of it, thwarting thought awhile, traveling thru the blue subterrain?— marine?—what? seeming tunnels of it, (utterly unable to photograph any of it), purposeless in my wanderlings around, seeming to be spiraling at times, timelessly, encountering shapes (indescribable), passing thru them, or were they passing thru me?[17]

The spectator of a Brakhage film feels as if his or her open eyes are seeing naturally, but at the same time has the sensation of ocular movements, dilating pupils and changes of focal distances that result in a kind of "mnemovision." In an interview, the film-maker said he wanted to reveal the essence of visual memory, the countless fragments of personal history that we unconsciously store throughout a lifetime. This idea suggests moving visual thinking, resulting from "feedback between neurons, the nervous system and visual music." These mental constructs appear as shadows, unreal colors, and variations of pace that overcome the viewer's spatiotemporal references.[18] They can trigger physical reactions of discomfort,

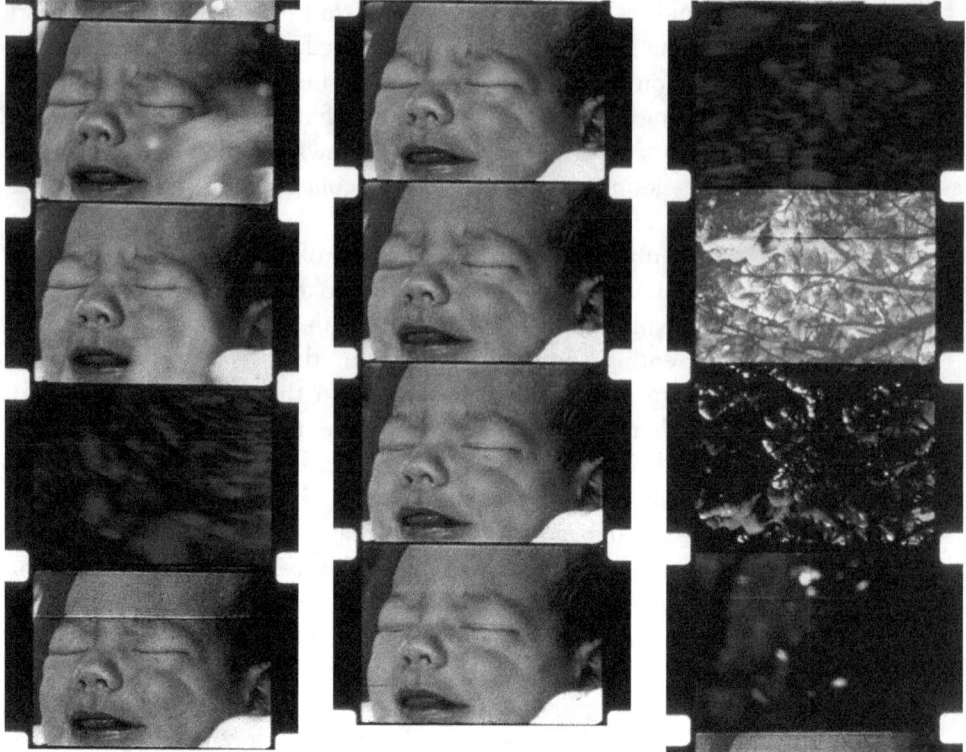

Figure 3.5 Stan Brakhage: still frames from *Dog Star Man: Part 2*, 1963. Courtesy of Marilyn Brakhage.

enjoyment, or drunkenness, as well as impressions of déjà vu, flashbacks, the sensation of living in a dream, and so forth.

Time-lapse

Experiences related to *palo monte* and NDEs share the fact that they begin with the same type of mental disturbance: a phenomenon in which the subject feels irresistibly drawn into another world. In *palo monte*, the subject is caught in a whirlwind towards the bottom of the sea. In an NDE, he or she is drawn into a tunnel towards a blinding light. In both instances, everything begins with intense feelings of intoxication and a time-lapse scrolling of images that seem to lead to death. Such a figurative dimension is generally foreign to experimental film; however, Brakhage also said that, when making his retinal experiments, he had the feeling of being caught in a kind of current and moving through a tunnel.

By going beyond normal viewing time, experimental film-makers captured the acceleration of time. This super-temporality destabilizes the viewers' common understanding by triggering a peculiar phenomenon of memorialization. Paradoxically, the high speed does not make them forget time. On the contrary, it makes them focus more intensely on memory and nostalgia, or perhaps on a past that has gone by too fast. It puts them in the presence of a "*dépassé*," of something overwhelming. Thus, the time-lapse sequences lead to the loss of images, to their disappearance. In *palo monte* or NDE, a whirlwind carries one irresistibly to the world of the dead; in experimental film, a time-lapse scrolling of images conveys the idea of death itself.

The *punctum*

How far can this "ultra" brain activity go? In *palo monte*, at a given moment, the possessed suffers from severe shivering, then falls to the ground as if fainting. The event lasts only a few seconds and may happen again. These peaks of intensity are triggered by a change in pace or an unintentional movement made by a participant or by the possessed himself—that is, during the whirlpool phase, called *cruce*, literally, "the crossing."[19] At that instant, the energy the possessed person is feeling seems to spread throughout the community and creates a palpable sense of bonding; some suddenly have chills, or burst into tears.[20] Symbolically, these signs represent the sudden arrival of a dead person who has come to enter the body of the possessed, or the coming of another person, unceremoniously hunting the first.

I propose to call this kind of excitation peak a *punctum*,[21] a term referring to Barthes's writings on photography. Barthes used the term to describe a visual detail that radically changes the way one reads a photograph. He defined it as an element that elicits emotion in the photographer while taking the photo, then in the viewer contemplating the photo. Each has emotions that come from the sense that his response is unique, that he alone is affected by this singular connection among heterogeneous elements.

In etymological terms, *punctum*, a Latin term, is the origin of the word "punctuate," and, in French, the word "point" (period), providing a full stop at the end of a sentence. But its Latin translation can also refer to a tiny hole (first century BC), or to a small puncture wound made with a sharp instrument (first century AD). Thus, concerning ritual, *punctum* could designate a rupture in the continuum of ceremonial ritual that radically changes its meaning, investing it with a higher order and giving it a collective dimension. In terms of experimental film, *punctum* could also represent the critical moment when the viewer, having abandoned the self—that is, after undergoing a change in visual and auditory perception—enters a new perceptual universe.

In addition, images are sometimes reworked to create long takes and slow zooms. This type of editing creates a surreal atmosphere: at times, a plane suddenly disappears, and, at others, a fluid movement is broken by a series of slow-motion frames. Each time, as Maya Deren had noted, they suggest an annotation, comment or hesitation, but also solemnity.[22]

In *Genius and Madness* (*Génie et Folie*),[23] Triny Prada strives to express the second state of the artist during creation. Images in fast-forward of an orchestra's conductor are periodically interrupted by still images of passers-by and pigeons on St. Mark's Square in Venice (see figure 3.6). In contrast with the moments of tension, the still images serve as moments of repose. Like *punctum*, they suggest reflection and critical distance.

By alternating between excessive speed and instantaneous vision, it questions the relationship between life and death. Strong emotion is stirred, plunging the spectator into a state of intense nostalgia, with feelings similar to those during a trance possession ritual. Like this visual sign in Barthes, which completely changes the meaning of a photographic image, the *punctum* ritual, which emerges in the ceremonial continuum, dramatically alters the meaning of the ceremony. Before being taken over by violent shaking, the subject is still engaged in the ordinary world. Afterward, the subject is transformed, and moves with extreme sluggishness. Although a few seconds still showing signs of extreme edginess, afterward the possessed suddenly goes limp. Movements become slow and disjointed; the voice, hoarse and raspy. Some—as is also the case in NDE—say they float in space. The *punctum* would be this moment of grace in which the subject shifts from "ultra-time" to "infra-time" and enters into a latency phase.

Figure 3.6 Triny Prada, "Je connais ma vérité (I know my truth)." Still frame from *Genius and Madness*, Lowave, 2013. Courtesy of Triny Prada.

Slow Motion

During a trance, slowing down therefore represents the other slope of time, but it also links *palo monte*, NDE, and experimental film. The latter—*a priori* far removed from the mystical *palo monte*—none the less shares not only its attraction for time-lapse seeing but also for states of consciousness associated with extreme slowness.

In *24 Hour Psycho* (1993) Douglas Gordon slowed down Alfred Hitchcock's *Psycho* (1960) so much that viewers are able to identify the sequences frame by frame. Bill Viola is also well known for his use of extreme slow motion. In *The Passions* (2003) he filmed groups of grieving figures whose facial expressions and gestures change so slowly that movement is almost imperceptible. The slow motion is so extreme that at first it is difficult to understand that the images are moving at all. Each in his own way, these two artists have tested the limits of the visible. The filmed characters appear weightless, as if moving through air. But beyond the poetic effect, the minimum transitional time between two frames can be interpreted, in less technical terms, as the minimal expression of an animation. The photograms create images that are not entirely motionless but are scarcely animated. This subtle "in-between" evokes a particular emotion, like the wonder we feel when we see life being born, or the passage from inertia to the living, as in germination, budding, and blooming.

In contrast to time-lapse, in which the succession and fading of images relates to the idea of death, slow motion suggests a beginning. It is a primordial expression of birth. Regarding the *palo monte* cult, it can be argued that slow motion is consistent with concepts of a "pre-world," of prescience and divinatory abilities. Is it possible to generalize? Concerning a shamanic Cuna Indian ritual used to facilitate difficult births, Claude Levi-Strauss compared his impression to watching "a film sequence projected in slow motion."[24] Birth and extreme slowness—it could certainly be dangerous to draw definitive conclusions, especially since experimental film is free of any symbolism and even asserts a certain ineffability. But one cannot help but ponder the unsettling similarities it shares with trance.

Parallel worlds

Additional thoughts about the notion of consciousness also come to mind. Profoundly affected by repeated trance sessions, the most devoted *palo monte* members no longer really separate their life on earth from the afterlife. By dint of distorting their voices, for example, they wind up sounding husky and hoarse. The most faithful have daydreams throughout the day, at moments briefly losing consciousness. They have visions of the dead, either as shadows, or, in contrast, flashes beneath their creased eyelids. The flashes occur suddenly—in the middle of the afternoon, during a walk or a family meal. They believe they can fall into a trance in their sleep, especially at daybreak, as if the dead, masters of the night, wanted to keep them in extremis before being chased away by the dawn. Still asleep, they emit incomprehensible sounds, which are interpreted as their continuing conversation with the dead.

As extraordinary as this is, living between two worlds merely enhances an ability we all possess. Everyone has experienced a more or less discontinuous consciousness upon waking. We can all shift from a keen sense of reality to daydream states of varying intensity, going from flashes to prolonged absences within a short time. When distracted, we rely on subliminal ways of thinking. On awakening, we may forget where we are, lose our sense of time and space, forget what we were doing, or lose the thread of a specific thought. What status can we attribute to these alternate records of human consciousness? Authors such as Luc de Heusch propose to differentiate the physiological state upon waking with that just before sleeping. The author distinguishes between, on the one hand, a waking state, related to activating the senses and the rational mind, and, on the other, a dream area associated with passivity. Trance, which he compares to a hypnotic state,[25] also pertains to sensory and cerebral inertia. But such differentiation is perhaps not as relevant as it might at first appear. In an article on the "efficiency of symbols," Lévi-Strauss was asked about the "intimate experience" of a shaman therapist. He replied that a shaman therapist does not merely reproduce or mimic events; he relives every moment completely. Bertrand Hell, who recently came back to this observation, states that the shaman, in his exhortations and his pantomime, goes well beyond simulation: he aims, according to the author, to put on a *"peau de possession"* (skin of possession).[26] This was recently confirmed in another way by neuroscientists. Having shown that reason and emotion sometimes interact in the same cerebral areas, they assert that a subject under hypnosis, despite apparent passivity, is still capable of having visions, experiencing sensations, and possibly even feeling the body move. Hypnosis, which is often compared to trance, is not inconsequential in terms of brain activity. Experiments have demonstrated that when the subject simply uses his or her memory, only the left and right temporal lobes become active. However, under hypnosis, much larger brain areas are used, reaching equally areas for vision (occipital lobe), for sensations (parietal lobe), and motor skills (precentral region). These laboratory observations suggest that the subject under hypnosis is not merely remembering a situation, but is literally experiencing it. Despite the passive appearance, the subject is intensely active.[27] These observations suggest first that we question an overly strict distinction between states of waking and unconsciousness. Moreover, in his *Anthropology of Time*, Alfred Gell wisely criticizes the vision of linear time that has long characterized anthropological studies.[28] Along with other authors, he considers it, on the one hand, necessary to move beyond this antagonism between the temporality of everyday life and mythological temporality; and, on the other hand, to envision time according to a sort of irregular flux in which states of consciousness alternate with states of unconsciousness. For Gell, time is apprehended in different "layers of subjectivity." Brakhage, who simultaneously uses multiple modes of vision, seems to demonstrate this.[29] The first nine minutes of his film *Dog Star Man* (1961–4) is a remarkable sequence (*Prelude*, 1961) that rejects any such linearity. His films belong to an unstable, cyclical time that plays simultaneously on multiple non-objective temporalities (see figure 3.5).

Unlike those of "classical" film, the intentions of experimental film have never been about telling stories but about provoking multiple sensations. In this way, it displays resistance to normative thinking. Today, such intentions continue to pose questions regarding acceleration and deceleration, simultaneous memory, and parallel consciousness, all of which suggest numerous paths for innovative research in the humanities, paving the way to an anthropology of hyperreality.[30]

Filmography

Dog Star Man, dir. Stan Brakhage, USA, 1963, 7 mins.
Genius and Madness, Triny Prada, Spain, 7 mins.
Psycho, dir. Alfred Hitchcock, USA, 1960, 109 mins.
24 Hours Psycho, dir. Douglas Gordon, UK, 1993, 1440 mins.

Video Installations

The Passions, Bill Viola, USA (Getty Museum), 2003.

Notes

1. Alfred Métraux, *Le vaudou haïtien* (Paris: Gallimard, 1958); Roger Bastide, *Le Candomblé de Bahia* (Paris: PUF, 1958); Michel Leiris, *La Possession et ses aspects théâtraux chez les Éthiopiens de Gondar* (Paris: Plon, 1958).
2. See Bertrand Hell, "Négocier avec les esprits tromba à Mayotte," *Gradhiva*, 7, 2008, from http://gradhiva.revues.org/1062 (accessed August 13, 2013).
3. See Gilbert Rouget, *La musique et la transe* (Paris: Gallimard, 1980).
4. The term *palo monte*, of Bantu origin, is primarily dedicated to the Dead (*nfumbi*). The priest, called *palero*, is bound by a pact with the spirit of a specific deceased person (*le muerto de prenda*). The person materializes through a "ritual caldron" (*caldero* or *ngangas*), which acquires increasing power as it is transmitted from generation to generation. It contains various objects: human bones, iron bars and sticks driven into clods of earth, fragments of skulls, wood, scrap metal, rope, nails, chains, shells, broken ornaments, herbs and stones collected in the water (on the sea floor or in a river), a cross, old dolls, an old shoe, or a miniature airplane. Scientific literature on *palo monte* is scarce. Less attractive, less exportable, and less comparable to Catholicism than *santeria* and spiritualism, the "African" and "witchlike" aspects of *palo monte* have contributed to its being kept in the background. One should nevertheless note the work of Lydia Cabrera *El Monte* (Miami: Ediciones Universal, 1954); *Reglas de Congo, Palo Monte, Mayombe* (Miami: Ediciones Universal, 1979), Natalia Bolivar Aróstegui and Carmen Gonzalez Diaz de Villegas *Ta Makuende Yaya Y Las Reglas De Palo Monte: Mayombe, Brillumba, Kimbisa, Shamalongo*,

La (Habana: Ediciones Union, 1998), Gonzales Bueno Gladys "An initiation ceremony in Regla de Palo" *AfroCuba: An Anthnology of Cuban writing on race, politics and culture* (New York: Centre for Cuban Studies, 1993), Todd Ramon Ochoa *Society of the Dead* (Berkeley: University of California Press, 2010), Fernando Ortiz *Los negros brujos* (La Habana: Ed. de Ciencias sociales, 1906 (2001), Figarola Joel James (*Cuba. La Gran Nganga.* Santiago de Cuba: Ediciones Caseron, 2006 and *La Brujeria Cubana: el Palo Monte. Aproximacion al Pensamiento Abstrato de la Cubania* (Santiago de Cuba: Editorial Oriente, 2001).

5. From mid-December to the beginning of the following year, stimulated by the many end-of-year holidays (*bembés*) organized under the auspices of St. Barbara and St. Lazarus, Cubans believe that spirits and the dead are especially likely to take possession of the individuals that solicit them. Although they are practiced throughout the year, trances and possessions experience their peak during this period.

6. Caterina Pasqualino, "Vocalization of suffering," in *Taken by Arts: Suffering in Culture and the Work of Aesthetics*, dir. Ratiba Hadj-Moussa and Michael Nijhawan (Montreal: McGill University Press, 2013). Caterina Pasqualino, "Metamorphoses des voix," in Bertrand Hell and Jean de Loisy (eds), *Les Maîtres de désordre* (Paris: Musée du Quai Branly, 2012), 202–3.

7. To introduce this phase, the possessed will greet the elderly, because he (or she) senses their strong affinity with the dead person that has taken hold of him (or her). Caterina Pasqualino, "Etre chose: marionnettes et pantins vivants, de la possession cubaine au théâtre de Kantor," in *La marionnette: objet d'histoire, oeuvre d'art, objet de civilisation?*, Editions du Cherche midi, 2014.

8. Jean-Jacques Charbonier, *Les preuves scientifiques d'une vie après la vie* (Paris: Editions Exergue, 2008), p. 81.

9. Raymond Moody, *Life After Life* (Covington, KY: Bantam Books, 1975), 21.

10. Clinical trials suggest that OBEs are cultural invariants "that have specific precipitating factors and that they can be investigated neuroscientifically." They are associated with "partial impairments of consciousness (such as epilepsy, migraine, and electrical cortical stimulation), supine body position, and disturbed own body processing. Silvia Bünning and Olaf Blanke, "The Out-of-body Experience: Precipitating Factors and Neural Correlates," in Steven Laureys (ed.), *The Boundaries of Consciousness: Neurobiology and Neuropathology* (Elsevier, 2005), 331–51.

11. In a highly controversial book, Jean Clottes and David Lewis-Williams suggest the existence of three stages of trance. Jean Clottes and David Lewis-Williams, *Les chamanes de la préhistoire* (Paris: Editions du Seuil, 1996), 16–20.

12. P. Dewavrin, *Les phénomènes de conscience à l'approche de la mort*, Dissertation en Psychiatry: Paris 5, Faculté de médecine Necker enfants malades, 1980, Paris.

13. Kenneth Ring, *Life at Death* (New York: McCann & Geoghegan, 1980), 95.

14. M. Thonnard, C. S. Chnakers, M. Boly, M. A. Bruno, P. Boveroux, S. Laureys, and A. Vanhaudenhuyse, *Expériences de mort imminente: Phénomènes paranormaux ou neurologiques?*, from http://www.coma.ulg.ac.be/papers/french/Thonnard_RMLg08.pdf (accessed January 17, 2014).

15. Jean-Michel Bouhours, "Avant-propos," in *Stan Brakhage, Métaphores et vision* (Paris: Centre George Pompidou, 1998), 5–6. See also Maurice Merleau-Ponty, *Le visible et l'invisible* (Paris: Gallimard, 1964), 181.

16. Fred Camper, *The Art of Vision*, a Film by Stan Brakhage, from http://www.fredcamper.com/Film/Brakhage7.html (accessed January 17, 2014).

17. Stan Brakhage, "My Eye," in *Metaphors on Vision* (New York: Film Culture, 1963).

18. Interview with Stan Brakhage on YouTube: *Brakhage on Brakhage 2*, YouTube.

19. Caterina Pasqualino, *Performance rituelle et artistique*, HDR, dir. Anne Christine Taylor (Université de Nanterre, October 2013), 73, 85.

20. In my previous work, I called attention to the concept of *duende*, a "force" that leads participants, at a specific time, to "become one" with the singer. The concept of *duende* is difficult to define. *Duendes* are a positive force, as opposed to *mengues*, entities that represent negative, diabolical forces. When they come out, they spread instantly, as if contagious (in forms musical and gestural) from one participant to another. This moment creates an intense sense of belonging. The public responds by encouraging the singer (*jaleos*) and clapping in rhythm (*compas*). All say the experience of *duende* passes through collectively shared physical sensations, which give everyone chills ("goosebumps"). When the singer's voice chokes, it is said, "he vomits blood, vomits his guts": the sound circulates from one body to another. Coming from deep inside the singer, it would penetrate in waves, deep inside the participants. See also note 6, and further references in note 44, chapter 1 in this volume.
21. Roland Barthes, *La Chambre claire: Note sur la photographie* (Paris: Gallimard, 1980, 2012), 49.
22. Maya Deren, "La cinématographie ou l'usage créatif de la réalité" (1960), *Ecrits sur le cinema* (Paris: Paris Expérimental, 2004), 93–4.
23. Triny Prada, *Genius and Madness* (*Génie et Folie*), "Human Frames" collection, directed by Silke Schmick (Paris: Lowave, 2012).
24. Claude Levi-Strauss, "L'efficacité symbolique" (The Efficiency of Symbols), in *Anthropologie structural* (Paris: Plon, 1958), 228.
25. Luc de Heusch, *La Transe et ses entours. La sorcellerie, l'amour fou, saint Jean de la Croix, etc.* (Brussels: Editions Complexe, 2006), 81.
26. Bertrand Hell, "Négocier avec les esprits tromba à Mayotte. Retour sur le 'théâtre vécu' de la possession," in *Gradhiva. Le possédé spectaculaire*, 7, 2008, 20–1.
27. E. L. Faymonville, G. D. Roediger, C. Fiore, C. Phillips Delgueldre, M. Lamy, A. Luxen, P. Maquet, and S. Laureys, "Increased Cerebral Functional Connectivity Underlying the Antinociceptive Effects of Hypnosis," *Cognitive Brain Research*, 17 (2), 2003, 255–62.
28. Alfred Gell, *The Anthropology of Time: Cultural Constructions of Temporal Maps and Images* (Oxford: Berg, 1992).
29. Stan Brakhage, "Metaphors on Vision," in *Essential Brakhage—Selected Writings in Filmmaking* (New York: McPherson & Company, 2001), 12.
30. The term *hyperreality* has had much success in twentieth-century philosophy and semiotics. This term refers to phenomena situated beyond the real. It is used here in its etymological sense. The term derives from: hyper, from the Greek *huper*, meaning above, beyond; and the word reality, from the Latin, *realitas*, meaning that which exists. I am not referring to its use by Baudrillard, for whom the term hyperreal has the meaning of simulacrum. For Baudrillard, the term refers to the confusion of consciousness between reality and imagination; their interaction engendered the production of worlds that have lost touch with reality. Like organized entertainment, such as Disneyland or pornography, Baudrillard asserts, the hyperreal world is a simulacrum of reality, whose appearance is more attractive and stimulating. My usage is closer to the meaning given by Walter Benjamin to evoke techniques for reproducing of a work of art, giving the viewer the ability to perceive it in a new light (see Jean Baudrillard, *L'Échange symbolique et la mort* (Symbolic Exchange and Death) (Paris: Gallimard, 1976) and Walter Benjamin, *L'œuvre d'art à l'époque de sa reproductibilité technique* (The Work of Art in the Age of Mechanical Reproduction) (Paris: Allia, 2012).

4

CONTEMPORARY EXPERIMENTAL DOCUMENTARY AND THE PREMISES OF ANTHROPOLOGY: THE WORK OF ROBERT FENZ

Nicole Brenez

Preamble: The Point of View of the Native

February 23, 2011. I discover the film version of *The Sole of the Foot*, the last work to date by Robert Fenz, which interlinks an ensemble of artistic gestures (photogram exhibit, book, installation). It's a shock. For the first time in years, perhaps since *Wheel of Ashes* by Peter Emanuel Goldman (1969) and *A l'ombre de la canaille bleue* ("In the Shadow of the Blue Rascal") by Pierre Clémenti (1978–85)—two fictions—I recognize in cinema, something of this place where I have resided for three decades: Paris. Suddenly—a phenomenon I realize retrospectively, for which I had completely lost hope—the cinema resonates with accuracy, when it comes to feelings, and the inescapable atmospheres that every Parisian immersed in the ordinary life of his city feels daily. Of course, there are as many visions of the city as there are blinks of an eye, dreams and psychic sketches, all of which coexist and rub against each other. But for the first time since Goldman and Clémenti's affective odysseys, during that first part of *The Sole of the Foot*, the experience of exactness overwhelms me, not in the sense of an impossible, objective truth, but as a venture at description, which completely freed itself from preceding images of an over-represented city, and which, modestly, courageously, seizes the ordinary with both hands. "To wrap gnarled reality in my arms!" as Arthur Rimbaud wrote in 1873, in the last section of *Une saison en enfer* (A Season in Hell), his own urban fresco after the Commune massacre, his own "meditation on revolution." Thus, while discovering the first section of *The Sole of the Foot*, it seemed I felt in the present what viewers might have experienced from two classics in controversial description, which also chose Paris as their figurative site for construction: *Nothing but Time* by Alberto Cavalcanti in 1926 and *Ali in Wonderland* by Djouhra Abouda and Alain Bonnamy in 1976. Cavalcanti, Abouda, and Bonnamy indulged in violent rectifications, they tore apart fallacious images in order to oppose them with what ideas left unaddressed, at which point it was necessary to begin the representation over again: misery, injustice, violence, exploitation, the merciless class struggle ... Their films unleashed a war of images and cultivated conflicts in editing. In the case of Robert Fenz—and this is true for the ensemble of his work—the images to which his films oppose themselves remain off-camera, off-topic: the descriptive energy concentrates in all entirety on the motifs to which it attaches itself. The work of Robert Fenz unfolds in an affirmative manner, and, as such, it adheres to the same sensitive logic as that of Jonas Mekas, but without having to add the poignant cards, "this is a political film," which punctuate the great elegy, *As I was Moving Ahead, Occasionally I Saw Brief Glimpses of Beauty* (2000), and which remind us of the stakes involved in every representation of a face, an animal, a river. The title of the ensemble of Robert Fenz's principal cycle, *Meditations on Revolution*, indicates the philosophical framework to which his image proposals adhere: biopolitics.

A Few Preconceptions on the Subject of Celluloid Film Description

Whether in fiction or documentary, essay or scientific, cinema is an art of description. And description, being first and foremost a literary form, finds forms of fulfillment, or even accomplishment, thanks to silver print. "Description is a figure of thought by development, which instead of simply pointing out an object, makes it somehow visible, with the vivid and animated exhibition of its most interesting aspects and circumstances."[1]

And yet, two preconceptions born of literary disciplines continue to reign over cinema.

First, the preconception of accuracy. Because it technically falls under the printing system, celluloid motion picture film would provide the most advantageous means of restituting a vestige of reality, both in time (the duration axis), in space (the axis of simultaneity and detail), and also outside all intentionality: it's "the intelligence of a machine," dear to Jean Epstein, capable itself of unveiling the unconsciousness of things, that the human eye wouldn't know how to perceive. On the foundations of such a premise, systems of objectivism have risen, which do not question the notion itself of "the real" nor that of reality, and content themselves with capturing the contours of a phenomenon: elaboration of the supposed transparency of an image toward its referent, thanks to the clarity of its contours, to proxemics and a coherent stability. This permits Marcel Mauss, for example, to view without any questions, cinema as a reliable instrument serving ethnography: "Cinema will enable the photography of life."[2]

The second preconception transposes the technical recording of contours onto the field of identity, and considers that the rendered description upholds a project of identification, or even of definition. If most film-goers satisfy themselves with such preconceptions, many film-makers have questioned them, by exploring the territory of visual art, the properties and paradoxes of filmic description. Numerous film-makers explore its visual territory, the characteristics, the paradoxes. Whether for confronting the cinema with traditional descriptive genres, like "The Portrait," or "The Landscape" (hence Charles Scheeler, Rudy Burckhardt ...). Whether to exhume unpublished themes from kinetic matter (Jean Epstein, Stan Brakhage ...). To feed our beliefs in the realm of objectivity (all scientific cinema, often very conscious of its visual virtues). To test a phenomenon with a descriptive analysis (Guy Debord, Jean-Luc Godard, Harun Farocki ...). Or to bring back the fable to its factual incandescence (Marcel Hanoun, Christian Boltanski). Since the end of the 1960s, this particular form—the description of images—has flourished (the ekphrasis), under its poetic and critical aspects (Ken Jacobs, Rafael Montañez Ortiz ...).

Robert Fenz, Trajectory

An experimental American film-maker, Robert Fenz was born in Ann Arbor, Michigan in 1969. He grows up in San Francisco, where he becomes a professional movie projectionist, notably for the Telluride Film Festival and for Anthropology Film Archives in New York, where he builds up a solid experimental culture. He begins studies in cinematographic directing at Bard College, NY, where he takes courses in particular by the master of film description, Peter Hutton. Graduating in 1997, he then obtains an MFA at the California Institute of the Arts in 2002. Robert Fenz meets Robert Gardner in Cambridge, MA in 1998, asks him to show him his work, and a written correspondence between the two artists follows. In 2003 Robert Gardner hires Robert Fenz at the Harvard Film Studies Center. Fenz finds himself in charge of restoring and transferring into 35mm, three films by Gardner originally shot in 16mm, and which become classics of visual anthropology: *Dead Birds* (1963), *Rivers of Sand* (1974), and *Forest of Bliss* (1986). In 2011, bolstered by a deep knowledge of his three films, their rushes, their out-takes, and their soundtracks, Fenz directs *Correspondence*, a return to the respective filming locations of Gardner's three films. He presents his endeavor thus: "*Correspondence* is not a direct commentary on Gardner's works, it is an elegy for a form of creating images that is at the brink of disappearing."

Desquamating Description

Film-maker, and film-lover, very conscious of his figurative heritage, and notably, a great admirer of Jean Vigo and Johan Van der Keuken, Robert Fenz works to desquamate description, to return, one-on-one with the world. For him, this implies meditating on his historic and psychological position at the moment of creating an image.

Let's start with the physical. Robert Fenz's work claims it belongs in the here and now, a localization, a science of the presence, which often leaves an explicit trace in the shot. In order to prove the concrete reality of a given confrontation, Robert Fenz, the virtuoso of cameramen, tireless bearer of his Bolex, and then his beloved Aaton, who doesn't refrain from distributing a film that highlights his own presence in the world: his shadow on the ground, motion blurs, occasional back and forth, consecutive swish pans when a difficult problem arises, in order to demonstrate confusion or suspense (the Israeli part of *The Sole of the Foot*, or a Papuan moment in *Correspondence*, 2011). Among his major films, *Greenville, MS* (2001) reveals perhaps best to what extent—far from appearances and outlines—the style of Robert Fenz rests first and foremost on gymnastics; the unique resource of a real body in movement, the craftsmanship of an "affective athlete,"[3] who formed himself through contact with Wadada Leo Smith, from whom he learned to play the trumpet, and the principles of improvisation.

Greenville, MS, a study of the kinetic energy deployed by the boxer Terry Whitaker during training, centers entirely on the athlete's gestures, described in their repetitiveness and their notion of series. The description strives toward a visual restitution, not as much toward physiological movement (which would be better accomplished with slow motion), as toward the vibrant energy triggered by the emergence and deployment of a gesture in time. The stakes involved in the real-time description concern very precisely the body's endurance, as it shapes itself through gesture, and, therefore, under our eyes. *Greenville, MS* presents a sort of equivalent for English boxing to what Phill Niblock accomplished in *The Magic Sun* (1966) for music, through other visual means, in other words: the optical transcription of physical virtuosity, transforming itself into great art. However, where *The Magic Sun* delves into the adherence, even the equivalence of bodies (fingers, mouths, arms …) and the instrument (saxophone, percussions …), of breath and sound, of optical and acoustic vibration, thus observing the magic of a transformation from gesture into music, from physical to sonorous, *Greenville, MS* observes a body that becomes its own instrument, whose power transforms the perception of time, whose duration becomes energy. *The Magic Sun* and *Greenville, MS* offer carnal reinterpretations, respectively to the cine-radiographies of Dr. McIntyre and to the original chronophotography of Etienne-Jules Marey.

Yet *Greenville, MS* also offers a description in turn of the way in which bodily energy structures Robert Fenz's style, bound to the concrete immersion of a living being in the here and now. His loyalty of the phenomenological order to "the flesh of the world"[4] also often manifests in the way the film resolutely abandons systems of objectivism (transparency, similar distance and stability, etc.) thus abandoning itself to a moment of vertigo. For example, it is the vertigo of euphoric drunkenness, with the palm tree dance, and especially the tele-visual images of Malcolm X in *Vertical Air* (1996), or, conversely, that of an accepted rage, as with the metronomic back and forth on the wall separating Mexico and the United States in *Crossings* (2006), which ends by mixing, and thus symbolically voiding the sides of the wall.

Figure 4.1 Robert Fenz, *Meditations on Revolution, Part IV: Greenville, MS*, 2001. Courtesy of Robert Fenz.

Collective Context and Voyages Within Singularity

However, far from impressionism, such a physical presence for oneself and others proves, in the case of Robert Fenz, not to be a condition of subjective possibility, or an arbitrary prerequisite for expression, but the practical consequence of a historical situation that is fully thought-out and acknowledged. What does this situation entail? It concerns the acute awareness of needing to work within the ebb of the great emancipation movements born in the 1950s, with the Civil Rights Movement in the United States, the liberation of Cuba in 1959, and the victories of Liberation Fronts in the colonized Third World. To be born in 1969, like Robert Fenz, means living one's life as an adult citizen in a world abandoned to a capitalist and neoliberal explosion after 1989, without any political perspective other than a resistance maintained at every step of the way, inch by inch, but without the possibility of a collective counter-attack—and this, until 2011, the start of the revolutionary blossoming, or the Arab Spring. Throughout these two interminable decades, political writing has gone through the reconfiguration of relationships between nature and man (Peter Hutton, James Benning ...), reconsideration of relationships between individuals and collective history (Lech Kowalski, Akram Zaatari, Wang Bing ...), transmission and remembrance of struggles (John Gianvito, Travis Wilkerson—who was a classmate of Robert Fenz), and, of course, daily recording of battles on the ground (Carole Roussopoulos, Lionel Soukaz, Florent Marcie ...). A large part of critical energy has been devoted to the analysis of representations, now becomes the main ground for the battle of images (Tony Cokes, Jayce Salloum …).

The ensemble of these concerns, practices and stakes spontaneously irrigate the lavishness and the stylistic exuberance of *Vertical Air*, all at once an hommage to freedom struggles (Malcolm X, Che Guevara), an extension of them, including several experimentations with relationships to landscape, a joyful search for the overflow of landscape into nature: a nature not yet untamed by a human point of view, but so diverse and immeasurable that she is already no longer possible to synthesize. The cycle, *Meditations on Revolution* (1997–2003), launches Robert Fenz on his own path: the solitary travels through places of battle in the Third World (*Lonely Planet*, 1997), the navels of injustice (*The Space in Between*, 1997; *Soledad*, 2001) and the ghettoes of wealthy countries (*Foreign City*, 2003). The voyage does not consist of one melancholic and nostalgic movement in search of great myths of emancipation, which would need to be reactivated, without hope, in the present, but of work on the concrete, on the individuality of the sites, of people and their gestures, whether unknown like the little Cuban children (*Lonely Planet*) or famous like Marion Brown (*Foreign City*). To travel, but not in order to find something we hunt, for example the revolutionary inspiration, or the path of a historic failure, but, on the contrary, to travel to start over with what can be demonstrated as tangible, concrete existence, in the name of which revolutions were and remain necessary. Thus, Robert Fenz's approach is similar to *Promenades in London* by Flora Tristan (1840), a concrete and documented description of the laborer's misery, prostitution, the exploitation of children, the lower classes—barring the difference that *Meditations on Revolution* entrusts itself entirely to the power of visual expression (and sound in *Foreign City*), leaving the intelligence of their premises and of their possible consequences to the freedom of the viewer.

In concretely affirming the shared presence of one remarkable entity (the author) to other remarkable entities, the shots highlight the characteristic aspects of fleeting movements (for unknown figures), or sculpt the detail of their earthly path (for Marion Brown, living in New York, but toward which it was also necessary to travel extensively—a superb handling of the subway route). Each film renews the portrait, the collective portrait, or the individual portrait. To what end? In the sense that it is never about identifying figures, assigning them to themselves by laying down a confining grid with a few, recognizable lines, but on the contrary, it is about revealing a vast visual plurality through them.

Plastics of Apparition: A Visual Declaration

Visible within (once) customary movie theater screenings, *The Sole of the Foot* first and foremost engages various current forms of film exhibition: shown in a gallery, it is accompanied by a series of enlarged photograms (the beginning and end of each shot), a soundtrack, and a book of reproductions.

Seen by projection, the beginning of *The Sole of the Foot* (0'50" to 5'01" mins) provides a treaty concerning forms of self-presentation, the visual art of presence, and the certitude that the motif is in no way equivalent to its referent. After a silent shot of the ocean, six very different sound shots succeed one another, forming a manifesto of cinematic apparition.

First shot (0'50"–1'21") *Congruity of set staging and the staging of oneself.*

Figure 4.2 Robert Fenz, *Sole of the Foot*, 2011 (shot 1)

In a doorway (probably of a café), a man framed at the bust smiles at the camera, moves slightly toward the light, turns his head to the right, to the left. His smile vanishes then reappears, he sometimes looks off screen, sometimes straight into the camera lens (as if seeing himself). Since the shot uses a hand-held camera, an overlaying occurs between the camera-gaze (into the lens) and the cameraman-gaze (into the face of the cameraman). The man most likely holds a cigarette in his hand, because smoke rises into the field of view. The image is granular, clear, and consistent, the colors deep, the palette green and yellow. The shot ends with a swish pan that shifts to the right. The shot describes the volubility of the face, the total willingness to offer one's presence to a camera, an equality in the co-creation of an image, produced as much by the film-maker, who masters precision and duration, as by the filmed subject, staging himself with jubilation and delivering what friendly, benevolent, delighted signs he wishes.

Second Shot (1'22"–1'33") *The machine.*

Figure 4.3 Robert Fenz, *Sole of the Foot*, 2011 (shot 2)

The urban sound of the preceding diurnal shot lengthens into a nocturnal image. In the background, a wide pan of green and white colors; in the foreground, a slim black bust, the ensemble is blurry, the subjects are brought back to a solid, cotton-like coating, vibrating in moving shades of color. The image goes dark, the frame oscillates: it appears the operator adjusts the lighting. A white flash, the black silhouette goes out of the field of view to the right. The shot captures a morsel of reality, prior to any realist orthoscopy, as if the film-maker hadn't yet established his frame, nor chosen the focal point, nor the diaphragm, and that the installation of the shot had been transformed into a proposal for visual art, through an editing decision. Following the humanity overflowing with emotions and the gestures of self-presentation described in the previous shot, this shot avoids anthropic points of view, and entrusts the depiction to mechanical unpredictability. However, in this quasi-abstract shot of a black mass on a green background, there clearly isn't less reality than in any other given realistic shot, and what is lost in terms of orthodox mimicry is won back in terms of textural density and haptic surprise. The extension of urban sounds into this image affirms that mechanical randomness—which also permits the understanding of events in terms of chromatic masses, and not as outlining contours—fully belongs to the realm of descriptive resources, it doesn't constitute a weak or faded version.

Third Shot (1'34"–2'26") *Dominance of the filmed subject.*

Figure 4.4 Robert Fenz, *Sole of the Foot*, 2011 (shot 3)

This shot concerns a sharply focused version of the previous shot. The black silhouette was that of a young boy, the green and white pan, a subway entrance and its lights. One by one, together or separate, three other boys enter the field of view and dance right in front of and for the camera, which they address and provoke with their gestures and movements. Due to their close proximity to the camera lens, the boys either remain blurry, or are "beheaded" by the frame, so that one especially distinguishes their chests, arms and legs. Their initiatives determine the clarity, the luminosity, and the depth of field. In this shot, the camera, the staging, and the operator let themselves be invaded and flooded by the dynamism of the filmed figures, they are the ones who create the image. The camera operator tries to focus on the children, but they move too much, so that several nuances of blurred shots succeed one another. When the young dancers depart, they leave behind the subway entrance all fogged, as if their dance succeeded in clouding the image. Therefore, this time the presentation of oneself does not merely constitute the principal motif of the shot (as in the first of this series, centered on the face), it creates the shot, in the sense that it chooses its optical and kinetic qualities. Here figures appear as subjects (and not as objects), and as subjects, they are less like individuals than vectors of visual energy.

Fourth Shot (2'27"–4'20") *Protocol of observation.*

Figure 4.5 Robert Fenz, *Sole of the Foot*, 2011 (shot 4)

The interior of a subway car. The lighting is stark, the image clear, in the gray, beige, and bluish tones of an old Parisian metro. A sequence shot records the route from one station to the next. The camera remaining stable, one can imagine it is mounted. At first, everything stays immobile; two seated male travelers punctuate the screen. A woman enters and sits right in the middle of the frame, as if she had been expected. But her behavior belies the hypothesis of a staged production. Bothered by the camera, the passenger acquiesces to its presence, lowers her eyes, withdraws, pretends not to notice. However, when the male travelers get off at the next station, she looks toward the lens, as if disappointed to realize that they didn't constitute the reason for the mechanical device, and that the filming continues. This ultra-realist shot (sharp focus, length of time indexed on a pro-filmic action, the theme of regular daily life), which brings to mind both Manet (for the absented face of the protagonist in *L'Absinthe*) and Chris Marker (for his stolen photographs of women in the subway) also constitutes an ordinary description: that of the explicit effects of observation on that which is observed, a disturbed observed subject, who withdraws into herself in order to escape the state of being visible, though it has become the very definition of her social existence in controlled society.

Fifth Shot (4'21"–4'51") *The figurative reservoir.*

Interior of a bus, night. After the icy lighting of the subway, its motifs gridded by society and its raw representation, the complex and mad softness of the lights and shadows in the city night. Seated across a window, the camera operator experiments with the optical nuances produced by different focal points on the window. A subtle palette of opacities and transparencies results, which confuses the bus interior and the street exterior, and notably does not permit the identification of the nature of a possible human shadow to the right, offering a chromatic counterweight to the warm oranges of the headlights. Is this shadow, a reflection, a silhouette? A traveler, the driver, the cameraman? There is no telling. As a result the visually rich textures, colors and lights which follow each other in the middle of the screen define this hypothetical phenomenon, no longer a euphoric face in connection with its visibility (shot 1), nor a haptic mass (shot 2), nor a kinetic body (shot 3), nor is it fleeting, in dysphoric relationship to the visible (shot 4), but an indefinite reservoir of figurative representation.

Sixth Shot (4'52"–5'01") *The "litotesque" portrait.*

Exterior night. The shot constitutes a visual paradox: to the right, a street is in perspective, in greenish colors, slightly blurry but discernible: in the foreground to the left, a bust frame, a man in focus, but whose features are barely distinguishable. In his hand something shines, maybe a lighter. Following a series of descriptive images so diverse and contrasting, his simple presence in the darkness becomes charged with mystery, it becomes etymologically "litotesque," in other words, of an inexhaustible simplicity.

The demonstration that results from such a paratactic series, indicative of a few potential cinematic descriptions, produces at least three conclusions: on the one hand, once one accepts to no longer adhere to mimicked codes of orthoscopy, no single descriptive tool possesses more legitimacy than another, concerning precision; second, visual resources are clearly unlimited, and each one of them provides new information and givens concerning the phenomenon at hand; finally, none of these techniques, nor their ensemble (infinite), echo the human being, but are merely forms of apparition, which our beliefs convert to impressions of presence. What matters, therefore, to cinema, concerns the exploration of descriptive resources, which is precisely to what the work of Robert Fenz is devoted.

Solo-forms

Such an ethical and aesthetic horizon determines two stylistic aspects of Robert Fenz. On the one hand, the textural diversity: transparent shots as well as thicker shots with gelatin-silver photo plates succeed one after the other, for the same figure or showing the same place—which is a way to visually insist that no image can claim to exhaust its motif, that every creature can beget an infinity of different impressions. And, on the other hand, editing without link shots: the shots juxtapose, more than dissolve into each other. This concerns one of the most noteworthy evolutions in the work of Robert Fenz: to increasingly abandon syntactical logic (such as in the case of the masters, Dziga Vertov or Artavazd Pelechian, who established it for the documentary) in order to continually move toward the radicalism and simplicity in parataxis. From *Vertical Air* to *The Sole of the Foot*, and *Correspondence*, the shots not only become autonomous in relation to one another, but cultivate the edges of their respective differences. For example, the very beautiful preamble in *Correspondence*, at first disconcerting, constitutes a declaration of the diversity of optical and tactile approaches, dealing with one motif: contemplative static shots follow, succeeding kinetic sequence shots, diurnal transparent shots, and nocturnal urban flashes, figurative restlessness and calm apathy, fulfillment in one shot (a man sleeps) and a cut in mid-movement (a dog gets up) ... The diverse realities handled here (Maine, West Papua, Varanasi in Uttar Pradesh/rivers, cities, men, animals) are resolutely captured according to their irreducible differences and not trapped in the nets of unfair comparisons, even if the figurative wealth of the images allows unexpected associations to emerge. The Correspondences remain, thereby, entirely to be established, and concern—not so much the relationships between locations (Papua New Guinea, Ethiopia, India) as that of the present filmed by Robert Fenz, with the past filmed by Robert Gardner (in his three films of reference, *Dead Birds* (1964), *Rivers of Sand* (1974), *Forest of Bliss* (1985)). The German philosopher, Georg Simmel (whose classes Walter Benjamin took) questioned the links between the artist and the traveler, and in 1911 he plotted out the Fenzien program: "It is well within the essence of a work of art to cut off a piece of the infinitely continuous sequences in the world, or in life, to free it from the groups that it forms, with everything that is above, or below it, and to give it a form that will only suffice its own self, and which is maintained as if by an interior core."[5]

"Liberate (the piece of the world or of life) what is pieced together"—Simmel's thoughts on liberating forms of division within continuous phenomena anticipate a notion used by Wadada Leo Smith, Robert Fenz's mentor and his first motif (he is the partner for *Duet For Trumpet and Camera* (1992), and the subject of the sublime shot—a sequence titled "Butterfly: Silver" which precedes *Vertical Air*): the *solo-form*, which associates the radical inventiveness of the musician to the unique character of improvisation. "Here the solo refers to the improvisor who performs complete improvisation as a soloist."[6] As the heir of free forms of documentary film, since the Lumière film-makers and Albert Khan, up to Peter Hutton (another of his professors) and including *The New York of Weegee* (and Amos Vogel (1948)), with every film, Robert Fenz invents a solo-form, or a freed form, from both structures and the links enforced within musical creativity; a unique form that we owe to the improvisation of a soloist, in other words, a liberated form including structures and bonds applied in *creative music*, a unique form, an *hapax*, susceptible of reporting the irreproducible character of the lived-in instant, captured in snippets (as opposed to the significant moment), seized according to an unattainable perception, and shared without instruction. Of course, real improvisation involves above all else the shooting; how to invest the here and now with the means of a perfectly mastered silver print instrument, mastered to the extent of its possibilities and not only in respect to its uses. Far from Benjaminian conceptions of photography and cinema as arts of reproducibility, Fenzian improvisation privileges celluloid film, defined as a permanent succession of differences, photogram by photogram: "Every frame of film is different. One frame of film has a million different pieces of grain. Every piece of that grain is different. Every frame then is different. So it vibrates,"[7] said Robert Fenz, an informed connoisseur of film properties and development.

However, improvisation also expands into forms of editing, in the sense where they work to respect the existence of each shot as if it were an *unicum*, a unique specimen, a conglomerate of the present that he makes sure not to confuse with any other, so that the film can legitimately make the shots flow one after another, and allow them to be thought of together, like so many specimens drawn with love from the world's immense murmurings. Such an individual, modest approach, non-definitional, non-authoritarian, affirms the infinite and vibrant character of every aspect of the real, however common or thankless it may appear at first, as is notably the case for the sad, empty lots in *The Sole of the Foot*, and for which the shot will only transmit one dimension, a specimen of visual art, which belongs as much to the characteristics of the mechanic device as to the motif itself.

The Infinite Volubility of Things

If Robert Fenz is among the "technical rebels" who keep silver print alive, it's because he knows that on every roll of film, every photogram possesses a different density, and, thus, specific exposure properties. The random variability of the silver print remains, to this day, the most respectful approach, when it comes to the infinite volubility of things—as long as it doesn't later become an object of industrial conformity through development and calibration. In the case of Peter Hutton, and then of Robert Fenz, who are part of the visual art research tradition led by the structural movements since the 1970s (notably that of Paul Sharits, Ken Jacobs, and Ernie Gehr on grain and speed), one witnesses the largest possible widening of the material palette. Until 2003, in order to conserve the richest textural palette possible, Robert Fenz worked with Mark Kosarik in a laboratory in Amherst, Massachusetts, where film development remained an artisanal, personalized craft. One can form the hypothesis that once the laboratory closed, Robert Fenz turned toward forms of discontinuity offered by film editing to elaborate the descriptive *hapax* which characterizes his research.

Conclusion in Loop Form

Georges Demenÿ (Marey's assistant), Alexandre Promio, Gabriel Veyre, and Félix Mesguisch (three of the Lumière film operators—we cannot mention them all) invented experimental forms of cinematic description. The following generations worked to elaborate its glorious and celebratory forms, including melancholic ones (from Rudy Burckhardt to Mako Idemitsu and Chick Strand); minimalist and serial forms (for example, *a.k.a Serial Killer*, by Masao Adachi (1969), *Too Early Too Late*, by Jean-Marie Straub and Danièle Huillet (1982)); plural and hybrid forms (Pierre Clémenti, Ange Leccia …). For his part, at a time when dominating documentary writing was demanded (one would have to say dominated), and bent into story-telling form, Robert Fenz elaborated with every shot and every film, ever unique and always radically simple structures; solo-forms linked to a political relationship, to the irreducible and incomparable existence of one another, who is not limited to all that is human, but spread toward the ensemble of phenomenon. As such, his work joins with the incomparable, collective inventiveness of the Lumière Vues films, Vues filmed by a virtuoso artisan of our presence in the world, who considers each phenomenon (whether an entity or connecting link) not as a universe, but as a multiverse.

Acknowledgments

Translation by Devorah Lauter.

An initial version of this text appeared in Robert Fenz, *The Sole of the Foot*, Berliner Künstlerprogramm des DAAD, Berlin, 2011.

Deep thanks to Robert Fenz and Katharina Narbutovic.

Filmography

a.k.a Serial Killer, dir. Masao Adachi, Japan, 1969, 86 mins, color, sound.
Ali in Wonderland (Ali au pays des merveilles), dirs. Djouhra Abouda and Alain Bonnamy, France, 1976, 49 mins, color, sound.
As I was Moving Ahead, Occasionally I Saw Brief Glimpses of Beauty, dir. Jonas Mekas, USA, 2000, 320 mins, color, sound.
Correspondence, dir. Robert Fenz, USA/Germany, 2011, 30 mins, color, sound.
Crossings, dir. Robert Fenz, USA/Germany, 2006, 10 mins, color, silent.
Dead Birds, dir. Robert Gardner, USA, 1963, 84 mins, color, sound.
Forest of Bliss, dir. Robert Gardner, USA, 1986, 90 mins, color, sound.
In the Shadow of the Blue Rascal (A l'ombre de la canaille bleue), dir. Pierre Clémenti, France, 1978–85, 84 mins, color, sound.
Meditations on Revolution Part I: Lonely Planet, dir. Robert Fenz, USA, 1997, 12 mins 30 secs, black and white, silent.
Meditations on Revolution Part II: The Space in Between, dir. Robert Fenz, 1997, 8 mins, black and white, silent.
Meditations on Revolution Part III: Soledad, dir. Robert Fenz, USA, 2001, 15 mins, black and white, silent.

Meditations on Revolution, Part IV: Greenville, MS, dir. Robert Fenz, USA, 2001, 29 mins 30 secs, black and white, silent.

Meditations on Revolution, Part V: Foreign City, dir. Robert Fenz, USA, 2003, 32 mins, black and white, sound.

Nothing but Time (Rien que les heures), dir. Alberto Cavalcanti, France, 1926, black and white, silent.

Rivers of Sand, dir. Robert Gardner, USA, 1974, 85 mins, color, sound.

The Magic Sun, dir. Phill Niblock, USA, 1966, 17 mins, black and white, sound.

The Sole of the Foot, dir. Robert Fenz, USA, 2011, 34 mins, color, sound.

Too Early too Late (Trop tôt trop tard), dirs. Jean-Marie Straub and Danièle Huillet, France, 100 mins, 1982, color, sound.

Vertical Air, dir. Robert Fenz, USA, 1996, 28 mins, black and white, sound.

Weegee's New York, dir. Arthur "Weegee" Felling, USA, 1948, 20 mins, color, sound.

Wheel of Ashes, 1969, dir. Peter Emanuel Goldman, France, 110 mins, black and white, sound.

Notes

1. "Description" from *L'Encyclopédie méthodique* of Panckoucke (Paris, 1872), cited by Philippe Hamon, *Introduction à l'analyse du Descriptif* (Paris: Hachette, 1981), 30.
2. Marcel Mauss, *Manuel d'ethnographie* (1947) (Paris: Payot, 2002), 35.
3. Antonin Artaud, *Le théâtre et son double* [1938], in *Œuvres complètes,* vol. XI (Paris: Gallimard, 1974), 585 et seq.
4. Maurice Merleau-Ponty, *Signes* (Paris: Gallimard, 1960), 22.
5. Georg Simmel, *La Philosophie de l'aventure. Essais* (1911), trans. Alix Guillain (Paris: L'Arche, 2002), 73.
6. Leo Smith, *Notes (8 pieces). Source a new world music: creative music,* published by Leo Smith, 1973, 10. Leo Smith studied the history of forms there, bequeathed by free-form jazz, and also demonstrates his philosophy of improvisation. Robert Fenz provided us with a copy of this text in 2004, noting its significant importance to him.
7. Robert Fenz with Wadada Leo Smith—*Reverberations* (August 2008), from http://VOORUIT.BE/NL/PAGE/2183 (last accessed June 29, 2011).

5

OUR FAVORITE FILM SHOCKS

Rane Willerslev and Christian Suhr

The medium of film has long been hailed for its capacity for producing shocks of an entertaining, thought-provoking, or even politically emancipative nature. But what is a shock, how and when does it occur, how long does it last, and are there particular techniques for producing cinematic shocks? In this text we exchange personal experiences of cinematic shocks and ponder over these questions as related to wider theories on human trauma, emancipation, and enlightenment. In conclusion we argue for a revision of anthropological notions of validity in terms of the efficacy of the cinematic shock rather than the perceived correspondence between cinema and the real.

The Montage Fist

Christian: In the history of cinema the notion of film shock has become almost synonymous with early Soviet montage. The idea of film as a kind of shock therapy was developed by Sergei Eisenstein with his somewhat radical concept of "cinema fist."[1] This implied film understood within the framework of dialectical materialism, proposing that artistic creation, like political progress, comes about from the interaction of contradictory opposites.

Rane: You mean the Hegelian–Marxist dialectic of thesis–antithesis–synthesis?

Christian: Absolutely, even though neither Marx nor Hegel used this phrase themselves. In any case, Eisenstein's principal thesis was that the single image is a "montage cell" and importantly not just an element of montage.[2] The creation of film is not just the piecing together of images as if they were bricks in a house. Within each frame certain dynamics are already present and when confronted with other montage cells these frames start to interfere and vibrate with one another causing various resonances and dissonances. So, the image gains its "punch" and qualitative leap through its placement within the wider dialectical montage structure, which again starts to resonate or dissonate through its insertion into even larger patterns of contradictory opposites. These clashes inflict a form of perceptual "wound" or "trauma," if you like, through which new and fresher perceptions might be born. I think that something along these lines was the idea behind Eisenstein's "Intellectual Cinema."[3] By way of radical montage, Eisenstein believed that humankind possessed a new powerful instrument for de-naturalizing social life by recasting it through unfamiliar eyes.

Rane: Can you give an example?

Christian: I have to confess that I like reading Eisenstein more than I like watching his films, but let me give an example that often has been highlighted. In Eisenstein's famous movie *October*,[4] celebrating the 1917 Revolution, we see Kerensky, the head of the provisional government, opposed by the Bolsheviks. Kerensky stands before the door of the czar's chambers and Eisenstein cuts from Kerensky to a gold peacock and back again. This leads us to see Kerensky as a peacock. So, an initial contradiction—contrasting images of Kerensky and a peacock—is followed by a revelation: as Gilberto Perez puts it, Kerensky achieves the vanity of a peacock, "a puppet whose illusions of grandeur are part of the machinery of exploitation."[5] In a similar way, weird looking bourgeois women are contrasted with a young revolutionary, and Kerensky's personal army is compared with wine glasses and tin soldiers. Through such juxtapositions the viewer is drawn into a new dialectic understanding of the world. What I like about Eisenstein is his insistence on using cinematic montage as a vehicle of revolutionary consciousness.

Rane: But do these montage shocks really work today? When I watch *October*, I cannot help wondering if Eisenstein's famous "montage fist" has lost its punch. His montage was supposed to shock the viewer into some altered state of consciousness, but have we not become immune to it? We see these techniques used all the time in MTV and in American movie trailers. There is not much novelty about this kind of montage. If it shocks us it does so only in the most conventional sense.

Christian: I guess these films had a different impact 90 years ago. But perhaps you are right, I also have this feeling. Having been raised with socialism, the exposure of the bourgeoisie in Eisenstein's films does not seem that radical to me either. So what would be a powerful montage shock in your opinion?

Rane: The montage cinema of Dziga Vertov is still really powerful. Although Eisenstein and Vertov were contemporaries and both were Russian Jews in culture and supposedly Marxists by ideology, their artistic visions differed quite profoundly. I don't regard Vertov as a political film-maker, at least not in the conventional sense. If Marxism involves the idea that actual or material processes inflect the course of human history, then Vertov may not really be a Marxist either. He oriented his masterpiece *The Man with the Movie Camera*[6] toward a contemplative and immaterial abstraction of human destiny, rather than toward something mediated by history. In this sense, he is more of a visionary, concerned with extracting cinema's capacity to reveal the potentiality of human creativity, than a traditional political film revolutionary. Vertov wanted to create a new reality modelled on a cyborg utopia, a high-tech reality where man and machine work together in perfect symbiosis.[7] We see his vision of peace between man and machine in several scenes: saws are made to dance at a sawmill and our eyes are made to spin like propellers. Most powerfully this is evoked in the recurring image of the human eye superimposed on the camera lens (see Figure 5.1).

Christian: I also like these weird camera angles and repetitions of shots. But what does this have to do with cinema's capacity for producing shocks?

Rane: I think that Vertov's vision of merging man and machine was as shocking then as it is now. At least I am shocked when watching his cyborg-reality, but shocked in a sort of thrilling way. His montages places us within the cinematic machine and provides us with an eye outside our ordinary organic eye, a super eye, whose power to see quite clearly surpasses our own human vision or perhaps adds to it a new cyborg dimension that fundamentally alters our perception of reality. We become a hyperbole of vision or just plain super vision![8] Suddenly, we see into the future or at least a version of the future. In this sense, Vertov's montages, though artificial constructs, are in an important sense more real than the present world that we experience outside the screen. In a sense, Vertov's film is itself situated in the future; its being is with a time that has not yet passed. This capacity of Vertov not

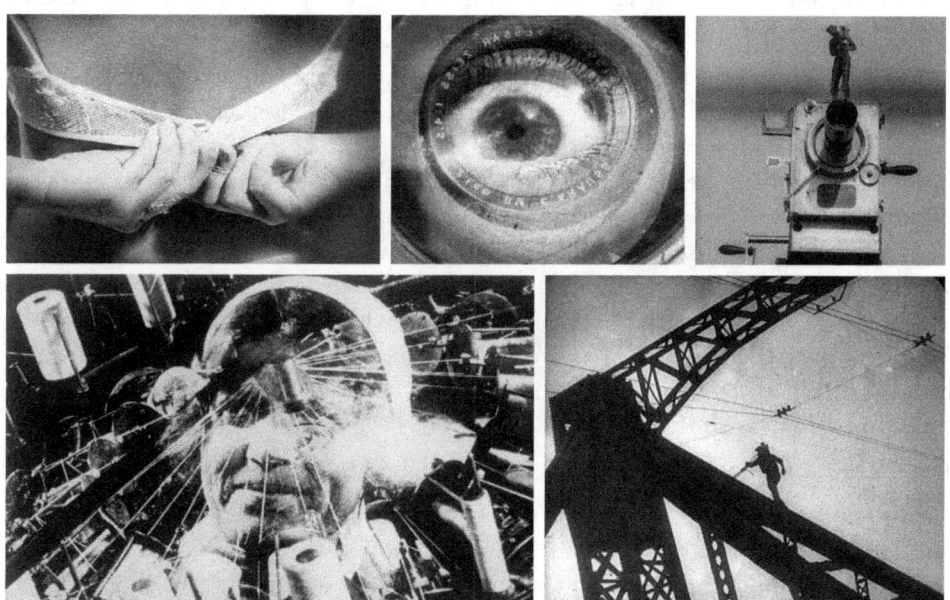

Figure 5.1 Dziga Vertov, *The Man with the Movie Camera* (Kiev: VUFKU, 1929), 68 mins.

simply to film in time, but *become* time, is truly shocking to me. The shock does not simply result from the pleasure of seeing into a time yet to come and which plays itself out in a surveillance-based reality, but also from the fear that I too am somebody to be seen, and that, indeed, the machine eyes are everywhere, watching me. In *The Man with the Movie Camera* we see a city full of eyes: cars, mannequins, and houses grow faces and stare at us. Being exposed to this strange place in which every object has a perspective of its own, is truly creepy. And this is why Vertov is at some pains to reveal what this technology—which enables vision to see without limits—is made of and how we can control it.

Christian: All this sounds a bit obscure to me. What do you mean?

Rane: The cinema of Eisenstein and the other montage theorists suffered from much of the same Hollywood imaginary as does conventional cinema of today. They all attract our attention to the story lines in the films, but not to the constructed nature of film itself. Thus, part of the power of these films lies in the covering-up of what could be called their "mode of production."[9] When watching these films, we tend to forget that they are orchestrated by humans. Even though they de-familiarize our commonsensical vision of things, they also resemble it by concealing the process of their own making. Vertov sought to expose this illusion by laying bare the devices of his film production so that we are encouraged to reflect critically on what we see. *Man with the Movie Camera* is about the making of a movie. Its sequences and the assembly of those sequences are continually made visible to us. The cameraman is shooting; we see the results of his craftsmanship. We also see the editor at work, putting film clips together that are then exposed on the screen. What Vertov is saying is that film is made by people and thus we don't have to fear it, because we can control it.

Christian: First of all I should say that I really appreciate the way in which Vertov draws our attention to the constructed nature of film—*Man with a Movie Camera* was and still is incredibly important in this regard. But what about his overall vision? Sympathetic perhaps, but not really a convincing vision. Have people taken control of the movie camera? Things seem to have gone quite the opposite way. Whereas satellites observe us from afar, nanotechnologies see our bodies from within. The mechanical vision that Vertov cherished is just as much a governor as a liberator of life. Mechanical eyes are everywhere and often we have little or no power over them. I think that Vertov was, despite his creative spirit and sober-minded ideals, a great romantic. The dreamy character of his vision is fascinating but also extremely shocking.

Rane: This is a bold statement. You have to elaborate further.

Christian: Well, I think it is clear that only few people, except perhaps intellectuals and avant garde artists, have found a revolutionary potential in Vertov's film. I like the film a lot and I can feel inspired and amused by it, but I'm not shocked. I am probably "thrilled" as you say, but I am suspicious about the way I am thrilled.

To what degree does the film really push my imagination? Do I like it because it reiterates my preconceptions or allows me to read them into its images, or does it really teach me something that I didn't know before? When you say that the film becomes time itself, I hear you reiterating a certain Deleuzian understanding of cinema, which to me is not revolutionary at all.[10] Why do you like this film? Is it because it allows you to linger on within these Deleuzian fantasies about the virtual, the pure time image, pure potentiality, and pure becoming? This superhuman becoming of vision sounds amazing, but I am not fully convinced. Perhaps you are right that Vertov was not a Marxist after all. If Vertov's film is to be received within such a Deleuzian framework, then it becomes nothing but a clothing of a suspiciously elitist, neo-liberal, and perhaps—as Catherine Russell says[11]—even sexist ideology. I can't see the critical potential. To me this view on Vertov's work fetishizes a fantasy of the human machine as a kind of boundless, free agency that I don't believe is possible or desirable.

Rane: You have a point here. But I still like Vertov's playful attitude to film-making more than I like the propaganda of Eisenstein. At least Vertov's intention was to liberate our minds, not simply to indoctrinate us.

The Long Take

Christian: So far we have talked about film shock in relation to montage. But we might also locate cinematic shocks in something that is not based in montage. Here I am thinking of the "long take." Put somewhat crudely, I would say that whereas montage in the radical version of Vertov is applied in order to produce new things and new futures, the long camera take allows us to look back at social life at the moment of its becoming.[12] In this way, long, uninterrupted takes can be shocking exposures of how concepts, ideas, emotions, ways of perceiving, ways of living, and ways of film-making are born in the midst of the interaction between humans and their environments. Often the concepts we use appear to acquire a life of their own. Often we naturalize our own way of understanding and perceiving the world as if this was the only one available. It's the task of anthropology to denaturalize such concepts and perceptions and I think film has a special way of doing this.

Rane: Can you give some examples?

Christian: As you know, I like the work of David and Judith MacDougall. Especially *Gandhi's Children*[13]—a three-hour-long film dwelling to the extreme on the everyday lives of children at a Delhi orphanage. We have discussed our disagreements about this film at length, so we need not reiterate all of it here. But I think the way in which the extended scenes of this film allow me to recognize these children as full human beings, in the sense of Emmanuel Levinas in his work on ethics[14]—that is, as people who are not reducible to any single projection or image—is truly shocking. Not thrilling, but astonishing, in the original meaning of the word as being struck by thunder. A testimony of an almost impossible manner of human survival in a world gone mad. We learn something about classic virtues such as humility. It's humbling to witness these children's ability to produce a life, despite the hardships of their circumstances.

Rane: I think that this film along with what you describe is not at all shocking, but boring; an endless line of long takes of the dire routines of everyday life. This monotony knocks me out completely. Nothing happens, and then even less of the same. Nothing like a stroke of thunder. How can you call this shocking?

Christian: But it has an effect on you. You yourself said that it "knocks you out." This is what thunder does. It infers a shock of some sort. It is so shocking that I believe you never managed to reach the end of this film.

Rane: Shock in this perspective is not at all the right word. Observational cinema's concern with the familiar, the everyday impulses of life takes the magic out of the image by making it imitate the human eye. Shock provoking cinema is about breaking away from the familiar regime of vision and its confrontation with the new and untested like what Vertov did. That is where cinema's magic is situated; its capacity to shock us.

Christian: Shocking cinema must be about breaking away from the familiar. So far we agree. It is true that some observational film-makers favor the long uninterrupted take for its way of simulating our normal field of vision.[15] But I think this is not correct. Often montage produces a better imitation of the rapid movements and constant reframings of a human eye. We simply don't perceive in the way a mechanical camera does. This is why long takes are so incredibly shocking—they insistently force us to continuously look at something and not to look away as we usually do when we get shy or bored. Actually, I think this is also what Deleuze means when he talks of "false continuity shots."[16] Such long takes destabilize our human habit of producing a world of perception that matches how we like to think of and act in it. Long takes set us aside from the possibility of action and render us into witnesses of life.

Rane: I agree with you on this last point. We were both flabbergasted when watching the first 11 minutes of Asch and Chagnon's film, the famous *The Ax Fight*[17] that broke out between different lineages of Yanomamö Indians (see Figure 5.2). This was basically a single take and it was almost impossible to see what really happened. Just a lot of odd Indians running around half naked with axes and spears, screaming incomprehensible insults at each other. I love this long take—it's by no means boring, but truly thrilling, revealing to us how scared anthropologists and ethnographic film-makers might get, when confronted with the radical impermeable alterity of others.

Christian: I totally agree. Also the montage of this film is absolutely astonishing. The subsequent efforts of Chagnon to render the fight intelligible in terms of kinship and alliance theory only add to the creation of bewilderment. This is anthropological theory thrown into the world by means of images, montage, kinship charts,

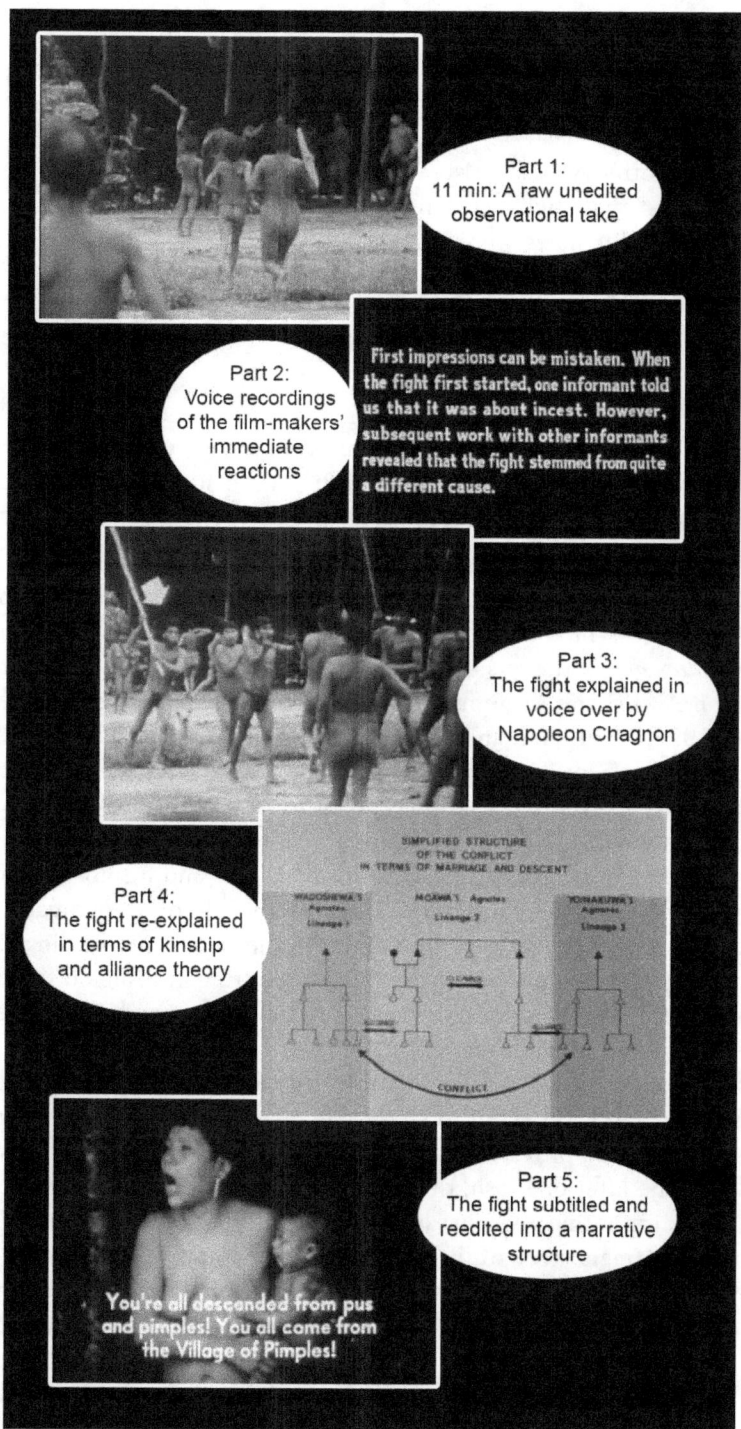

Figure 5.2 Timothy Asch and Napoleon Chagnon, *The Ax Fight*, 30 mins, 1975, Watertown, CT: Documentary Educational Resources.

and voice-over. In the clashes and misfits between theory, film aesthetics, and pro-filmic "reality," truly thought-provoking and critical potential arises. This is why we still keep discussing this odd film. Too bad there are so few films like *The Ax Fight*—it's a model to follow.

Rane: I like Timothy Asch's insistence on keeping the mistakes in the film like strange "gargoyles" that stick out. This is what makes it so difficult and thrilling to watch. As he said, "its flaws were instructive to students—they stick out and you say, what's this?"[18]

Seeing Spirits

Christian: Let us now discuss this question: Can cinema, which is only concerned with the visible world, show us the invisible?[19] And if so, is this of any importance for its capacity for producing shocks?

Rane: I think cinema may give us access to the world of spirits in that it can make us behold a world "turned inside out" or perhaps it even "turns us inside out" in the process of looking—which is, I would say, rather shocking. Take the film *The Journals of Knud Rasmussen*.[20] It depicts the relationship between an Inuit shaman, Avva, of the Canadian Arctic, and some famous Danish explorers during their "Great Sled Journey" of 1922.[21] The shaman must decide whether to accept the Christian faith that is converting the Inuit across Greenland and Canada. Avva and his community are starving and he eventually decides to bring his people to Igoolik, the place where the Christian Inuit live. As they arrive, a line of Inuit walks out to meet them, singing a hymn. Avva is given to understand that if he and his group join the new faith, they can eat with the community of Christians; if not, they must starve. One by one, the shaman's people leave him and join the Christians, placing themselves in line, kneeling, ready to pray. In the end Avva is sitting in his igloo surrounded by only three persons. You wonder: who are these folks that stay loyal to the shaman? And indeed, you find out at the end of the film, when Avva finally decides to join the Christian community. Standing alone in the endless landscape, he calls out to his helping spirits and asks them to leave. Weeping and moaning in despair, we see the three persons, who previously sat around him in the igloo, walk away, over the snow and into the interior. Gosh, these are his helping spirits, who are now leaving him! The shock is not that Avva has lost his spiritual allies; his meaning as a shaman. We all know the tragic story of disappearing indigenous cultures all too well. The real blow rests with the fact that what all along we took to be ordinary persons, something immediate organic, turns out to have been spirits. What is revealed at the moment the spirits are lost to the shaman is what has been concealed all along—namely, that the material and the spiritual constitute the otherside of each other; they are interchangeable. This is what I mean when saying that the interior and exterior are turned inside out in the process of watching this film.

Christian: It reminds me of David Lynch's films. He operates in the same kind of spirit economy that you describe. Also here we encounter the spiritual and material, dream, and reality as mutually entangled. Take the mystery of the murdered Laura Palmer in *Twin Peaks*.[22] As Bent Fausing points out, we are constantly confronted with a double perspective, something which Lynch often exposes by showing the same thing twice.[23] In the series' introductory still image we see the road leading into the town Twin Peaks with the two mountain peaks in the background. At the edge of the road stands a placard showing an image of the same two mountain peaks. The placard is the ideal fiction about Twin Peaks—a fantasy about everything being transparent and nothing hidden. By contrast, the real Twin Peaks on the screen is covered in dark shadows and is surrounded by dead trees and telephone poles with no wires.[24] What is real and what is phantasy swim in and out of focus. Likewise, at the end of each episode, we see a photo of the murdered Laura Palmer's smiling face. Her eyes are always covered by credit list names. Her actual identity is hidden, what is not there to be seen, the dark side: the violence and the sexual abuse. We are confronted with the two parallel universes, which mirror and echo one another: the apparent visible and transparent world, and the hidden and twisted world.

Rane: I agree. This is typical for *Twin Peaks*, the characters are constantly questioning who they are and what is happening to them; again and again they find themselves deceived, deluded, and misled by appearances. What is shocking about *Twin Peaks* is not the violence, though that is quite ugly, but that the realness of the hidden side—the shadow side—identifies what is uncanny and twisted about the perceptible and known side of life. The two are so ensnared that I cannot help getting confused about the basic existential question of what counts as reality.

Christian: We both like to be shocked by *Twin Peaks*. At some point I guess we need to consider whether we are really shocked by it or only thrilled. Can I mention yet another observational film that I think offers some shocking scenes?

Rane: Okay, go ahead, but don't make me bored again.

Christian: I'm afraid that I need to bore you again. I want to mention *Koriam's Law and the Dead Who Govern*[25] by Gary Kildea and Andrea Simon.

Rane: Gosh, I knew you would talk about that film—it's not shocking.

Christian: The film explores the Kivung Movement in Papua New Guinea—a movement commonly referred to as a Cargo Cult. In the first part of the film, we are presented with long takes of ritual participants serving food and offering money to their forefathers. A performance that at first glance—at least to non-Melanesianists—may appear somewhat incomprehensible, irrational, if not outright silly. Nevertheless, over the course of watching the whole film—which lasts nearly two hours—what first seemed empty becomes charged with something rather other-worldly. What at first appeared to be a waste of fine food becomes comprehensible as real food for the ancestors.

Figure 5.3 Gary Kildea and Andrea Simon, *Koriam's Law and the Dead Who Govern*, 110 mins, 2005, Canberra: ANU RSPAS Film Unit and Ronin Films. Courtesy of Gary Kildea.

Rane: I don't agree that anything gets charged in this film. At least, I can testify that it completely drained my energy.

Christian: Okay, I'll omit the "we" then and only speak for myself. What for me enables an experience of some kind of charged atmosphere or sense of the invisible presence of the ancestors is the few but well posited montage effects of the film. Some of these effects come about as the result of the commentaries of the anthropologist Andrew Lattas and his key informant or co-anthropologist Peter Averea. A turning point, however, comes about in a scene around 30 minutes into the film, where we are shown a German missionary preaching at the local Catholic church prompting the locals to stop wasting money and food on their ancestors and instead give it to their children. After criticizing the natives for their occult beliefs, he reads from the bible, conducts communion, offering the local churchgoers a piece of the "body of Christ." The scene establishes itself as an allegory to or even caricature of indigenous beliefs. At one level it points to occult beliefs in Western culture. At another level it contextualizes why these people may have come to think that whites are hiding the true knowledge from them. By upturning such assumptions and stereotypes, the juxtaposition of shots produces a different experience of what goes on—a possibility for conceiving that the food served for the forefathers might not just be a waste of food.[26] At a later stage in the film, we are forced into watching extremely slow pans from an open window to a table where ancestors are offered food. While such shots in the beginning of the film initially appeared empty, they are now filled with a pretty dense feel of ancestral presence (see Figure 5.3).

Rane: Okay, I see that you like this film, but do you remember when we screened a scene from it as part of our joint presentation at the UCL [University College London] weekly seminar in 2006? People were completely bored and confused.

Christian: This is true, but that was because I made the same mistake as we make now, namely of explaining the shock. Once the shock has been explained it's gone, it has ceased to exist. Explanation is a form of killing, and film theory is a method of killing films, making them numb, making them succumb to some tangible analytic frame.

Film as Ritual Technique

Christian: The problem that film has as a ritual technique that somehow may conjure the invisible is that it is fixed in a certain form and therefore can be endlessly reviewed and explained. Real "ritual," if we can speak of such a thing, is not possible to capture and pacify so easily since it has the capacity to shift its form in each and every repetition. This is the loss of "aura" that Walter Benjamin described.[27] The problem with film is that, except for the shifting context of viewers and viewing environments, the repetition is always identical.

Rane: This is true. Repetition of the same in the exact same way is extremely painful, not thrilling at all. Actually, now we speak of Deleuze and repetition. He points out how a repetition can never be the same; it always does something extra through its insertion into new contexts.[28] It transmutes itself. Perhaps "aura" could still be found to exist in these transmutations of repetitions of the same, but in constantly new variations.

Christian: One really disturbing film experience I once had concerns exactly this. I was watching Philip Gröning's film *Into Great Silence*—yet another very long and slow film about the everyday doings at a monastery in France.[29] It was late at night so I was quite exhausted. At some point the film became really creepy. Somehow scenes started to repeat themselves—then suddenly again the monks had their lunch in the sunshine on the small veranda with birds singing from above, the only time in the whole film when talking was allowed, but then once again these monks walking down the silent halls, then lighting the candles again, it looked as if exactly the same candle was being lighted over and over, and then again this monk kneeling down to perform a small prayer. Even the same Bible citations were repeated. As I said, it was really late at night that I was watching this film so my consciousness was swimming in and out—neither being fully asleep nor awake. All these repetitions produced something like a waking nightmare. This monastic world felt truly horrifying. It seemed not at all like a life; more like death or hell or perhaps the intermediate space between life and death. Then I finally discovered that the DVD player had started to repeat a sequence of approximately 20 minutes. I guess this whole sequence was repeated three or four times before I discovered what was wrong. This mechanical reediting of the film was shocking in a really frightening way.

Rane: What you just describe is in some important sense the definition of "melancholia" in Freud's conception—endless unconscious repetition of an unrecognized trauma.[30] I'm glad you survived because sometimes melancholia leads to suicide. As said, for Deleuze this is not possible since repetitions can never be exactly the same. But perhaps it is in fact possible with these new technologies of film and DVD players. As you say, in the age of mechanical reproduction, a precise mechanical repetition is in fact possible. Bruce Kapferer has discussed Deleuze's theory of film as a model for understanding ritual.[31] In fact following Deleuze's own theory we must recognize that ritual is more cinematic than cinema, exactly for its way of bending and changing its form in each and every repetition.

Christian: Yes, that's true. There are ritual repetitions that always and necessarily must be repetitions on a path and then there are mechanical repetitions and here we have the loss of aura—a risk of suffocating the possibility of ritual. Film is a bad replication of real ritual. But perhaps there are a few exceptions. Do you remember Sasha Rubel's[32] film experiment with film and spirit possession [see Figure 5.4]? Following Kapferer and Deleuze she constructs what she calls a sacrificial cinema ritual. On the basis of a kind of cloth embroidered with decorations of ritual

Figure 5.4 Sasha Rubel, *Vertigo, Vodoun, Vérité*, 25 mins, Paris: NIMBY Films. Courtesy of Sasha Rubel.

intervals of an African spirit possession cult she edits her film as a precise translation of ritual time—a translation from live ritual to printed cloth, which then is measured and reapplied as a system for film editing. The film switches back and forth between a number of possession dances, traditional performances in African villages, performances of modern dance companies, sacrifices of goats, purifications of water—a pretty mesmerizing cacophonic constellation of diverse images, film styles, and sounds.

Rubel is herself a dancer and participant in a spirit possession cult. At the time of editing the film she suffered from a paralysis making it impossible for her to dance. She sees her film as a way of accessing the space of the "virtual" that she couldn't access within her own body due to her paralysis. The link between the film subjects and their actions is completely dismantled in this film in favor of a radical alterity beyond human control that acts out a certain display.[33] As Michael Taussig puts it in his discussion of *Les Maîtres Fous*[34] montage becomes a manner of "interruptedness"—a device for provoking a zone of imaginary possibility where any sense of stable identity is turned upside down and made strange.[35] Rubel calls it a way of citing spirits. A kind of film choreography of alterity becoming alterity.

Rane: Yes, I also like Rubel's experiment, but now I wish to be the critical voice. You mentioned *Les Maîtres Fous*. Paul Henley has an important point about the montage of this film.[36] Especially about Rouch's juxtaposition of a shot featuring performers in the *hauka* spirit possession cult cracking an egg on the head of a statue, representing the British governor, with a shot of the real governor wearing a white plumed helmet. This juxtaposition was celebrated by Taussig and others as a kind of subversion of imperial power.[37] For Henley the montage and the interpretation of the montage simply mirror certain political preferences of French academics and avant garde artists in the 1960s. In actual fact the cracking of an egg is about achieving the powers of spirits in order to cure a problem of infertility. So, as in your point previously regarding my understanding of Vertov, we need also here to ask to what degree such film montage works to reiterate our preconceptions and to what degree we are pushed beyond them.

The Effective Shock

Rane: By way of conclusion perhaps we could say that cinema's capacity for producing shocks of an entertaining, thought-provoking, or even politically emancipative nature is situated in "efficacy" rather than in the medium's capacity to reflect what we conventionally take to constitute the socially real. In other words, being shocked by film, whether through montage, the long take, or even the interplay between the material and the spiritual, has little to do with realism in the conventional sense of the word, but everything to do with *effect*. This is essentially an anti-representationalist insight, which, I think, is in accordance with Deleuze, who claims that an image is not a representation of a physical reality, but a movement in the world of the mind—that is, "The image is the spiritual life," all by itself.[38] Our eyes are, so to say, *inside* the images themselves and so, too, do we participate directly in the creations of the shocks that we are said to perceive on the screen. The imaginary images of the film shock and our perception of them is indiscernible. All of this implies that the film shock effect becomes a kind of virtual spectacle—a purely contemplative and essentially dematerialized spiritual affair.[39] The effective film shock, we could say, forces us out and away from the traditional representationalist position trapped in realism to a position invested with the power to liberate the human eye from the world.

Christian: This notion of efficacy works well with Charles Taylor's criticism of the correspondence theory of truth.[40] What he basically argues is that since a theory about social practice is itself social, it inevitably changes its object of study in some way. For this reason validity cannot be based in a notion of truth as correspondence. The studied practices would simply have transformed by the time the validity of a theory could be assessed. Taylor proposes that instead we should value a theory for its way of producing what he calls "better practices." What we seem to suggest here is that (1) film can be understood as a theory and (2) that its validity lies in its way of pushing the limits of our perception, to make us see and understand other things, and somehow not only enlarge our field of perception but perhaps even produce the object of perception in preferable ways. I like this idea. I just wish to say two things. First, there is something strange about the way we constantly return to a notion of failed correspondence when we validate the efficacy of these film shocks. We like films when they seem to fail to correspond to or in some way turn upside down what we thought was the "real"—be it the "realities" of Yanomamö Indians, Laura Palmer, the organic spirits in the Knud Rasmussen film, or the invisible forefathers of the Kivung movement in Papua New Guinea. To what degree have we removed ourselves from a correspondence theory of truth? It seems simply to have become a theory of truth in terms of failure of correspondence. The other point I wish to address is that, while we both have a tendency to highlight films in terms of such a failure of correspondence, there also seems to be a way in which these films correspond pretty well with some standard theoretical preferences that we also have. You like Deleuze, I like Levinas. You like to be shocked by futuristic propellers, rapid crosscuttings and montage, I like to be shocked by slow revelations of "full" human beings who, despite being displayed through multiple and often long camera takes, somehow still are left to me as a mystery. I guess for our next discussion we need to force each other into watching films that we don't like to watch. We need to experience forms of shocks that are not just likeable and to which we don't have a proper vocabulary ready to explain away the mechanisms of how we are shocked.

Filmography

Gandhi's Children, dir. David MacDougall, Australia, 2008, 185 mins.
Into Great Silence, dir. Philip Gröning, UK, 2005, 162 mins.
Koriams Law and the Dead who Govern, dirs. Gary Kildea and Andrea Simon, Australia, 2005, 110 mins.
October: Ten Days that Shook the World Eisenstein, Sergei, Soviet Union, 1928, 104 mins.
The Ax Fight, dirs. Timothy Asch and Napoleon Chagnon, U.S.A. 1975, 30 mins.
The Man with the Movie Camera, dir. Dziga Vertov,, Soviet Union, 1929, 68 mins.
The Journals of Knud Rasmussen, dir. Zacharias Kunuk, Canada, 2006, 112 mins.
Twin Peaks, dirs. Lynch, David and Mark Frost., U.S.A., 1990/1991, 47 mins.(97 episodes / TV Drama).
Vertigo, Vodoun, Vérité, dir. Sasha Rubel, France, 2011, 25 mins.

Notes

1. Sergei Eisenstein, *Selected Works* (London: BFI, 1988), 64.
2. Sergei Eisenstein, "The Cinematographic Principle and the Ideogram," in *Film Form—Essays in Film Theory* (London: Meridian Books, 1963), 37.
3. Ibid., 30.
4. Sergei Eisenstein, *October: Ten Days that Shook the World* (Moscow: Sovkino, 1928), 104 mins.
5. Gilberto Perez, *The Material Ghost: Films and their Medium* (Baltimore, MD: Johns Hopkins University Press, 1998), 154.
6. Dziga Vertov, *The Man with the Movie Camera* (Kiev: VUFKU, 1929), 68 mins.
7. Dziga Vertov, "Kinoks: A Revolution," in Annette Michelson (ed.), *Kino-Eye: The Writings of Dziga Vertov* (Berkeley, CA: University of California Press, 1984), 17.
8. Nicholas Baume, *Supervision* (London: Institute of Contemporary Arts, 2006), 32.
9. Gilles Deleuze, *Cinema 2: The Time Image* (London: Continuum, 2005).
10. Terry Eagleton, *Literary Theory: An Introduction* (Oxford: Basil Blackwell, 1983), 171.
11. Catherine Russell, "Women in Cities: Comparative Modernities and Cinematic Space in the 1930s," in Christian Suhr and Rane Willerslev (eds), *Transcultural Montage* (New York: Berghahn, 2013).
12. See, e.g., Paul Henley, "Putting Film to Work: Observational Cinema as Practical Ethnography," in Sarah Pink, László Kürti, and Ana Isabel Afonso (eds), *Working Images: Visual Research and Representation in Ethnography* (London: Routledge, 2004), 109–30. See also David MacDougall, *The Corporeal Image: Film, Ethnography, and the Senses* (Princeton, NJ: Princeton University Press, 2006).
13. David MacDougall, *Gandhi's Children* (Canberra: Ronin Films, 2008), 185 mins.
14. Emmanuel Levinas, *Collected Philosophical Papers*, trans. Alphonso Lingis (Dordrecht: Martinus Nijhoff Publishers, 1987).
15. Paul Henley, "Putting Film to Work," 114.
16. Gilles Deleuze, *Cinema 2: The Time Image*, 41.
17. Timothy Asch and Napoleon Chagnon, *The Ax Fight* (Watertown, MA: Documentary Educational Resources, 1975), 30 mins.
18. Timothy Asch in Jay Ruby, *Picturing Culture: Explorations of Film & Anthropology* (Chicago, IL: University of Chicago Press, 2000), 129.

19. The question has been discussed by a number of authors, see, e.g., Christian Suhr and Rane Willerslev, "Can Film Show the Invisible: The Work of Montage in Ethnographic Filmmaking," *Current Anthropology*, 53 (3), 2012, 282–301; Arnd Schneider, "Expanded Visions: Rethinking Anthropological Research and Representation through Experimental Film," in Tim Ingold (ed.), *Redrawing Anthropology: Materials, Movements, Lines* (Burlington, VT: Ashgate Publishing, 2011), 177–94; Wilma Kiener, "The Absent and the Cut," *Visual Anthropology* 21, 2008, 393–409; George E. Marcus, "The Modernist Sensibility in Recent Ethnographic Writing and the Cinematic Metaphor of Montage," in Lucien Taylor (ed.), *Visualizing Theory: Selected Essays from V.A.R. 1990–1994* (New York and London: Routledge, 1994).
20. Zacharias Kunuk, *The Journals of Knud Rasmussen*, 112 mins (Montreal: Isuma, 2006).
21. Knud Rasmussen, *Den Store Slæderejse* (The Great Sled Journey) (Copenhagen: Gyldendal, 1932).
22. David Lynch and Mark Frost, *Twin Peaks*, 29 episodes of 47 mins, TV Drama, Lynch/Frost Productions, 1991.
23. See the discussion of *Twin Peaks* in Bent Fausing, *Synet som sans* (Copenhagen: Tiderne Skifter, 1995).
24. Ibid., 27–33.
25. Gary Kildea and Andrea Simon, *Koriam's Law and the Dead Who Govern* (Canberra: ANU RSPAS Film Unit and Ronin Films, 2005), 110 mins.
26. Food offered to the ancestors in the Kivung can be eaten by the family after the spirits have dined on its essence. In *Koriam's Law* we learn how fireflies land on the food as a sign that the dead have feasted.
27. Walter Benjamin, "The Work of Art in the Age of Mechanical Reproduction," in Hannah Arendt (ed. and trans.), *Illuminations* (London: Fontana, 1968).
28. Gilles Deleuze, *Difference and Repetition*, trans. P. Patton (New York: Columbia University Press, 1994).
29. Philip Gröning, *Into Great Silence* (New York: Zeitgeist Films, 2005), 162 mins.
30. Sigmund Freud, "Mourning and Melancholia," in Leticia Glocer Fiorini, Thierry Bokanowski, and Sergio Lewkowicz (eds), *On Freud's Mourning and Melancholia* (London: Karnac Books, 2009 [1917]).
31. Bruce Kapferer, "Montage and Time: Deleuze, Cinema and a Buddhist Sorcery Rite," in Christian Suhr and Rane Willerslev (eds), *Transcultural Montage* (New York: Berghahn, 2013).
32. Sasha Rubel, *Vertigo, Vodoun, Vérité* (Paris: NIMBY Films, 2011), 25 mins.
33. Gilles Deleuze, *Cinema 2: The Time Image*, 272.
34. Jean Rouch, *Les Maîtres Fous*, 24 mins (Paris: Films de la Pléiade, 1955).
35. See Michael Taussig, *Shamanism, Colonialism, and the Wild Man: A Study in Terror and Healing* (Chicago, IL: University of Chicago Press, 1986), 441–3; Michael Taussig, *Mimesis and Alterity: A Particular History of the Senses* (London: Routledge, 1993), 243.
36. Paul Henley, "Spirit Possession, Power, and the Absent Presence of Islam: Re-viewing *Les maîtres fous*," *Journal of the Royal Anthropological Institute*, 12, 2006, 731–61.
37. Michael Taussig, *Mimesis and Alterity: A Particular History of the Senses* (London: Routledge, 1993), 243; Catherine Russell, *Experimental Ethnography: The Work of Film in the Age of Video* (Durham, NC and London: Duke University Press, 1999), 224.
38. Gilles Deleuze, *Essays Critical and Clinical*, trans. Michael A. Greco and Daniel W. Smith (Minneapolis, MN: University of Minnesota Press, 1997), 169.
39. Peter Hallward, *Out of this World: Deleuze and the Philosophy of Creation* (London: Verso, 2006), 116.
40. Charles Taylor, *Philosophy and the Human Sciences: Philosophical Papers 2* (Cambridge: Cambridge University Press, 1990).

6

DO NO HARM—THE CAMERALESS ANIMATION OF ANTHROPOLOGIST ROBERT ASCHER

Kathryn Ramey

Finally Adair felt that it was time to bring up the subject of our visit. Adair explained that we wanted to teach some Navajo to make movies and mentioned Worth's part in the process several times ... When Adair finished, Sam thought for a while, and then turned to Worth and asked a lengthy question which was interpreted as, "Will making movies do the sheep any harm?"

Worth was happy to explain that, as far as he knew, there was no chance that making movies would harm the sheep.

Sam thought this over and then asked, "Will making movies do the sheep good?" Worth was forced to reply that as far as he knew making movies wouldn't do the sheep any good.

Sam thought this over, then, looking around at us he said, "Then why make movies?"

From the introduction of *Through Navajo Eyes* by Sol Worth and John Adair explaining how they asked the Navajo chief Sam Yazzie for permission to teach film in the community.

... Even the most carefully planned and executed live action filming in another culture is in some way intrusive. I may take missteps in my interpretation of myths, but sitting alone in front of my light box involves zero intrusion in the lives of others.
From "Myth into Film" by Robert Ascher in the volume *Anthropological Film and Video in the 1990s* edited by Jack Rollwagen.

Introduction

In 1966 Sol Worth and John Adair, along with a graduate student Richard Chalfen, conducted research among the Navajos, Native Americans in the southwestern United States. Part of their research was to teach 30 indigenous people, two of whom did not speak English, how to use motion picture cameras to document themselves, their community and their traditions. I begin this essay with a passage from their monograph about this research because the central problematic poised by tribal elder Sam Yazzie, why make movies if they do no good for the community they represent, remains a concern for contemporary anthropologists. It is also at the heart of the series of rationales anthropologist Robert Ascher employed as he moved from more traditional anthropological and archaeological pursuits and methods to photography, sculpture, and finally direct animation as a means to represent anthropological knowledge. This chapter explores the development of Ascher's practice and analyses the four animated films that comprise his entire cinematic oeuvre. Because animation in general and direct, camera-less animation in particular is such a unique pursuit for an anthropologist, this writing also provides a brief history of the practice and those film-makers who influenced Ascher.

Robert Ascher is an American anthropologist who graduated from the University of California in 1960 and published several articles in the 1960s and early 1970s contributing to the emergence of post-processual archaeology in the United States.[1] He taught his entire career in the Department of Anthropology at Cornell University and remains a professor emeritus there. Outside of his contributions to rethinking archaeology, Ascher is best known within the field for his work with his wife, Marcia Ascher, on decoding the Quipu, an Incan mathematical recording device.[2] Ascher came to his use of direct animation as a means to communicate anthropological ideas after spending several decades conducting more traditional anthropological and archaeological research in the United States, Mexico, Ecuador, Peru, Chile, Turkey, and England. His desire to express himself artistically in response to anthropological research can be dated specifically to work he conducted in the late 1960s and early 1970s on Cumberland Island, Georgia, when he started to feel confined by the limitations of the anthropological write-up as a means to convey the full experience of an archaeological dig. The excavation was of a slave cabin from a plantation. There are several photographs accompanying the essay and Ascher asks the reader to imagine using all of their senses as he describes events and locations.[3] In this way Ascher presages an area of research known as sensuous ethnography or anthropology of the senses that would come to prominence in anthropology in the 1990s with practitioners such as Paul Stoller.[4]

After his essay of the Cumberland Island research, Ascher felt that he had gone as far as he could within the framework of the traditional anthropological write-up. He began to experiment with other ways of representing anthropological knowledge. He became increasingly interested in looking at American culture and asked himself what had informed his understanding. His list of influences consisted primarily of artists, musicians, and writers: people who, Ascher reasoned, because of their positionalities as "partial outsiders" had developed what he called an "oblique perception so necessary to the interpretation of culture."[5] Ascher notes that this subjectivity, what might be described as being both with and in a culture, is also the objective of the anthropologist. Ascher concludes that because the artist takes a more holistic and symbolic approach in their interpretation and representation of culture, their work is more easily received by a lay audience than that of the average anthropologist.[6] Thus, in the early 1980s Ascher spent a few years making representational sculptures as a means to symbolize Americans and American social practice. Human in form, these sculptures, with titles such as *Candidate for Vice-President* and *Mrs. K*, were responses by Ascher to broader social and cultural dialogues and were received by anthropologists and others as a representative aesthetic response to American culture.[7]

It was after a few years of producing wood-carvings that Ascher began to think about film-making as another aesthetic response to anthropological understandings. Initially Ascher was discouraged by the seemingly high cost of film production and he did not want to give over any authority in the image making process to other individuals such as cinematographers, editors, sound recordists, or lab technicians.[8] Ascher insists that the anthropological film-maker should assert as much or more control over his/her films as s/he would over writing.[9] He also believes that there was no way a Western film crew could go into a non-Western setting and be anything other than intrusive. In his writing about his own work, Ascher frequently invokes the now infamous exchange between Sol Worth, John Adair, and Sam Yazzie quoted at the beginning of this essay as foundational for his way of making films. Thus, because of his strong sentiments that live action film-making within a culture is invasive and frequently perpetuates misreadings of the culture instead of sympathy, traditional documentary was not an option for Ascher.[10] Knowing nothing of the tradition of cameraless/direct animation, Ascher began to draw directly on clear motion picture stock. He showed his friend Don Fredrickson in the Department of Theater Performance and Dance at Cornell University where they both taught; it was Fredrickson who exposed him to the work of artists Norman McLaren and Len Lye.

Direct/Cameraless Animation

Direct animation, also known as cameraless animation, is so-called because it is made by working directly on the celluloid without any camera or photography in the creation stage. However, because of the frailty of these original drawings, direct animation is almost always rephotographed onto film through a device called an optical printer. Sometimes there are significant interventions that are made at this stage of the process, color shifts, superimpositions (layering of images one on top of the other), looping (reusing the same animated sequence over again), and/or other techniques. Cameraless film-making emerged in both Europe and the United States at a time of great experimentation in the arts. In a 1912 essay, Italian Futurist Bruno Caro calls for an abstract cinema of color. Many cite these films, now lost, as the first direct animation.[11] American pianist Mary Hallock-Greenwalt produced hand-painted films as a part of her color organ, although they were not projected in the standard sense but viewed within her musical device. Man Ray extended his direct photographic technique known as the "ray-o-gram" to cinema in his 1926 film *Emak-Bakia* where he put a whole variety of objects on unexposed film and then flashed the film with light so that the items left their imprint on the celluloid.

The first artists to draw on film were New Zealand film-maker Len Lye and Canadian film-maker Norman McLaren. According to biographer Roger Horrocks, Len Lye's first cameraless film was an uncompleted scratch animation (scratching into black leader to produce white images) made during his free time while working at Filmads in Sydney, Australia, in the 1920s.[12] Lye moved to London in 1926 and there began working as an animator making commercials, eventually gaining enough experience to make his own cel-based animated work. Lye's nine-minute film *Tusalava* (1929) drew on his exposure to and interest in aboriginal art from Australia and New Zealand and was well-received by the European art and avant garde communities. Because of the economic downturn of the 1930s he had a difficult time gaining funding for new projects and returned to his experiments with working directly on the celluloid, acquiring the raw materials (clear 35 mm film) cast off as waste by other film-makers. The resulting film, *A Colour Box* (1935), featured abstract images painted directly on film. Lye would continue to make cameraless films but it was *A Colour Box* that convinced Canadian film-maker Norman McLaren, also working in London at the time, to invest in direct, abstract animation.

Both of these film-makers were supported by funds from Great Britain's General Post Office film unit and Lye would go on to make a number of abstract films there. Later McLaren would return to Canada and, funded by the National Film Board, would become recognized world-wide for his direct animation and pixelation work. Both Lye and McLaren worked with musicians as a part of their practice. Such a film is McLaren's and Evelyn Lambart's 1949 *Begone Dull Care* made to illustrate the scores of jazz musician Oscar Peterson who improvised music for the piece. McLaren worked back and forth with Peterson to create a visual interpretation of Peterson's improvised jazz.[13] The work of Lye and McLaren was so influential to Ascher that he would bring works by McLaren and Lye to show alongside and provide a context for his own creations. Although these works were abstract, Ascher states, "I showed the abstract films to demonstrate the contrast with my work and to honor those who went before me. Almost all of direct animation had been abstract."[14]

After Frederickson exposed him to McLaren's work, Ascher contacted the Canadian film-maker. Although McLaren tried to dissuade Ascher from trying to create narratives with direct animation, he did send him a flip book of a bird made from film cels, showing how representational (as opposed to completely abstract work) was possible in that form. Most importantly McLaren sent Ascher a 35 mm film strip that was graphed with 16 vertical lines and 12 horizontal ones per frame. Ascher cut a strip into a light box and embedded posts for sprockets to hold the film in place. Figure 6.1 is an image of Robert Ascher at work. It is possible to see the size of the film strip on the light table and how he worked by looking through a magnifying glass. Before he retired, Cornell University recorded a series of web-based lectures with Ascher about his process and also put all of his films online, albeit at very poor resolution. These short lectures illustrate the mechanics of how Ascher made his films as well as the theories behind them.[15]

In the video from this series, *Making the Films You Will See*, after explaining his rationale for working in direct animation, he demonstrates his process of drawing directly on 35 mm film with technical pens that could be loaded with a variety of inks.[16] Backgrounds and large areas of color are painted in by brush or applied with a sponge. You can see the graph and framelines that he was sent by McLaren still in use as he works on his most recent film. This graph allowed him to create very slight gradations in movement between his drawings. Ascher says he watches conventional live action films and would count the duration of certain types of movements. How long does it take someone to walk across the screen? For an eye to blink, for the moon to rise in fast motion?[17] Ascher used this information to create his animations. What is fascinating about this process is that there are dozens, perhaps even hundreds of textbooks on animation that teach such things, but Robert Ascher never approached learning animation in a conventional manner. Indeed it is almost as though he reinvented it himself solely for the purpose of communicating his vision of putting myths onto film.

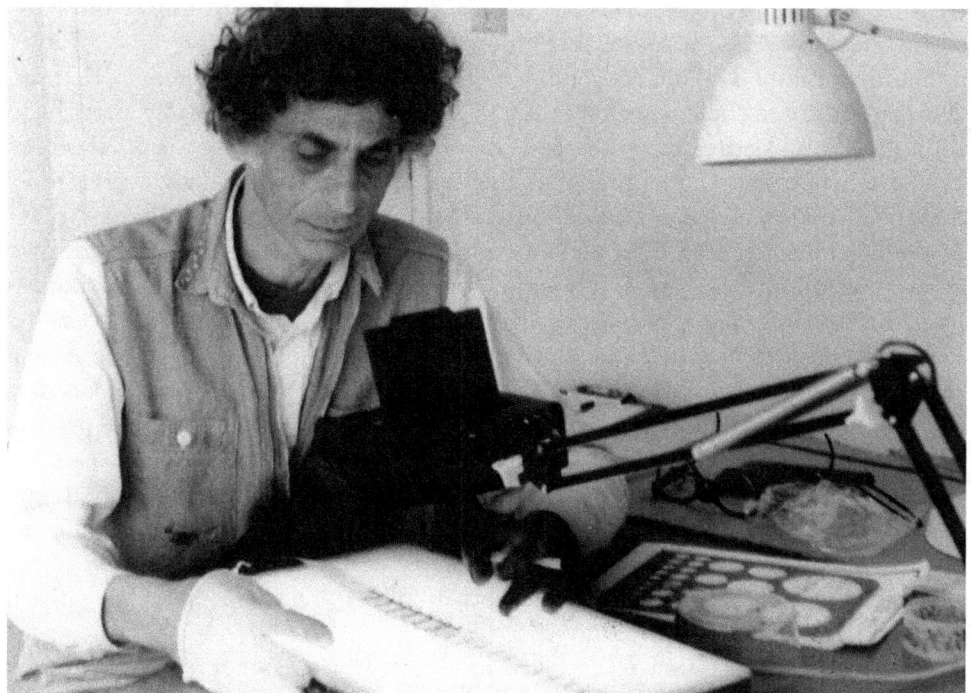

Figure 6.1 Robert Ascher at work. Courtesy of Robert Ascher.

Traditional film-making, says Ascher, is entirely disruptive, extracting something from people who may or may not see any cultural value in having their own image exhibited on screens and in classrooms half a world away. Instead, he argues, why not focus on something that is central to all cultures, myths, and try to make something out of it that neither completely communicates nor lies beyond understanding, but rather operates in the field of abstraction and of dreaming. In order to support his rationale, Ascher takes two theoretical constructs and brings them together. First Ascher asserts that myths are primary to human culture; they compose what Malinowski called the charter, "a people's orally transmitted mythology."[18] Ascher states: "Myth has been seen as a kind of map that directs and guides people through everything from property rights to behavior towards the gods. It has also been viewed as an expression of the unconscious … The glue that binds the people of a community."[19]

For Ascher, myth is larger than Western perspectives on how to explain it and it exists in all human cultures. It also shares space with the dream world. This is his second theoretical position taking. Ascher argues that dreams are also central to all humans and all cultures. All humans dream, and there are archetypical experiences in all dreams. The laws of time and space do not adhere and fantastical things happen. Drawing on Balzac and Christian Metz, among others, Ascher argues that in films the relation of the viewer to the film screen induces a kind of dream state. Films, like dreams, are able to render things impossible in our time and space and "At the heart of the connection is a poetics. What seems absurd in the 'ordinary' world becomes perfectly reasonable."[20]

Ascher's method of drawing on film is an attempt to "render a myth from another culture in such as way that it is comprehensible to us, but not thought to be of us."[21] It is like dreaming someone else's dream without trying to understand it. While the images are representational, they are also abstractions, drawn very simply due to the extremely small size of the canvas on which they are rendered. Ascher made four films inspired by myths—two from Ascher's culture, Judaism, and two from other cultures. Figure 6.2 is a still from his first film, CYCLE. The story is based on an Australian aboriginal myth about a boy who runs away from home. As his family pursues him he climbs into a tree where he becomes the moon. When the moon wanes it falls into the sea and becomes a shell and when the moon rises the shell becomes the moon again. Ascher picked this myth because of its cyclical nature and how it is such a ubiquitous origin story in its region. It is also a story that is never told precisely the same way, with tellers free to alter the geography and objects. In this rendering the tree becomes a lotus that grows to become the evening star. The important aspect of the story, that Ascher hopes to convey, is the way in which the "never ending cycle symbolically relates people, the spiritual world, and the natural environment."[22]

Although the film was well received in the art world, Ascher was criticized by anthropologists for using a myth from a culture not his own, so for his next project

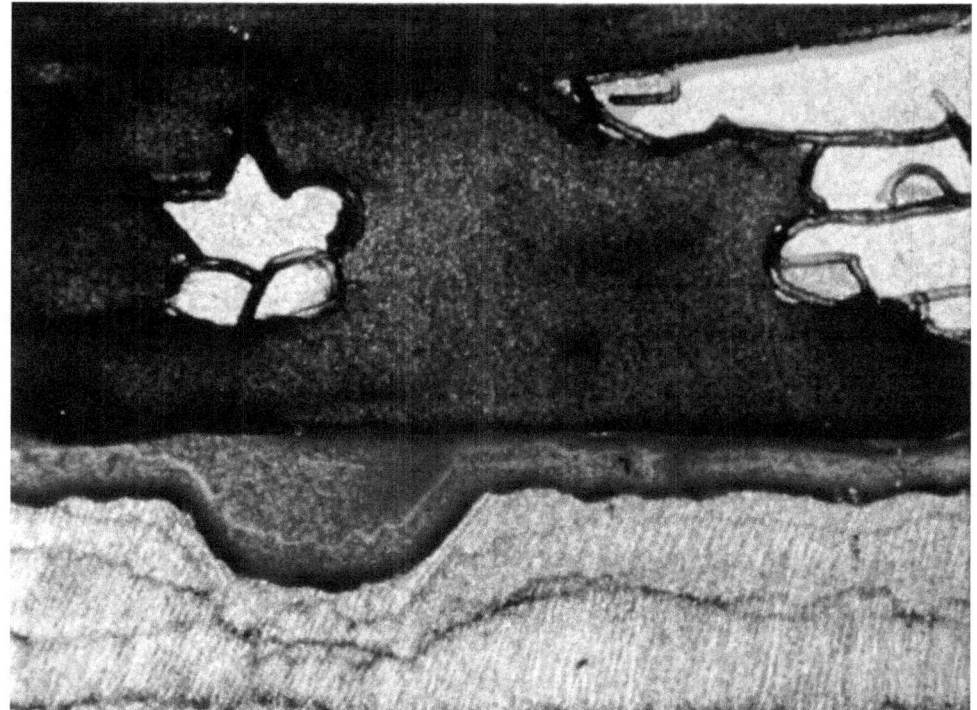

Figure 6.2 A still from the film CYCLE, a lotus turns into the evening star. Courtesy of Robert Ascher.

he began by participating, along with 2,000 others, in the celebration of the second-century mystic Shimon Bar Yohai at his burial site on Mt. Meron in Israel. Bar Yohai is thought to be the author of the Zohar, one of the primary books of Kabbalah, and Ascher spent two years reading these texts as he drew the images for his 1988 film *Bar Yohai*. He felt that this immersive experience of reading the texts would lead to his imaging them not so much in a literal fashion but that his creative efforts would embody his intellectual concerns. Figure 6.3 is an image from the photographs that he took at the event that inspired his drawings. Figure 6.4 is a still from *Bar Yohai* in which he draws nine figures, leaving the tenth space for the viewer to become the final witness. This film works to represent the symbolic language of the Zohar via symbolic visual language, where ten people become a ten-branched menorah, and then rays of light.

Following *Bar Yohai*, Ascher made *Blue: A Tlingit Odyssey* in 1991 based on a Pacific northwest coast Native American hero myth. In the myth four brothers go in search of the color blue, venturing out to sea and encountering various creatures and hazards. They eventually find the color and begin to take it back to their people but one brother is lost in a storm on the way home. The film is divided into three parts. In the first part, a trickster raven brings the gift of daylight to the world. In the second part four brothers go on a search encountering many monsters (see

Figure 6.3 A photo of pilgrims to the tomb of Shimon Bar Yohai on Mt. Meron, outside Safed, Israel. Ascher used this and other stills from his pilgrimage at the end of his film *Bar Yohai*. Courtesy of Robert Ascher.

Figure 6.5) and, finally, in the third part, the brothers find and take the color blue, angering nature who sends a storm in which one brother dies.

The last film in the group, *The Golem* (1995), tells another myth from Jewish folklore about a man made of clay. The soundtrack was made with graduate students chanting in Ascher's studio where he constructed his film, much like the mythical rabbis of old chanted over a man of clay. Ascher asserts that "a major theory of myth holds that its power rests in language" and that myth is a form of poetry.[23] The consideration of sound, its treatment, and the role it plays in the transmission of meaning to the audience is an essential communicative aspect of Ascher's films. Instead of translating the myth into English and/or subtitling the film, Ascher uses a language and a method of telling closest to the culture of the myth. Thus in CYCLE, "only the barest outline of a story is indicated in keeping with the way the myth is told."[24] In *Bar Yohai* a song is sung in Hebrew in praise of Shimon Bar Yohai. In *Blue* a Tlingit woman speaks in the beginning of the film and the rest is silent. In all aspects the sound is used as a corollary to the visuals, not in an explanatory mode. Thus the whole presentation is meant to draw the viewer into a dreamlike contemplation in which some sense is achieved, some recognition

Figure 6.4 A still from the film *Bar Yohai* of the pomegranate tree and nine people. The viewer is meant to become the tenth and thus form a minyan, or a quorum of ten adults necessary for religious services. Courtesy of Robert Ascher.

of a story is gained that is like us but not of us. Or as another film-maker, Trinh Minh-ha, said, not "speaking about" another culture, but "speaking nearby."[25]

Reception In The Field(s)

In 1973 Robert Ascher wrote an essay called "How to Build a Time Capsule" about the practice of making and unearthing time capsules in twentieth-century America.[26] In terms of the reception of Ascher's work within anthropology perhaps it is instructive to think of the films like a time capsule. In all the world, I know of no other anthropologist who chose direct animation, the painting of images directly on film, as a means to represent anthropological knowledge. Much like a future generation deciphering a time capsule, a successful reading of these films in relationship to the field of anthropology at the time is significantly aided by extra textual information and a brief history of the context of their creation.

I compare Ascher's films to time capsules for two reasons: (1) as he himself said, "time capsules are attempts to present a civilization or part of it in a remarkably

Figure 6.5 A still from the film *Blue: A Tlingit Odyssey*. The four brothers encounter a sea monster. Courtesy of Robert Ascher.

compact way" and (2) because a time capsule is a "carefully prepared message" from a previous generation to a future one.²⁷ Similarly, films have a message and an intended audience. Although we tend to think of motion pictures as rather contemporary communicative efforts they are rapidly shifting into a historic tense in which their means of production and contexts of reception will have to be explained in order to render them comprehensible. Thus films become time capsules, the social and historical significance of which shifts as they move from the present to the past tense in terms of their cultural value and the communicative circle in which they are exhibited.

This is painfully obvious in the work of Robert Ascher. He made his first film in 1986 and finished his most recent in 1995. His films had a brief public life, were favorably reviewed, shown at major festivals and institutions, and in circulation through film cooperatives and small distributors, and then, but for a few brief mentions in visual anthropology texts, Ascher's work went out of public view. Ascher's work existed on the periphery of two small and seemingly discrete fields of research: experimental film, and visual anthropology. In other places I compared these arenas of scholarship as similarly marginalized and self-marginalizing from their larger and more public kin, mainstream cinema and socio-cultural anthropology respectively.²⁸

For several years Ascher's films were distributed by Canyon Cinema cooperative, one of two distributers of experimental film in the United States. Ascher's work is mentioned in essays by Cecille Starr, co-author of the book *Experimental Animation*, and for a time she distributed his films through her company in New York City.[29] His films showed at major experimental film festivals and at the 1987 Flaherty Film Seminar, a nexus for the creative and intellectual interchange between documentary, ethnographic, and experimental film-makers.[30]

At the same time, Ascher's work was supported and reviewed within anthropology. He received a Wenner Gren grant to complete *CYCLE*. In writing about Ascher's films, anthropologist Paul Stoller said that *Blue: A Tlingit Odyssey* was highly appropriate for screening in undergraduate and graduate courses on myth and religion. Further, he argues that Ascher grapples successfully with the question poised by Sam Yazzie, by turning inward toward contemplation and poetic visual representation of a myth rather than intruding on a culture to film.[31] Fred Myers, who was initially suspicious of Ascher's film *CYCLE*, came to see that "The imaginative visual continuity of the myth *is* valuable for challenging overly word and logic centered approaches to symbolic forms, which among aborigines, are often as much ritually constituted as they are verbal forms."[32] Both Stoller and Myers saw these films as adding important questions to the discourse around image making and the traditional anthropological subject, but, beyond their reviews, Ascher's work was not significantly picked up for discussion among other anthropologists. Ascher is mentioned in Jay Ruby's book *Picturing Culture*: "Rouch is not alone in pushing the boundaries of documentary realism. For example, US anthropologist Robert Ascher experimented by drawing directly on film to produce a 'cameraless' interpretation of myth—a technique found in experimental films (Ascher 2000). As with Rouch, his efforts have been ignored."[33] It is worth noting that this is the only mention of Ascher in the entirety of the book and thus Ruby also basically ignored him.

As someone who studies the economics and distribution networks of the film avant garde, I hypothesize that the reason Ascher's films "disappeared" despite their critical acclaim was that both Ascher and his films existed on the periphery of the two distinct exhibition networks, experimental/art cinema and anthropological film mentioned above. Reception and continued resonance of films in both networks depend most on their being taught within college and university classrooms.[34] To a smaller degree, being written about in texts used within academia also contributes to a film's continued exhibition life. Although exhibition at festivals, galleries, museums, and other venues can also raise the profile of a film and artist, if they aren't made part of a significant collection, either at a museum or research facility, these screenings frequently only have relevance for the time frame surrounding them.

Despite the fact that Ascher's films had been distributed briefly in the 1990s, in 2006, when I was conducting research for an essay on the interconnections between experimental film and anthropology, the only way for me to see his work was to make a pilgrimage to Ithaca, New York where he still lives and arrange for a private viewing of his films with the projectionist at Cornell Cinema.[35] What I saw that day and learned through conversations with Bob Ascher, as I would come to know him, inspired me to write about his films but also to work toward preserving them and finding distribution for them. I know that this surprised Ascher. He had often had people interested in his work, but never someone who existed firmly in both of the worlds that his films had emerged from—that of experimental or art cinema and anthropology. My subject position as both an experimental film-maker and an anthropologist allows me to communicate across both spheres and give context for his modes of production that is based on personal experience with similar techniques.

For example, not only do I understand how Ascher makes his work, direct animation is something that I teach as a part of my alternative production classes as a faculty member in film-making at Emerson College in Boston, Massachusetts. Direct animation continues to be a vibrant part of experimental film-making. Since I have been in contact with Ascher, I have shown his work to other animators and they are amazed with its visual quality. Perhaps it is possible that Ascher will find a resurgence in his work, this time with historians of animation. Like items taken from a time capsule buried in the 1990s, his work will be viewed *in historical and social context*. The question that will continue to be asked is: why make (these kinds of) films? The answer, I hope, is that instead of making the viewers think they *know* something about a different culture, they create a desire to learn, a will to reach across cultural difference.

Continued Resonnance/Conclusion

In the Spring of 2012 I was contacted by an animator and author of books on animation, Maureen Furniss, about my work with Robert Ascher. Part of my project has been to preserve the films of Ascher by transferring them to raw digital movie files and making a short run of DVDs to share with other artists and scholars. It has been my ambition to find a distributor for Ascher's films so that they do not fade into obscurity.[36] Through contact with Furniss I learned about the *Yanyuwa Animation Project* in which anthropologists collaborating with Australian aboriginals and animators produced animated stories from oral history. The anthropologists were inspired to suggest such an approach to cultural memory by viewing the series *Raven Tales*, a narrative computer animation produced by a team that includes Winadzi James, an indigenous Kwakwaka'wakw from the northwest coast of Canada, when it screened at the 2004 Margaret Mead Film festival.[37] Moving images, be they animated or live action, are increasingly an important tool for teaching and remembering our cultural heritage. More and more traditional anthropological film "subjects" are gaining the tools to represent themselves. In societies where photographic representation may be problematic because it conflicts with cultural beliefs about representation, animation may be a way to make films that "do no harm."

Filmography

A Colour Box, dir. Len Lye, Light Cone, France, 1935, 4 mins.
Bar Yohai, dir. Robert Ascher, Israel, 1988, 6 mins.
Begone Dull Care, dirs. Evelyn Lambart and Norman McLaren, National Film Board of Canada, 1949, 8 mins.
Blue. A Tlingit Odyssey, dir. Robert Ascher, USA, 1991, 6 mins.
CYCLE, dir. Robert Ascher, USA, 1986, 5 mins.
Emak Bakia, dir. Man Ray, Images Film Archive—distributor, Mamaroneck, NY, 1926, 19 mins.
The Golem, dir. Robert Ascher, USA, 1995, 4 mins.
Making the Films You Will See, Cybertower, Cornell Cast, Cornell University, Ithaca, NY, 2011, 12 mins.
Raven Tales (TV series), dirs. Chris Kientz, Colin Curwen, and Winadzi James, Raven Tales, Alberta, Canada, 2004–11.
Reassemblage, dir. Trinh Minh-ha, Women Make Movies, USA, 1982, 40 mins.
Tusalava, Len Lye. Light Cone, France, 1929, 11 mins.

Notes

1. Ascher's contributions to the emergence of post-processual archaeology in the United States can be deduced from many references to his 1961 publication "Analogy in Archaeological Interpretation," *Southwestern Journal of Anthropology*, 17, 1961, 317–25. Also of note is his 1961 essay "Experimental Archaeology," *American Anthropologist*, 63 (4), 1961, 793–816.
2. These books are Marcia Ascher and Robert Ascher, *Code of the Quipu: Databook* (Ann Arbor, MI: University of Michigan Press, 1978); and Marcia Ascher and Robert Ascher, *Code of the Quipu: A Study in Media, Mathematics, and Culture* (Ann Arbor, MI: University of Michigan Press, 1980).
3. Robert Ascher and Charles Fairbanks, "Excavation of a Slave Cabin, Georgia U.S.A.," *Historical Archaeology*, 5, 1971, 3–17; this essay continues to be used in contemporary anthropological courses.
4. The term "anthropology of the senses" can be traced back to a 1986 book by Alan Corbin titled *The Foul and the Fragrant* (Cambridge, MA: Harvard University Press). While there were many ethnographies that focused on a sensual or sense centered approach to research in the 1980s (e.g. Michael Jackson's essay "Knowledge of the Body" (*Man*, 18 (2), 1983, 327–45) and Paul Stoller's book *The Taste of Ethnographic Things* (Philadelphia, PA: University of Pennsylvania Press, 1989), it coalesced as an area of study in the mid-1990s with Constance Classen's article "Foundation for an Anthropology of the Senses" (*International Social Science Journal*, 49 (153), 1997) that illustrated the historical basis for the sub-discipline.
5. Robert Ascher, "Sculpting Americans," *Anthropology and Humanism Quarterly*, 10 (1), 1985, 16–17.
6. It is important to note that Ascher is speaking about artists in the most general sense here, including musicians, folk artists, painters, sculptors, and so on. While it can certainly be argued that certain artistic production is created for very elite and/or educated audiences, Ascher's own artistic production was trying to tap into a tradition of wood folk sculpture. See Ascher, "Sculpting Americans," for representative work.

7. Ibid.
8. In 2006 I met with Robert Ascher in Ithaca, NY and conducted an interview that would contribute to my essay "Productive Dissonance and Sensuous Image Making" in Jay Ruby and Marcus Banks (eds), *Made to Be Seen* (Chicago, IL: University of Chicago Press, 2011). Any information regarding Ascher not attributed to others was gained through this initial interview or through successive email and phone exchanges with him.
9. Robert Ascher, "Myth and Film," in Jack Rollwagen (ed.), *Anthropological Film and Video in the 1990s* (Brockport, NY: Institute Press, 1993) 67–75. "Most filmmaking is a group effort. We insist upon naming the director of a film as its author even in the knowledge that a soundperson, an editor, a cinematographer and often a writer, among others, share control through heavily influencing the final version of a film. By contrast, I exercise near total control over my films. This applies even to the lab work. An optical printer (basically, a camera on one side of a platform and a projector on the other) is required to reduce my 35mm. original to a 16mm. negative. This machine is capable of many additional cinematographic tricks. I request only a negative that is the truest possible rendering of my original. In my view, anthropologists and other scholars should have as much control over the films they make as they insist upon having (or should insist upon having) when it comes to the words that are published under their names. The direct cameraless technique brings me close to this ideal" (73–4).
10. This perspective has been argued substantially within the subfield of visual anthropology in the United States. See, for example, Wilton Martinez, "Who Constructs Anthropological Knowledge? Toward a Theory of Ethnographic Film Spectatorship," in David Turton and Peter Crawford (eds), *Film as Ethnography* (Manchester: Manchester University Press, 1992), 130–61; Wilton Martinez, "Critical Studies and Visual Anthropology: Aberrant vs. Anticipated Readings of Ethnographic Film," Commission on Visual Anthropology Review, Spring, 1990, 34–47.
11. The manifesto can be found translated into English in the collected volume *Futurist Manifestos* edited and with an introduction by Umbro Apollonio (New York: Viking Press, 1973).
12. See Roger Horrock, "The Life and Work of Len Lye," in Ian Cornrich and Stuart Murray (eds), *New Zealand Filmmakers* (Detroit, MI: Wayne State University Press, 2007).
13. See Robert Russett and Cecille Starr, *Experimental Animation* (New York: De Capo Press, 1976) as well as Terence Dobson, *The Film Work of Norman McLaren* (Eastleigh: John Libbey Publishing, 2006).
14. This information is from an email between the author and the film-maker from January 2012. In the late 1980s and early 1990s Ascher showed his four films at many venues such as the Museum of Modern Art in New York. On February 8, 1993 Ascher screened Len Lye's *Free Radicals* (1958, revised in 1979), a film scratched on black leader, and Norman McLaren's *Serenal* (1959), a hand-painted film, along with his films *Bar Yohai* (1988) and *Blue: A Tlingit Odyssey* (1991). Also see Museum of Modern Art press release, Barbara Marshall, *CINEPROBE CONTINUES ITS TWENTY-FIFTH SEASON AT THE MUSEUM OF MODERN ART* (New York: Museum of Modern Art, January 1993).
15. There are seven videos available on Cornell University's website. The three films *Bar Yohai, Blue: A Tlingit Odyssey,* and *CYCLE* and four short lectures: *Introduction: The Centrality of Myth; Making the Films You Will See; Myths, Films and Dreams;* and *Myth, Film and Dream: Conclusion.* These are currently archived on Cornell Cast, Ithaca, NY: Cornell University. http://www.cornell.edu/video/people/robert-ascher (accessed August 19, 2013).
16. See "Ascher, Robert, 'Making the Films You Will See", in *Speakers: Robert Ascher* on Cornell Cast, Ithaca, NY: Cornell University. http://www.cornell.edu/video/myth-film-and-dream-3-about-cameraless-animation (accessed August 19, 2013).

17. *Ibid.* Towards the end of *Making the Films You Will See* Ascher notes that when he watches a movie he counts how many seconds each scene is.
18. Robert Ascher, "Approach, Theory and Technique in the Making of *Bar Yohai*," *Visual Anthropology*, 3, 1990, 111.
19. Robert Ascher, "Myth and Film," in Jack R. Rollwagen (ed.), *Anthropological Film and Video in the 1990s* (Brockport, NY: Institute Press, 1993), 70.
20. Ascher, "Approach, Theory," 113.
21. *Ibid.*
22. Ascher, "Myth and Film," 72.
23. *Ibid.*, 68.
24. *Ibid.*
25. Minh-ha says this in the voice over in the film *Reassemblage* (1982). Trihn Minh-ha, *Reassemblage*, 16mm, col/snd. Film. (New York: Women Make Movies, 1992).
26. Robert Ascher, "How to Build a Time Capsule," *Journal of Popular Culture*, 8, 1975, 242–53.
27. *Ibid.*
28. Kathryn Ramey, "Productive Dissonance and Sensuous Image-making: Visual Anthropology and Experimental Film," in Jay Ruby and Marcus Banks (eds), *Made to be Seen: Historical Perspectives on Visual Anthropology* (Chicago, IL: University of Chicago Press, 2011).
29. Russet and Starr, *Experimental Animation*.
30. Ascher was a Flaherty Film Seminar grant recipient in 1987.
31. Paul Stoller, "Film Reviews—*Blue: A Tlingit Odyssey* Produced by Robert Ascher," *American Anthropologist*, June, 1992, 521.
32. Fred Myers, "Film Reviews—*Cycle*," *American Anthropologist*, March, 1988, 245.
33. Jay Ruby, *Picturing Culture: Explorations of Film and Anthropology* (Chicago, IL: University of Chicago Press, 2000), 13.
34. Michael Zryd explores the dependence of the film avant garde on academia in his essay "The Academy and the Avant-Garde: A Relationship of Dependence and Resistance," Cinema Journal, 45 (2), 2006, 17–42. I also explore this in my "Is the Film Avant-Garde Still *Avant-Garde?*: Economics and Culture of Artisanal Moving-Image Makers," Kathryn Ramey, Unpublished Doctoral dissertation, Temple University, Philadelphia, PA (2006).
35. I would like to thank the director of Cornell Cinema in 2009, Mary Fessendon, the projectionist Paul, and my friend and experimental film-maker Jason Livingston, a former student of Ascher's, for helping to set up this meeting. Of course I also thank Ascher for his ongoing willingness to answer all my questions.
36. As of this writing, Bob and I are co-signing a contract for distribution of his work with Documentary Educational Resources in Watertown, MA, USA (http://www.der.org). I have taken on the responsibility of making a high definition transfer of his films and created a DVD for them so that subsequent generations of anthropologists will be able to see this work. As DVDs are significantly cheaper to purchase than film prints, this distribution will make his work available to college and university libraries where it can be accessed by faculty and students. This is how art and scholarly films survive.
37. Amanda Kearney, John Bradley, Brent Mckee, and Tom Chandler, "Representing Indigenous Cultural Expressions through Animation: The Yanyuwa Animation Project," *Animation Journal*, 2012, 4–29.

7

ASYNCHRONICITY: RETHINKING THE RELATION OF EAR AND EYE IN ETHNOGRAPHIC PRACTICE

Jennifer L. Heuson and Kevin T. Allen

Anthropologists are the sojourners of "the between."[1]

Commitment is not a category of art. This does not mean that art is apolitical. It means that aesthetics has its own politics, or its own metapolitics.[2]

Introduction

Listening and looking often go together and—along with touch, smell, and taste—shape our encounters with the world. These encounters, in turn, give rise to knowledge claims, to affective states, to remembered pasts and imagined futures, to politics and social relations. Sometimes the linking of ear and eye is made strange—by bodies that do not work, by unfamiliar landscapes, by media that "tune in" to one sense or another—but usually it is not. Usually, ear and eye are "in sync," are synchronous. What is heard and what is seen are close. Sounds stay near their visible sources. Media makers generally attempt to replicate the synchronous sensations of daily life, the apparent synchronicity of ear and eye. In an everyday sense, "synchronicity" refers to the simultaneous occurrence of two events, events that seem causally linked. Carl Jung called "synchronicity" an "acausal connecting principle"—a "meaningful coincidence" that offered evidence of a collective unconscious.[3] The presumed causal link between ear and eye ultimately reveals much about a society, about its modes of sensing, feeling, and knowing. Yet this link—the synchronicity of ear and eye—is rarely interrogated.

What would it mean to propose *asynchronicity* as a mode of ethnographic practice? What would this uncover that the synced ear–eye does not? What would such a method sound like ... what would it look like? How would it challenge the sedimented styles of anthropologists and experimental film-makers alike?

This chapter will explore these questions by offering examples of the authors' own asynchronous ethnographic practice. Importantly, this is an attempt to theorize an organic practice we have engaged in for nearly two decades and it is informed heavily by our training in experimental film and philosophy, respectively. Our theorization is concerned both with how tools and techniques borrowed from experimental film-making might alter ethnographic encounters, including fieldwork and its representation, and with how these encounters might offer a "critical phenomenological" account of the relationship between knowledge, sensation, and representation.[4] Borrowing from Jacques Rancière, we hope our asynchronous practice will challenge "the distribution of the sensible" normalized in both anthropological practice and experimental film-making.[5] Our intervention will emphasize the ear–eye relation, but will also consider how experimenting with this relation might produce more or less dynamic experiences of time and space.

"Asynchronicity" is a term used variously by communication theorists to describe asynchronous circuits or processes of data transfer and by education scholars to discuss asynchronous learning or distance education. The former refers to a data circuit that does not use a digital clock (or quartz oscillator) to standardize the transfer of information.[6] The latter is a model of pedagogy (primarily for online-based distance education) where the classroom is no longer bound by traditional notions of time and space.[7] In both cases, the asynchronous is presumed to directly oppose the standardized temporality ("clock time") and spatiality ("coeval presence") of synchronous experiences. For some media theorists, asynchronicity is an inherent aspect of new media technologies and works to uncouple, loosen, or even abandon "previously compulsory time and space patterns."[8] While theorists like Ursula Franklin find this "unravelling of social and political patterns" troubling, we believe it offers artists and anthropologists a unique engagement with the aesthetic and sensorial politics shaping knowledge production and its representation, including a reframing of the "synchronic–diachronic" debate.[9] The primary "social and political" pattern we intend to critique involves the conceptual and practical distinction between synchronous and non-synchronous techniques and their resultant representations. While the synchronized ear–eye depends upon "clock time" and "coeval presence," the non-synchronous presumes to clearly separate ear and eye, placing them in distinct temporal and spatial zones, creating a relation of action–reaction, of randomness or commentary.[10] In contrast, the asynchronous moves *in between* these two modalities, offering an ear–eye sometimes "in sync," sometimes not. Aporetic gaps, uncertainties, disruptions, and durations are crucial. Thus, our use of "asynchronicity" is not meant to evoke clear demarcations between sync and non-sync ear–eye techniques or representations, but to explore movements between the two.

We hope in these pages to offer an adequate account of how asynchronicity shapes our practice. This account will attempt to define asynchronous techniques and representations (largely through example) and will discuss the critical, political, and ethical impacts of these practices and products for the larger fields of non-fiction film-making and anthropology. Before we offer examples from our practice, we want to briefly hint at some of the sedimented styles (and joined ear–eye relations) we work against.

Notes on the Sedimentation of Style

By "sedimented style" we mean the normalized "ways of doing and making" that approach ear–eye relations as *either* synchronous or non-synchronous, as seamlessly joined or concretely separated.[11] Roughly, these correspond to the "realist" and "anti-realist" strategies of anthropologists/documentarians and experimental artists/film-makers. Simply put, on one hand, the ear and eye share time and space; on the other, they do not. There are outliers, of course, and most films contain asynchronous moments throughout. Our claim is that "sync and/or non-sync" strategies have become mostly standardized styles of both ethnography and film-making, of fieldwork encounter, and its representation. These "sedimented styles" recur along three lines: (1) the synchronous direct or observational recording of an event (where ear and eye share the same time and space); (2) the non-synchronous pairing of sound and image (where ear and eye exist in juxtaposed or countered times and/or spaces); and (3) the reflexive use of sound and image (where a non-sync ear–eye is used to interrupt synchronous time and/or space). Each of these depends upon specific ear–eye relations that we believe do not adequately reflect or reproduce the ambiguity and ambivalence of everyday perception.

In anthropology, "sync and/or non-sync" styles are manifest in and reinforced through disciplinary distinctions that either conflate or clearly demarcate ears and eyes. Often divisions between "textualists" and "sensualists" or between a "sounded" and a "visual" anthropology fail to engage the collusion and collision of the various senses and of sensing and knowing and representational tools and techniques.[12] Consider, as an example, the following claim made by Steven Feld and Donald Brenneis in 2004:

> Until the sound recorder is presented and taught as a technology of creative and analytic mediation, which requires craft and editing and articulation just like writing, little will happen of an interesting sort in the anthropology of sound.[13]

We believe our work responds to recent calls for "a sounded anthropology" by engaging it "as a technology of creative and analytic mediation," and as "a meaningful form" beyond data source.[14] What we want to challenge, however, is the continued separation of "the sound recording" from other ethnographic methods and technologies—oral, visual, textual, archival, and archeological—and the presumption of intelligibility embedded in claims that sound recording is "articulation." Asynchronous ethnography experiments with relations between sound and sound recording and other ethnographic practices of looking, writing, collecting, touching, and so on.[15] These experiments question the effectiveness of sedimented anthropological practices and publications in generating "a sounded anthropology" that is both critical and engaged. Importantly, our approach also counters current examples of experimental and ethnographic "sensory immersion" and "intersensoriality" through incorporating representational *and* sensorial politics.[16] In other words, we argue that a study of the senses in relation can better reveal the politics of sensing undergirding knowledge claims and their link to aesthetic practices.

The asynchronous sound–image strategies of early film-makers, based upon technical limitations and reception styles, point to some of the ways asynchronicity can be understood as both aesthetic and political. Lack of sync-sound recording equipment and standardized frame rates allowed early film-makers to more critically and creatively relate ears and eyes. In some cases, asynchronous strategies even radically transformed fieldwork encounters, challenging the dominant role of synchronized time and space in anthropological representation. Jean Rouch's *Jaguar* (1967) is a pivotal example.[17] While asynchronous moments may occur in many anthropological and artistic works, here asynchronicity shapes the entire time–space of the film and the encounters it affords. We mention *Jaguar* for two reasons. First, we hope it will give readers a concrete sense of the sorts of films and practices the term "asynchronicity" encompasses. Second, we want to acknowledge a history of asynchronous ethnography, while also hinting at its relative absence today.

The Asynchronous Document

We turn now to trace the basic outline of an asynchronous document. How does it represent peoples, places, and things differently? How does it use time and space reflexively? How does it challenge sedimented styles? What might asynchronicity do to the stories anthropologists tell or to the peoples, places, and things they encounter? Our discussion will hinge on two experimental non-fiction films—*Still Life with Ho Chi Minh* (2008) and *Luthier* (2010)—and will sketch how each documents and reproduces asynchronicity. It is important to keep in mind the relationship between technical limits and sensory ones. Like Rouch, we embrace the technical restraints of our tools and use these limits to force or evoke conditions of aesthetic and representational pause and contemplation. It is our view that through the use of such asynchronous tools, ethnographers, subjects, sites, and audiences will engage in sensory relations "made strange" through form and uncertainty.

Our films vary in subject, yet our asynchronous approach to sound and image clearly unifies our work. We attempt to produce documents that evoke "being here" but that also explicitly signal that a film (or other type of recording) is an artifact, not a *re*-presentation, of experience. In other words, our films attempt to asynchronously document our everyday (ambiguous and ambivalent) experience of presence, while reminding that "presence" is itself a production.[18] We use a number of strategies to produce these "artifactual reminders" in our films. Our audience is reminded both through the materiality of the media we use (Super 8 mm film) and through the fluctuating (temporal and spatial) interaction of ear and eye. Most of our films are structured around the integrity of the Super 8 mm camera roll.[19] Images are sequenced in the manner they are recorded in the camera. This structure includes camera flares, accidental tilts, false starts, or other artifacts of representation at the head and tail of each shot. Sound is recorded separately, usually during the intervals between shots, but occasionally at disparate times and spaces. This intermittent engagement of ear and eye, combined with the discontinuity of the camera-roll structure, transforms our encounters into asynchronous documents.

Our first example, *Still Life with Ho Chi Minh*, chronicles an encounter with Ho Chi Minh's personal photographer Mr. Bảy, a 92-year-old man we met in the streets of Hanoi.[20] The film consists of an intact (roughly three-minute) camera roll spanning the hour we spent at his home, talking and exploring his collection of historical photographs. As we talk, Mr. Bảy becomes more and more emotional, recollecting the past and the suffering endured by his people. We record image and sound during this period of time, yet not at the same moment. This positioning between synchronous and non-synchronous recording creates a tension. Time becomes relative, elastic, and intermittent. The footage is hand-processed. Packed into a canister, drowned in chemicals, one section of the film scratches and physically imprints itself upon the others. The film, thus, bears the mark of its own material history (see Figure 7.1). Through the noise of these interventions, we see a man in conversation, and we hear him speaking. We have some context, but the language is foreign. No subtitles translate the encounter. We soon stop listening to his words and hear, instead, his voice. The voice quivers and breaks, slowly transitioning to emotional and violent sobbing. We meet this transformation as a purely affective state. Rather than interpret, we are urged to experience his emotion, to embody and become embodied by his grief. Yet, we are simultaneously distanced from Mr. Bảy, reminded through scratches, flares, and un-translated language of the time and space separating us.

Luthier follows in a similar vein, but its techniques differ.[21] The film is a portrait of an aging Patagonian instrument maker at work. We see time passing through exterior time-lapse images of his workshop, and we hear the tuning of guitars. Footage was often shot in extreme close-up, the texture and graceful movement of his callused hands telling a narrative far richer than could words (see Figure 7.2). This is as much a study of the maker's hands—his tools and materials—as of the maker himself. Sound and image were again recorded during the same period of time, yet not at the same moment. Sound and image are close, but not quite "in sync." We see the hand pushing a planer, and we hear the scraping of wood giving way. The sawdust settles, and the hand is still, but the sound continues. At other moments throughout, atop this asynchronous sound–image environment, we hear

Figure 7.1 Film strip of three frames from *Still Life with Ho Chi Minh*, 2008, by Kevin T. Allen, 3 mins, Super 8mm film, © Small Gauge, Ltd.

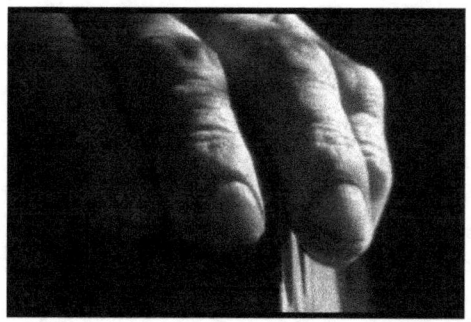

Figure 7.2 Film still from *Luthier*, 2010, by Kevin T. Allen, 6 mins, Super 8 mm film, © Small Gauge, Ltd.

the maker speaking about his "alchemical" craft. These recordings were made off-site prior to filming. We see the maker on screen and acknowledge that the voice is his, yet his lips do not move. His voice, thus, references and creates a different time and space, one that exists between the film-maker and film, between the film and audience, between the maker and his materials. "They begin in a semi-solid state," he says, "and transform over time into hard material."[22] This is a voice that comments on the "alchemical" experience of making, while in the midst of being made.

Another temporal–spatial intervention in both these examples is the use of titles. In both films, titles doubly sound the film-maker's presence and voice and the voice of the men speaking, while also providing needed context for our encounters. Traditionally this context might be introduced through voice-over. Such a technique, however, fails to challenge audiences' knowledge assumptions, allowing them to be "omnisciently present." What we wanted, instead, was to provoke some of the ambiguity of our own encounters, encounters shaped through words misunderstood or meanings lost in translation. In *Still Life with Ho Chi Minh*, intertitles precede the film, describing the events leading up to and following the encounter in minimal language yet leaving much that is said "unintelligible." In *Luthier*, the action proceeds with little context; we hear only comments spoken by the maker about his craft. An intertitle toward the end of the film reveals that the film-maker has brought the instrument maker a piece of wood from his family home to shape into a guitar. We then see a close-up image of a hand playing a guitar, presumably now the film-maker's. Although we hear guitar music, the sounds of hands at work continue. In this case, two sonic narratives in two sonic time–spaces intersect to evoke the sounded history of this material artifact. As film-makers, we exist in both films through these titles, dwelling both inside and outside of the diegesis, in between our roles as makers and participants of a shared experience.

Asynchronous Making and Sensing

The tools we use inform both the experiences we record and our own encounters in and with the field. Our asynchronous practice arises primarily from our use of

Super 8 mm film. Because the Super 8 mm camera does not record synchronous sound, sights and sounds must be recorded separately with distinct strategies.[23] A camera that does not record sound might seem disadvantageous, but such a "limitation" discourages a totalizing approach to representation and affords encounters "made strange" through the initial separation of eye and ear. The eye frames the world through the lens. The ear precedes or follows through the microphone. Each modality functions in its own time and space, on its own terms. This temporal–spatial separation between eye and ear allows a deeper engagement with how each sense uniquely interacts with a place or with a people. It also offers an alternative approach to synchronic fieldwork with time-based media that gesture toward the diachronic. Multiple senses operate both in and *in between* multiple times and spaces to offer a singular, yet asynchronous, experience.

We regard the temporal and spatial interventions made possible by the Super 8 mm camera, including practices such as time-lapse photography, as techniques that call attention to the practice of film-making as a sensory reconstruction of experience, in turn, revealing the fragmented, asynchronous nature of experience itself. Film-making is not a linear or synchronized form, but an intermittent series of fragmented frames over time. Generally, it is used as a tool for constructing synchronicity, what we believe to be the continuity of lived (temporal and spatial) experience. Yet, lived experience is far from synchronous. Shaping the perceptual and representational aspects of film experience in this way fails to engage the gaps and confusions of everyday life and the political aspects of narrating sense. Experimental film-maker Nathaniel Dorksy puts it this way:

> Life is full of gaps. We try to make the whole thing seem continuous and solid, but it's actually more intermittent than we often want to admit. In a sense, for a film to be true, it has to trust this intermittence … If a film fills in too much, it violates our experience.[24]

Film-making as a sensory tool must construct a film experience that works in tandem with the intermittence of lived (temporal and spatial) experience. Furthermore, by reflexively calling attention to itself as a temporal and spatial construction, a film becomes a participatory environment that elicits sensory and political engagement from its audience.

Although the relationship between the ear and eye is a key concern in our practice, it is also pertinent to discuss the hand. The Super 8 mm format is a tangible medium that can be both seen and touched. A small strip coated with silver-halide transforms into translucent film grains that dance on screen to form an image. It is vulnerable to materialities such as solar flares, scratching, and other physical markings. Super 8 mm cameras, often old, consumer grade, and prone to mechanical malfunction, make their own unpredictable physical interventions. The film may also be hand-processed, adding yet another layer of tactility. In the processing can, sprocket holes overlap with the frame and imprint themselves on the image; chemicals are unevenly distributed and polarize portions of the film. Even with a high-fidelity digital transfer of these images, their materiality is writ large. The surface of the screen becomes as tactile as the physical objects it represents, begging the eye to reach out and touch.

But when not bound to the camera, the ear too can touch. Over the past few years, our practice has evolved to include the use of contact microphones. These instruments do not record the compression and rarefaction of air molecules, or what we humans hear as "sound," but rather the oscillation of the physical objects themselves. Piezoelectric discs, often made of ceramic or crystal, are placed in direct physical contact with an object. What they record is not the sound of the object per se, but sound traveling through the object. By listening to these objects, we can imagine material ears transducing the soundscapes that surround us. Our ears, no longer confined to air, touch the ground or even submerge underwater, offering new avenues of sensory knowledge. Wearing headphones and listening through a microphone itself elicits a heightened and engaged sensory experience. Additionally, recording with contact microphones offers a tactile relationship with the field. Like a stethoscope, these tools are placed by hand on a physical body to sound a presumed "invisible" and "unknowable" sonic world. Such a practice not only engages an asynchronous relationship with one's own senses, but also forces an openness to other modes of sensing. It demands a fieldwork of discovery—informed by eye, ear, and hand—most explicit in our recent film *Bridge* (2012).[25]

The genealogy of *Bridge* begins with the ears. We were conducting research on a project called *Sonic Geologic* (2011) that investigated the geologic properties of contact microphones.[26] We needed a test site to put these microphones into practice. The Brooklyn Bridge was an easy choice because it is part of our everyday commute and because it is a particularly resonant structure. One interesting outcome came from attaching contact microphones to the suspension cables of the bridge. The cables moved so forcefully that vises were needed to secure the microphones in place (see Figure 7.3). In other locations, it was easy to hear vibrations made by humans, but here, the sonic material from the suspension cable sounded as if it were coming from within the structure, as if the bridge itself were a massive living organ. Such results allowed us to imagine the bridge as an anthropological body, sounded additionally by human ears. Our sampling extended from a single bridge to the three bridges that connect Brooklyn and Manhattan. Over several months, recordings were made at these bridges at various times of day. Sound recording with contact microphones was the primary means of engagement. After repeated listening, image gathering began. The materiality of Super 8mm film greatly suited a film about such physical objects. Images were often framed in extreme close-up to reinforce the materiality of the sound recording method (see Figure 7.4). However, long shots were particularly affective in tandem with the intimate soundings of the bridge, the close ear paired with the distant eye to form a dissonant negotiation.

Figure 7.3 Production still from *Sonic Geologic*, 2011, by Kevin T. Allen, handmade contact microphones secured with vises, © Small Gauge, Ltd.

Figure 7.4 Film still from *Bridge*, 2012, by Kevin T. Allen, 11 minutes, Super 8 mm film, © Small Gauge, Ltd.

Bridge is not only a good example of asynchronous fieldwork, it also demonstrates asynchronous practice in the editing room. As with many of our films, editing began with asynchronous projection. When footage returned from the lab, we screened it on a Super 8 mm projector along with edited sequences of field recordings. Because Super 8 mm projectors play back at variable speeds, it was impossible to predict the resultant sound–image associations. Furthermore, each screening yielded unique results, depending not only on projector speed, but also on human interventions such as the exact moment the playback button was engaged. While this is not a realistic way to distribute work, it provides a great method to freely brainstorm asynchronous eye–ear associations. Notes from these screenings informed the final cut of the film in its current digital form.

The asynchronous techniques employed in our films are informed by the tools we use. Importantly, we do not want to suggest that one tool is "better" than another or that asynchronous practice is restricted to particular technologies. We also want to avoid nostalgia for tools that seem advantageous because of their "retro" pastiche. What we value are the limitations implicit in non-sync technologies, especially in relation to the dominance of synchronous "point-and-shoot" media. Non-synchronous technologies persuade us to rethink sedimented assumptions about the relationship between eye and ear. We could use varied tools to do this. We are excited by a surge in popularity of DSLR (digital single lens reflex) cameras that have limited shooting time and require external sound recording. We are also encouraged by the proliferation in critical thinking about sound in tandem with the overwhelming number of high quality, affordable audio-recording devices now available. The tools we use dramatically affect how we think about time, space, and the senses, yet it is important to note that an asynchronous shift in thinking can transform whatever tools are at an ethnographer's disposal.

The Politics of Asynchronous Encounters

> ... [I]t is only in holding open the gaps and tensions in cultural representation itself that we can glimpse an "other" mode of cultural critique that speaks from a "place" of contingency, vulnerability, and felt impact.[27]

A common interest in peoples and politics is crucial to our understanding of the ability of asynchronicity to challenge the sedimented practices of some anthropologists and artists. Specifically, we want to make a case for the reflexive and critical encounters that we believe our approach offers. Challenging eye–ear relations both through practice and through representational techniques and tools can enable us to engage the politics of aesthetics, sensation, and place in new ways. This engagement hinges on generating "gaps and tensions" in the "primary aesthetics" of these disciplines. For Rancière, "primary aesthetics" involves "a delimitation of spaces and times, of the visible and the invisible, of speech and noise, that simultaneously determines the place and the stakes of politics as a form of experience."[28] In this section, we want to develop the potential of asynchronicity to interrupt the "sync and/or non-sync" aesthetics that shape much ethnographic, documentary, and experimental film work as well as the implication of this interruption for political and ethical encounters. Our discussion will focus on *Immokalee, My Home*, an experimental non-fiction film completed in 2009.[29]

Immokalee, Florida, is the heart of industrial agriculture in the U.S. and home to its largest population of migrant farm workers. The much publicized conditions of migrant farm labor, particularly Florida tomato pickers, highlights both the low wages and the slave-like working conditions of many migrants today. A Florida farm worker, for example, must pick two and a half tons of tomatoes in a single day to earn a living wage.[30] And, because more than half of all migrant farm laborers live and work illegally, they have little to no protection.[31] Some farm bosses, taking advantage of this fact, beat, enslave, withhold food or water from, or refuse to pay their migrant laborers.[32] Our work in Immokalee began in early 2008 and was initially an attempt to document the story of the Coalition of Immokalee Workers, an organization laboring to improve working conditions in and around Immokalee.[33] This project involved mostly didactic interviews with CIW members.[34] And, while we wholeheartedly supported their struggle for "human rights," something seemed missing. Our preliminary work failed to capture the complexity of food production and consumption today. It seemed to offer a one-line slogan—Pay a penny more for a pound of tomatoes!—as a solution for global conditions and experiences of inequity.[35] It also seemed to avert, or even cover over, crucial narratives of displacement, loss, and hope. What we wanted, instead, was to speak "from a 'place' of contingency, vulnerability, and felt impact."[36] What we wanted was to generate "gaps and tensions" in the normalized story of Immokalee so that the "felt" or "not yet" narrated experience of actual, living human beings might peek through.

Our central dilemma involved how to engage Immokalee as what Kathleen Stewart calls "an occupied place" but to filter our engagement through the experience of the displaced, itinerant workers who both occupy and are occupied by it. Importantly, our dilemma hinged on somehow interrupting the usual flow of "cultural representations" of migrant work or workers. CBS productions such as *Harvest of Shame* (1960) and *New Harvest, Old Shame* (1990) are pivotal examples. We could add many more. Our point here is to consider how these representations have come to occupy both Immokalee and migrant workers, structuring possible narratives and encounters. For example, both "human rights" and "fair food" models must define when, where, and for whom "rights" and "fairness" exist. In the case of CIW, this limit extends only to those tomato farms around Immokalee who have signed CIW's Code of Conduct or to those corporations who have agreed to pay increased tomato prices.[37] This occupation by narratives, stereotypes, and other cognitive or perceptual schema is manifest (and reinforced) in the primary "sync and/or non-sync" aesthetics used to represent the story of Immokalee and its workers. In other words, time and space play a crucial role in how "occupation" is normally narrated and countered. Thus, to us, representing the temporal–spatial experience of migrant labor seemed politically crucial.

Through our encounters with migrant workers, we noticed that a number of temporal–spatial divisions undergirding the normalized story of Immokalee were not, in fact, consistent with workers' daily experiences or with their "ways of talkin' and "doin'."[38] For example, "work" is normally either bound temporally by the "clock time" of the workday or spatially by the "coeval presence" of workers "in the field." And, while this bounded model of work clearly structures discussions of migrant rights, representations of "work" also come to stand in for the larger life world. Consequently, work is either understood to occupy all times and spaces of migrant life, or crucial instances of work—such as waiting to work—are omitted (see Figure 7.5). Importantly, dominant narratives of migrant life also rely upon the bounded time and space of (in this case) "Immokalee now." This denies migrants' past stories of migration and presumes a "settled" future. In effect, it transforms all migrants into immigrants. Language is just one form of this denial and subsequent transformation—the assumption, for example, that Spanish is the native tongue of all migrant workers in Immokalee. The temporariness of migrant life and the lived (temporal and spatial) experience of language and culture are also denied. Ultimately, what we found missing from the normal story of Immokalee were the fluid, ambiguous, and ambivalent experiences of time and space that recurred in our discussions and encounters with Immokalee migrants.

Figure 7.5 Film still from *Immokalee, My Home*, 2009; by Kevin T. Allen and Jennifer Heuson, 16 mins, Super 8 mm film, © Small Gauge, Ltd.

In this example, asynchronous ethnography offers a strategy for intervening in the normalized or "primary aesthetics" of representations of Immokalee and of migrant work and workers more generally. We will note just two asynchronous moments in the film as illustration. The first moment responds directly to the synchronized experiences of "work" just discussed, the second to the asynchronicity of linguistic and cultural displacement. *Immokalee, My Home* contains a single representation of tomato-picking work.[39] The one-and-a-half-minute sequence follows a male worker through a series of picking, collecting, carrying, and delivering tomatoes and tomato buckets. We follow him closely with medium moving shots, cutting next to a series of static shots of fields, buses, and other workers. This sequence is bookmarked on either end by examples of "waiting work" ... workers waiting for buses and tomatoes waiting for sale. We use a number of visual strategies to interrupt normal perceptual patterns—such as hand-processed Super 8mm images, solar flares, "exposed" segments of film reels, and slow-motion cinematography—but we also employ asynchronous sound–image techniques. This includes the use of sounds recorded at the same "time and space" as images but manipulated to represent fluid movements between interior and exterior temporal–spatial experiences of tomato fieldwork. A second example occurs during our depiction of a CIW *Radio Consciencia* broadcast.[40] In this case, what we see and what we hear are not quite "in sync," calling attention to the temporal and spatial disruptions of speech experienced through foreign language and culture, political agenda, and radio broadcast technologies.

While there is much more to write about the asynchronous moments scattered throughout *Immokalee, My Home*, we would like to conclude this section with a few thoughts regarding the political and ethical impact of asynchronicity upon the fieldwork encounter. In this example, the most pressing of these involved the actual safety of both ethnographer and informant. By using small, portable "async" equipment and conducting mostly off-screen interviews, we were able to spend minimal time in the (heavily guarded) tomato fields. And, by dividing our attention and equipment to ear and eye separately, we could utilize that precious time effectively. However, this division of ear and eye also afforded more intimate interviews and the possibility of protecting our informants' identities. Furthermore, by isolating documentation techniques and tools—emphasizing image or sound or text—we were able to focus our own attentions and more deeply engage with our subjects' stories and lived (temporal–spatial) experiences. Out of this focus came our desire to resist and even counter the now standard use of migrant voices, bodies, and experiences for specific didactic statements or political agendas.

Conclusion—What Does Asynchronous Ethnography Offer Anthropology?

With these pages, we suggest our asynchronous practice as a way to challenge the "historical sedimentation" of traditional ethnographies, of the numbing embedded in either/or relations between the senses and their modes of representation and inquiry. We have sketched our practice and its resultant representations, including the tools and techniques we use and how both influence our encounters in and with the field. Our goal has not been to discount "sync and/or non-sync" strategies, but rather to challenge their overuse. Following C. Nadia Serematakis, we think asynchronicity will allow the "dustiness" of normalized eye–ear relations to be engaged. She writes:

> The relation between dust and what it covers is not a relation of appearance and essence. It is a relation of historical sedimentation. *Dust is not deposited only on the object but also on the eye.* Sensory numbing constructs not only the perceived but also the perceiving subject and the media of perception; each of these are reflexive components of an historical process.[41]

We offer asynchronous ethnography as a way to deposit dust on the eye in order to remove it from the ear (and vice versa). Can we think of asynchronicity as a reversal of the usual anthropological impulse to "dust off" peoples, places, and things? What new circuits—of encounter, sensation, and knowledge—does the creation of dust generate? Does it offer alternative ways to engage "the politics of aurality" in relation to looking, writing, or field recording?[42] Does it offer links between sensory and representational politics? Our approach to these questions involves re-thinking the relation between ear and eye in ethnographic practice in the hope that new relations between the two senses will provoke and promote new engagements between anthropologists and their fields, tools, and collaborators. We think the timing of this provocation particularly crucial.

On one hand, anthropology is in the midst of what David Howes calls a "sensual turn" with an expanding interest in modes of sensing (especially looking and listening, but also tasting, touching, and smelling) across its varied sub-disciplines.[43] This is coupled with an increased attention to the artistic and experimental nature of ethnographic practice.[44] Both have the potential to disrupt the normalized aesthetics that have become what we refer to as the "sedimented styles" of anthropology. It is our claim, however, that this disruption can only occur through a shift in representational practices, including such things as field recording tools and techniques as well as modes of publishing. To get at "sensory politics" thus requires radically new approaches to *how* anthropological research is conducted and distributed. On the other hand, an increasing number of experimental film-makers, sometimes explicitly framing their works as anthropological or ethnographic, engage in just such a shift, challenging the usual styles of "experimental" films. We have positioned our practice in between these two concerns. Synchronicity ("clock time" + "coeval presence") and its non-synchronous opposite have come to define the two disciplines and their methods. We offer "asynchronicity" as a provoking response.

Acknowledgments

An earlier version of this chapter was presented at the "Sound Studies, Sound Traces" panel we organized for the American Anthropological Association's Annual Meeting in Montreal in 2011. We would like to thank our fellow participants and attendees and are especially grateful for the feedback of our two respondents: Jonathan Sterne and David Novak. We would also like to thank Arnd Schneider for attending this talk and for finding our work interesting enough to invite us to contribute to this collection. Finally, we would like to thank the people whose images, voices, and lived experiences contributed to the works and ideas discussed throughout this chapter.

Filmography

Bridge, dir. K. T. Allen, New York: Small Gauge Ltd., 2012, 11 mins.
Immokalee, My Home, dir. K. T. Allen, and J. Heuson, New York and Florida: Small Gauge Ltd., 2009, 16 mins.
Jaguar, dir. J. Rouch, France, Niger and Ghana: Les Films de la Pléiade, 1967, 110 mins.
Leviathan, L. Castaing-Taylor, and V. Paravel, USA: Arrête ton Cinéma, 2012, 98 mins.
Luthier, dir. K. T. Allen, New York and Argentina: Small Gauge Ltd., 2010, 6 mins.
Still Life with Ho Chi Minh, dir. K. T. Allen, New York and Vietnam: Small Gauge Ltd., 2008, 3 mins.

Notes

1. Paul Stoller, *The Power of the Between: An Anthropological Odyssey* (Chicago, IL: University of Chicago Press, 2009), 4.
2. Jacques Rancière, "The Janus-Face of Politicized Art: Jacques Rancière in Interview with Gabriel Rockhill," in Gabriel Rockhill (ed.), *The Politics of Aesthetics*, trans. Gabriel Rockhill (London: Continuum, 2004), 60.
3. We mention Jung as a springboard for engaging with how the synchronous has been theorized. Carl Jung, *Synchronicity: An Acausal Connecting Principle* (Princeton, NJ: Princeton University Press, 1973).
4. For an example of the sorts of "critical phenomenologies" that interest us, see Kathleen C. Stewart, "An Occupied Place," in Steven Feld and Keith Basso (eds), *Senses of Place*, (Santa Fe, NM: School of American Research Press, 1996), 137–65.
5. Jacques Rancière, "The Distribution of the Sensible," in *The Politics of Aesthetics*.
6. For more about asynchronous circuits, see Chris J. Myers, *Asynchronous Circuit Design* (Hobokon, NJ: John Wiley, 2001).
7. For more about asynchronous learning, see Frank Mayadas, "Asynchronous Learning Networks: A Sloan Foundation Perspective," *Journal of Asynchronous Learning Networks*, 1 (1), 1997, 1–16.

8. Ursula M. Franklin, *The Real World of Technology* (Toronto: House of Ananzi Press, 2004), 151.
9. Franklin, *The Real World of Technology*, 146–56. For an overview of diachronic, synchronic, and interactive perspectives in anthropology, see Alan Barnard, *History and Theory in Anthropology* (Cambridge: Cambridge University Press, 2000), 8–9.
10. For more on the "audio–visual" contract, see Michel Chion, *Audio-Vision: Sound on Screen*, ed. and trans. Claudia Gorbman (New York: Columbia University Press, 1994).
11. Rancière, "The Distribution of the Sensible," 13.
12. David Howes, *Sensual Relations: Engaging the Senses in Social and Cultural Theory* (Ann Arbor, MI: University of Michigan Press, 2003); David W. Samuels, Louise Meintjes, Ana Maria Ochoa, and Thomas Porcello, "Soundscapes: Toward a Sounded Anthropology," *Annual Review of Anthropology*, 39, 2010, 329–45.
13. Steven Feld and Donald Brenneis, "Doing Anthropology in Sound," *American Ethnologist*, 41 (4), 2004, 461–74, 471.
14. Feld and Brenneis, "Doing Anthropology in Sound," 471; Samuels et al., "Soundscapes: Toward a Sounded Anthropology", 330.
15. As an example, see Jennifer Heuson, "Hearing the Hills: An Acoustic Encounter with South Dakota's Black Hills," *Sensate: A Journal for Experiments in Critical Media Practice*, April, 2011, from sensatejournal.com/2011/03/jen-heuson-hearing-the-hills (accessed December 16, 2013).
16. The "sensory immersion" techniques of recent works such as *Leviathan*, and the "intersensorial" approaches of sensory studies more generally, must more fully engage the role of aesthetic and representational tools in producing "sensory ideologies." David Howes, "Introduction: Empires of the Senses," in *Empire of the Senses*, ed. David Howes (Oxford: Berg, 2005), 9; Lucien Castaing-Taylor and Véréna Paravel, *Leviathan* (USA: Arrête ton Cinéma, 2012).
17. Jean Rouch, *Jaguar* (France, Niger and Ghana: Les Films de la Pléiade, 1967). *Jaguar* was shot in the 1950s when portable sync-sound recording equipment was not available. Rather than record non-sync sound or attempt to create synchronicity, Rouch embraced this limitation and used it to creatively probe the experience he was documenting (three men traveling from their rural villages in Niger to the cities of Ghana) and the experience of documenting (Rouch as ethnographer).
18. For more on the "production of presence," see Hans Ulrich Gumbrecht, *Production of Presence: What Meaning Cannot Convey* (Stanford, CA: Stanford University Press, 2004).
19. A roll of Kodak Super 8 mm film contains 50 feet of film or approximately three minutes and 20 seconds of screen time (at 18 frames per second).
20. Kevin T. Allen, *Still Life with Ho Chi Minh* (New York and Vietnam: Small Gauge Ltd., 2008). Material for this film was gathered incidentally while making another film in Vietnam in 2006. As a photographer, Mr. Bảy was drawn to our anachronistic equipment and invited us to his home to discuss photography and Vietnamese history.
21. Kevin T. Allen, *Luthier* (New York and Argentina: Small Gauge Ltd., 2010). Produced in the workshop of master luthier Raúl Orlando Pérez in Bariloche, Argentina, in 2009. Pérez has crafted custom instruments for musicians around the globe since 1962. For more about his work, please visit http://www.sinfoniagemela.com.ar/turismo/WEBRAUL/Roperez2.htm (accessed December 16, 2013).
22. The segment begins at 0:03:03 and runs until 0:03:10.
23. Although Super 8 mm sound cameras do exist, film stock was discontinued in 1997.
24. Nathanial Dorsky, *Devotional Cinema* (Berkeley, CA: Tuumba Press, 2005), 31.
25. Kevin T. Allen, *Bridge* (New York: Small Gauge Ltd., 2012). Produced in cooperation with Michael Gitlin's 'Microcultural Incidents' graduate course at Hunter College for the Integrated Media Arts.

26. Kevin T. Allen, *Sonic Geologic: The Secret Life of Material Objects* (New York: Small Gauge Ltd., 2011). A sound installation produced in cooperation with Smudge Studio for an exhibition and book launch at Columbia University's Studio-X for *Geologic City: A Field Guide To The GeoArchitecture of New York* (New York: Smudge Studio, 2011). For more about Smudge Studio, visit: http://smudgestudio.org (accessed December 18, 2013).
27. Stewart, "An Occupied Place," 140.
28. Rancière, "The Distribution of the Sensible," 13.
29. Kevin T. Allen and Jennifer Heuson, *Immokalee, My Home* (New York and Immokalee, FL: Small Gauge Ltd., 2009), produced by Kim A. Allen.
30. Coalition of Immokalee Workers, "Farmworker Facts and Figures," from http://ciw-online.org/101.html#facts (accessed April 27, 2013).
31. U.S. Department of Labor, "Findings From the National Agricultural Workers Survey (NAWS) 2000–2001," *U.S. Department of Labor* (2005), from http://dol.gov/asp/programs/agworker/report9/toc.htm (accessed December 7, 2008).
32. Coalition of Immokalee Workers, "Anti-Slavery Campaign," from http://ciw-online.org/slavery.html (accessed April 27, 2013). CIW, "Guilty! On Eve of Trial, Farm Bosses Plead Guilty to Enslaving Immokalee Workers in Tomato Harvest," *CIW Online Headquarters: Breaking News* (September 3, 2008), from http://ciw-online.org/news.html (accessed December 7, 2008).
33. The roots of this project began in October 2006 when CIW co-founder Lucas Benitez visited St. Luke's School in New York City to speak to producer Kim Allen's middle-school students. These visits sparked a friendship between Benitez and Allen that resulted in two trips to Florida in 2008. For more about the Coalition of Immokalee Workers, visit http://ciw-online.org/ (accessed December 18, 2013).
34. To view our campaign work, see Kevin T. Allen, *CIW Films*, New York and Florida: YouTube, March 30, 2008, from youtube.com/user/CIWfilms/videos (accessed December 16, 2013).
35. Coalition of Immokalee Workers, "The Campaign for Fair Food," from http://ciw-online.org/101.html#cff (accessed April 27, 2013).
36. Stewart, "An Occupied Place," 140.
37. Coalition of Immokalee Workers, "Fair Food Program FAQ," from http://ciw-online.org/FFP_FAQ.html (accessed April 27, 2013).
38. Stewart, "An Occupied Place," 138.
39. The scene discussed begins at the 0:02:20 mark and runs until 0:04:04.
40. The scene begins at 0:06:15 and runs until 0:07:40.
41. C. Nadia Seremetakis, "Memory of the Senses, Part II," in C. Nadia Seremetakis (ed.), *The Senses Still: Perception and Memory as Material Culture* (Chicago, IL: University of Chicago Press, 1994), 38.
42. Samuels et al., "Soundscapes: Toward a Sounded Anthropology," 339.
43. Howes, *Sensual Relations*, 29.
44. For more on collaborations between art and anthropology, see Arnd Schneider and Christopher Wright (eds), *Between Art and Anthropology: Contemporary Ethnographic Practice* (London: Bloomsbury, 2010).

8

MEMORY OBJECTS, MEMORY DIALOGUES: COMMON-SENSE EXPERIMENTS IN VISUAL ANTHROPOLOGY

Alyssa Grossman

Unpacking the secrets encoded in images and objects, we find the memory of the senses.[1]

Introduction

Visual anthropologists who actually make films, as opposed to those who solely write about them, face a dual set of expectations from the academic community. Like all anthropologists, they must articulate their arguments and findings through the conventions of scholarly writing. But they must also master, to a certain extent, the technical, conceptual, and material challenges that accompany any work with visual media.

Recent debates have underlined the need to extend anthropological uses of film beyond the realm of "visual communication," to treat it as more than just a means of conveying "pictorial" translations of anthropological ideas. It has been argued that being sensitive to such alternative approaches can lead to a different type of ethnographic knowledge: a sensory and bodily knowledge generated through the act of using a camera.[2] Yet even with increasing numbers of anthropologists working with visual media in new ways, it is widely acknowledged that there has been a "certain collective failure of the imagination" within the discipline.[3] Often visual material still serves as a mere illustration of anthropological concepts, with the camera functioning as a tool for recording the pictorial equivalent of field notes.

Because most visual anthropologists are trained as anthropologists, rather than as artists, it is to be expected that their films might not conform to the "standards" of what is produced in the film industry or the art world. But this need not prevent them, if and when the occasion arises, from exploring innovative or unconventional approaches to their work with visual media. As Arnd Schneider argues, any anthropological incursions into experimental film-making should not be performed for their own sake, but rather must make theoretical and contextual sense, and be somehow "linked to the experience of the subjects of anthropological research."[4] Yet anthropological films that do venture beyond conventions of the "narrowly realist paradigm" are still too often discouraged in academic contexts, or viewed as highly "contentious."[5]

This chapter focuses on one such film that counters traditional ethnographic norms of visual representation. *Memory Objects, Memory Dialogues* (2011), a collaboration between Selena Kimball (a visual artist) and myself (a visual anthropologist), plays with the boundaries between anthropology and art, and uses material objects and the medium of film to generate, rather than merely reflect, different modes of anthropological understanding. The film consists of a dual-screen projection, juxtaposing a sequence of ethnographic interviews about a collection of artifacts with a series of 16mm stop-motion animations of these same artifacts.

I am hesitant, however, to categorize this project as "experimental" just because it incorporates visual elements that anthropologists might shy away from or regard as overly "artistic." If we understand experimental film as "challenging major codes of dramatic realism" and using certain formal techniques to point to the illusory nature of visual representation,[6] then *Memory Objects, Memory Dialogues* could indeed be considered to fall within such a category. It does contain animations of ordinarily inanimate objects. It does use a double projection format to convey multiple perspectives, times, and spaces. It does subvert linear narratives and play with temporal gaps through repetition and the recurrent use of black screen. But these features alone do not make this film experimental. It is rather the ideas and approaches mobilized in the processes of its conception and realization that land it on experimental terrain within the field of visual anthropology.

I steer away from the notions of "borrowing" from art practices or "applying" artistic methods to my anthropological activities.[7] Instead, I regard anthropology as a discipline that possesses inherently artistic dimensions and capacities, which need only be recognized and embraced by its practitioners. In this case, I let the very subject matter of my research open up different lines of inquiry, contributing to the formation of a work that might not meet traditional expectations of what an "anthropological" film is or should do. Rather than adhering to a particular formula or a given set of shooting and editing conventions, I allowed material objects themselves to direct my research, thereby supplementing *and* transforming its direction, form, contents, and theoretical implications. Such tactics are surely more "logical" or "common-sense" than "experimental" (to return to Schneider's stipulation, these pursuits should make "theoretical and contextual sense"), and hopefully, as the discipline of visual anthropology continues to mature, will become more and more mainstream.

Background

My fieldwork primarily has been in post-communist Romania, focusing on sites and practices of memory in the urban context of Bucharest. Looking at how ongoing changes in Romania's global framework impact and reflect remembrance processes on local and individual levels, I have been exploring the contemporary dynamics of "transition" two decades after the 1989 revolution that ended 45 years of communist rule. Instead of focusing on explicitly commemorative, "official" arenas of memory production, such as archives, monuments, or museums, I am more concerned with "non-commemorative" memories[8] that occur in "unofficial," often unexpected contexts—unnoticed corners of the city, interiors of people's homes, the all-too-underexplored realms of everyday life. I am interested in when and where such memories surface and how they manifest in tangible and intangible forms, including objects, images, discourses, and public and private landscapes.

Researching the topic of memory requires a departure from traditional participant observation practices. Simply interviewing someone about his or her memories is not enough to evoke the multi-layered, visceral processing activities involved in the intricate workings of memory itself. As Maurice Bloch writes, we perceive experience in "conceptual clumps" of visual, sensory, and linguistic information, which, to be made fully comprehensible, must be rearranged into logical and sequential thoughts and words.[9] But while memories are often described through narratives or discourses,[10] such accounts are only "re-representations" of the very complex sets of activities occurring during actual processes of recollection.[11]

Bloch maintains that it is possible to come close to "living through" another person's memory if, as you encounter it, you flesh it out with your own experiences and emotions—an activity that involves you in processes similar to what the other person undergoes as they are doing the remembering.[12] I personally did not experience Romanian communism first-hand; so in order to supplement my intellectual understanding of this particular past, I needed to facilitate my own sensory and emotional recollections "by proxy," or by "knowing *through*" other people's accounts.[13] These memories need to be more than explanatory accounts or descriptions of the past. They must leave room to stir the imagination—that of the person doing the remembering and that of the person doing the listening.

In this vein, central to my methodology are imaginative experiments I devise to actively provoke memories in my interlocutors, to revive in them the experience of remembering, and to produce similar experiences in myself. Inspired in part by the Mass Observation movement,[14] which combined artistic and scientific sensibilities and focused on the "primacy of reality" through investigating the textures of everyday life,[15] I treat objects and places not as records or reminders of the past, but as "inducers of reminiscence,"[16] setting further processes of recollection in motion and allowing me to grasp their sensory and corporeal implications. Such an approach defines my fieldwork as a dynamic and relational process that profoundly influences and shapes—rather than merely aids or facilitates—my research.

In my investigations of memory traces within urban, domestic interior spaces of Bucharest, I asked a set of individuals to go through their household possessions, revisit their storage areas, and find an object to donate to me. I wanted things that were somehow associated with the past—specifically with the communist period in Romania before the 1989 revolution. I was not seeking explicitly political artifacts or souvenirs that had been preserved for sentimental reasons. Because I was looking for memories connected to the banal realms of everyday experience, I asked for items that were not worth much money and that people would be willing to part with permanently. I wanted ordinary things that had been tucked away or forgotten, objects considered outdated, shabby, no longer significant or relevant.

I filmed people as they rummaged through their cupboards and closets. Many of them initially insisted that they had nothing left from "back then." But once they started looking, they often were surprised by what they found. Accompanying them around their cellars, balconies, pantries, and attics, I watched them rediscover items from their pasts, examining once familiar household goods with different eyes. After they chose an object to give to me, I asked them to write a few sentences about what it was and what it meant to them. I then filmed them reading these statements, which frequently led to several more hours of filming as further reminiscences surfaced.

As my interlocutors' memories were triggered through finding the objects, so were my own. I was led into spaces of recollection not only through my physical contact with the artifacts, but also through the social and emotional experiences arising from these encounters (with the objects and with their donors). By helping to locate these artifacts and conjure forth their stories, I became part of the generative and constructive processes of recollection. Participating in such an experience offered me a more embodied understanding of the intangible elements of people's memories, and deepened my empathic connections to the objects affiliated with these memories.

The Objects

The items that I collected were relatively unremarkable in and of themselves. They included objects such as a glass inkwell still partially filled with blue ink; a hand-dyed silk scarf; a polyester school uniform; an aluminum ice cube tray; a hand-crocheted shopping bag; a miniature porcelain figurine; a heavy manual typewriter; a hand-made wooden darning mushroom; and a pair of wire-rimmed eyeglasses missing some parts.

As my collection expanded, I realized that it was not a collection in the conventional sense of the word. It rather consisted of inadvertently accumulated bits of domestic clutter that had been long neglected, and in some cases completely forgotten. Nicolette Makovicky writes that household collections may be seen as sites of practical, non-discursive memory work, as their accumulation involves not only explicitly constructed narratives but also unspoken assumptions and recollections.¹⁷ Many of my interviewees remarked that, until they had started searching for these objects and telling me their stories, they had not stopped to reconsider the multitude of associations and memories they had about them.

> Manual typewriter (Figure 8.1):
> I wouldn't have thought of a typewriter [to donate], something I've been familiar with since childhood, if in the 1980s, people hadn't become so obsessed with these machines. In order to discourage their use as a means of producing anti-Ceaușescu propaganda, there was a law that all owners of typewriters had to register them at their district's militia office ... During those years, this was the strangest queue of all. The typewriter queue in front of the militia office ... (Zoltán, aged 61)

> Ice cube tray (Figure 8.2):
> This is from the "Fram" fridge, also called the "Polar Bear"; our old refrigerator that used a lot of energy, in which I made cantaloupe ice cream for the first time. It spilled all over the fridge because the freezer didn't work. When we bought another fridge, an "Arctic" from Găești, in 1978, our poor "Fram" ended up as a chicken coop in the countryside. (Fotinica, aged 55)

> Seltzer bottle (Figure 8.3):
> Back then, seltzer water was the ordinary person's mineral water. It was never absent from the table ... When I was little, I was often sent to the seltzer bottle shop to exchange the cartridges, which I didn't enjoy doing ... There were several types of seltzer bottles. The older models were made of glass and wrapped in a mesh bag. This object is one of the everyday things I grew up with, but now it provokes in me a funny nostalgia. (Mónika, aged 37)

I came to see these artifacts as Benjaminian points of rupture, as they had lain dormant for many years, sparking unexpected recollections in a later present—a "historical awakening" providing fresh insights into contemporary perceptions of the past and the future. As Benjamin noted, our encounters with devalued and abandoned objects allow us not simply to remember the past, but also to better understand the current context where the past is read, as well as our lingering dreams, wishes, and projections.¹⁸ In this sense, mining storage areas and their forgotten contents could serve as an avenue for accessing old memories and provoking new ones, as well as for gauging people's feelings about the present and their expectations about the future.

Animated Collaborations

Just as I sought alternative methods for gaining a more intimate and embodied understanding of my interlocutors' recollections, I needed to find a way to appropriately treat this material through film. I did not wish to use the medium to merely

Figure 8.1 Manual typewriter. Digital film still by Alyssa Grossman.

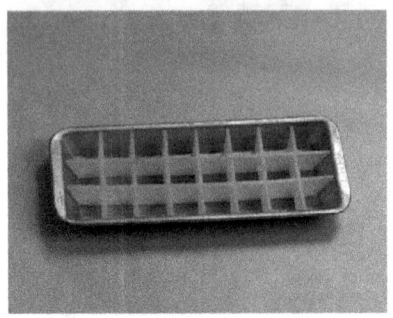

Figure 8.2 Ice cube tray. Digital film still by Alyssa Grossman.

Figure 8.3 Seltzer bottle. Digital film still by Alyssa Grossman.

present my collection of objects and relay their histories, but rather to evoke the sensory, affective aspects of recollection.[19] I wanted to emphasize memory's generative, constantly evolving qualities, and question the use of documentary images as an easy means of calling up a static past through mechanical processes of information retrieval.[20] I wanted the film's form and contents to convey the idea that individual memories are selected and transmitted through fluctuating and contingent social meanings and values, not handed down as a given set of biographical facts or fixed personal data.[21]

This was where my long-time friend and collaborator, Selena Kimball, stepped in. Selena and I had already worked together on a number of projects over the previous 15 years. Our work in Romania began in 1997, when we first traveled there to investigate the dynamics of the early post-communist period. After I received a Fulbright grant two years later to work with an ethnographic museum in Bucharest, Selena and I produced an exhibition of objects, paintings, and texts stemming from the year-long postal correspondence we maintained while I was living in Romania and she was working out of her studio in New England.

In 2005, Selena joined me at a Romanian Orthodox nunnery where I was filming and researching the everyday lives of the nuns who lived there. Selena brought her 16mm Bolex camera along, and made a series of stop-motion animation sequences of me, alluding to some of my daily struggles with fieldwork and film-making. I incorporated her animations into my film, *Into the Field* (2005), using them as reflexive structuring devices that repeatedly interrupted (and interrogated) an otherwise observational exploration of the daily routines and rhythms of monastic life.

I wanted to incorporate similar stop-motion techniques into *Memory Objects, Memory Dialogues*, with my collection of household objects as the subjects of the new animations. In 2007, after I had completed another year of fieldwork in Bucharest, Selena joined me there for a few weeks with her Bolex camera.[22] Initially, Selena deliberately kept herself in the dark about the objects' origins and their stories. She decided to read the donors' texts and watch the interviews only *after* filming and editing the animations. Rather than being concerned with conveying the objects' "actual" memories and narratives, she was more interested in their universal qualities as "auratic" objects.[23] She wanted to focus on the substance, form, and feeling of the artifacts themselves, and involve them in new activities that would add to their role not as vehicles for transmitting or illustrating their given histories, but as objects that could speak for themselves. Such an approach parallels what Henare, Holbraad, and Wastell describe as the anthropological shift from seeing artifacts as illustrations of social or historical systems, toward letting materials themselves "enunciate" their own meanings and "dictate the terms of their own analysis."[24]

It took us two weeks to film ten animations. Using the balcony of my Bucharest apartment as an improvised studio, we spent hours shooting each object in short vignettes that Selena conceived in response to the collection I had assembled. Stop-motion filming requires the exposure of a single frame at a time, repositioning the object just a fraction between each shot in order to create the illusion of movement when the film is played back at 24 frames per second. Often it would take an entire day to film a sequence that in its finished form would last no more than 10 or 20 seconds.

Making the animations required us to physically intervene, placing the objects in new settings and circumstances. Selena and I became involved with them in ways that most curators or handlers of ethnographic material do not ordinary allow themselves. While altering and dismantling objects was part and parcel of Selena's artistic practice, I had been taught that field collections must be preserved, handled with gloves, and displayed behind glass cases. Yet as I watched in horror as she cut a hole in one of the donated socks so she could film my hands sewing it up with the aid of the donated darning mushroom, I found myself reconsidering the value of such "destructive" acts. As we cultivated our own relationships and affinities with these objects through direct, bodily contact, I became increasingly attuned to their material presence, recognizing them as much more than mere symbols or triggers of particular narratives about the past.[25] As Laura Marks argues, objects encode meaning not only metaphorically but also through physical contact.[26] Putting these objects to use allowed me to bodily connect with them and to engage not just with the narratives recounted by their donors, but also with their very forms, textures, and materials.

For instance, in order to make an animation showing trails of melting ice, Selena and I first froze water in the donated ice cube tray. Accustomed to using more "modern" trays made of plastic, we struggled with its inflexible metal frame to extract unbroken cubes that were large and uniform enough to film. Returning to my interviewee's account of her "Fram" refrigerator, an infamous Romanian communist brand, I could draw upon this experience to relate to the frustration she must have felt when it failed to properly function. After my own battle with the ice cubes, I found myself echoing her wry appreciation of the fact that, after it became defunct, it was at least put to some use as a makeshift chicken coop in the countryside.

In another instance, as Selena and I carried the heavy manual typewriter around the streets of Bucharest, searching for an appropriate setting in which to animate it, my aching arms gave me a more physical understanding of the literal burden it must have been to have to lug these typewriters to the police station to be registered. The donor had explained to me that, since the keys wore down with use, in order for any dissident manifestos to be properly traceable, all typewriters had to be brought in to the militia for inspection every single year. Until that point, I had understood this memory as a narrative account, but now I had a more embodied knowledge of the responsibility involved in owning a typewriter in that particular context, and of the absurdity of having to stand in long, cold queues every winter for the sake of such a machine.

Manipulating objects and engaging with them in such ways evokes Robert Ascher's accounts of the "imitative experiments" conducted by archaeologists in the 1950s. In these instances, archaeologists would put objects and materials to work in manners "simulative of the past" in order to test hypotheses and establish "legitimate inferences" about their previous roles and functions.[27] Unlike these archaeologists, Selena and I were not attempting to come closer to how these objects were originally used. But our unusual physical interactions with them sparked deeper understandings of their social and cultural relevance, and gave us unexpected insights into their ironic and poignantly humorous qualities. We brought several of the objects around the streets of Bucharest, filming them in landscapes where they could enter into new conversations with their surroundings. The donated porcelain bibelot almost seemed to grow in size and importance when we filmed it strolling down the sidewalk in front of Ceaușescu's Palace of the People, the second largest building in the world. Although the Romanian media (and much of the local population) tends to disparage the Palace as an abominable eyesore and an unwelcome reminder of Ceaușescu's totalitarian regime, the cute kitsch of the figurine somehow made the appalling kitsch of the Palace seem more laughable and less ominous (Figure 8.4).

To be able to laugh at the Palace of the People, rather than be crushed by it, resonated with my findings that Romanians' recollections included varied and strategic treatments of communist power structures. Rather than demonstrating either full complicity with or total resistance to the system, my interviewees had the capacity to work around it, even to mock it, with self-conscious and deliberate wit. Such a complex response is not the message conveyed by dominant memory discourses circulating in Romania's public spheres. Disseminated through the media, politics, and academic and cultural institutions, these official narratives tend to be more black and white, depicting the communist past either as something to be criminalized and condemned, or as having provided a sense of security and stability in people's lives, leading it to be romanticized and viewed with nostalgia. As sensory memories are particularly important when "official" histories fail to fully illuminate personal realms of experience,[28] my own embodied encounters during the process of making the animations gave new layers of meaning to my interlocutors' nuanced (and sometimes idiosyncratic) recollections.

Figure 8.4 Porcelain bibelot in front of the Palace of the Parliament in Bucharest (formerly known as Ceaușescu's Palace of the People). Photograph by Alyssa Grossman.

Haptic Dialogues

In its finished form, *Memory Objects, Memory Dialogues* consists of ten interviews, which I edited into a 26-minute-long sequence, and ten short animations, which Selena edited into a repeating 6-minute loop. The animations and the interviews play simultaneously, though they are not synchronized according to a particular plan, and rarely reference the same objects at the same time. They are intended to be projected either as a split image on one wall (for cinema and festival viewings), or on two screens on adjacent walls of a room (as a gallery installation) (Figure 8.5).

On one side of the projection, the animations present episodes that contain suggestive and sometimes unfinished narratives. The wooden darning mushroom hurtles through a sock stretched horizontally from one side of the frame to the other. The inkwell leaks a puddle of blue ink that forms a wavering shadow, then shrinks and disappears. Miniature cookbooks pile up in a stack, with one opening to reveal its illustrations dislodging themselves from the page to perform a tightrope act. The animations have retained their grainy, shadowy, flickering 16mm quality, and are silent, with no added sound track. Each one flashes by quite quickly (most last less than a minute), and between the scenes Selena inserted bits of film lead in bursts of blurry color that add to the film's "haptic" qualities.[29]

As Marks argues, haptic images require the viewer to pay more attention to their material presence than to their meanings as representational narratives.[30] In order

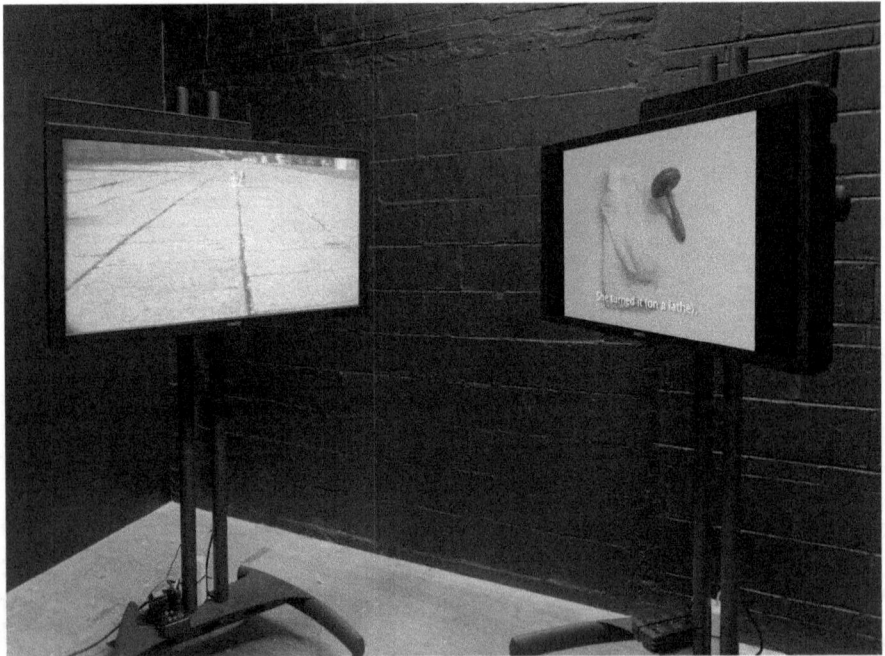

Figure 8.5 Dual-screen installation of *Memory Objects, Memory Dialogues* (2011). Photograph by Rachel Topham for *Ethnographic Terminalia* 2011: Field, Studio, Lab.

to decipher such images, the spectator cannot rely on vision alone; the eyes must operate like organs of touch,[31] giving rise to visceral responses that engage not just the intellect, but also the memory and other senses. This embodied act of looking propels the viewer to question the illusion of cinematic representation, and to participate in "shar[ing] and perform[ing] cinematic space dialogically."[32]

The corresponding interviews also invite haptic attention. While the voices of the speakers are heard as continuous narratives, for the most part people's faces are not seen. Each interview begins with a black screen and a voice describing an object, which appears for several seconds, photographed on a plain white background. The object then gives way to black screen again, and we are brought into the donor's personal stories, thoughts, and reminiscences, with the speaker's image breaking through the black for only a few brief instances. The coherent flow of the aural narratives, together with the fragmented glimpses of the narrators themselves, draw upon but also subvert the documentary "talking heads" convention. As the stories unfold, the stretches of black allow for closer scrutiny of the other screen featuring the animations, but at the same time suggest the limitations of understanding or remembering through visual images alone.

As the animations loop four times during the course of the interviews, the images, objects, and stories diverge and overlap, producing new and unexpected dialogues. Chance encounters, where one donor's animated object emerges and resonates with another donor's memories, add new layers of significance and irony to the film. While the donor of the darning mushroom recalls her nervousness during her first day as a teacher, an animated school uniform appears, rapidly expanding and contracting as if it were breathing, seeming to reflect some of the anxieties and fears of the narrator on the other screen. While the donor of the cookbooks speaks about the gradual disappearance of food during communist times, another animation shows ice cubes slowly circling around and melting, leaving a dark, expanding ring in their wake. Occasionally, the animation of an object will appear while its own donor is speaking about it (another chance meeting), and the viewer may experience a flash of recognition, the way a memory can flare up in the mind. But then it quickly passes as the story changes and another animation flickers into sight.

The objects and narratives reference and speak to one another, but they do not represent or illustrate each other. While they offer glimpses into past and present material realities and human subjectivities, they do not provide definitive explanations or conclusions. As Marks reminds us, auratic objects can never be reduced to narratives, and they can never satisfy our wish to recover a memory in its entirety.[33] These open-ended dialogues and remnants echo what Elizabeth Cowie describes as cinema's ability to activate the desire to see ("scopophilia") and the desire to know ("epistephelia"), through never wholly fulfilling these desires.[34] They allow for gaps in the idea of completeness, saying more through their disjointed syncopations than through a linear, continuous story.

The multiple projections in *Memory Objects, Memory Dialogues* literally create a life-sized stereoscope, requiring the viewer to shift back and forth between them;

though in this case, a single, distinct image never comes into focus. The "incoherence of vision"[35] resulting from such a viewing arrangement may be destabilizing, but it is this very fact that makes it not just a visual experience, but a sensory one as well. The decentering of perception in stereoscopic vision, as film scholars have noted, physically impacts observers, making them more conscious of their unusual spatial position in relation to the objects on the screen, and drawing their attention to the very mechanisms of visual representation.[36] By cultivating such physical disjunctures and discontinuities, *Memory Objects, Memory Dialogues* opens up new spaces for affective engagement with the ambiguities and complexities of the remembrance process itself.

Conclusions

In a cautionary essay on documentary treatments of the phenomenon of memory, David MacDougall warns against film's tendencies to convey memory as fixed or unchanging, particularly in its misleading and uncritical use of objects and images as signs of a "recoverable past."[37] Many films, he argues, erroneously depict such "secondary representations" of memory as if they were memory itself, simplifying its "multidimensional" qualities and "stripping the representation of memory of much of its breadth and ambiguity."[38] While the existing repertoire of ethnographic films about memory was likely more limited when his article was published in 1992 than it is now, MacDougall's concerns reflect ongoing debates about the materiality of remembrance work and the challenges of using visual media in relation to issues of memory.

These debates appear to revolve around three main poles. One position considers objects to be "relics" that serve either as "witnesses of the past" or as vehicles for communicating people's ongoing narratives about the past.[39] The second position challenges such assumptions, suggesting that material artifacts function more often as aids of forgetting than of remembering.[40] The third acknowledges that material forms cannot ever directly illustrate or give access to the past, and suggests that new strategies are necessary for experimenting with the evocation, rather than the representation, of memory.[41]

It is this third position that *Memory Objects, Memory Dialogues* takes as its starting point, though it uses the impossibility of memory's representation to articulate a slightly different thesis. Rather than shying away from the use of material artifacts because of their potential to be mistakenly read as literal "signs" of memory, this project embraces the capacity of objects (as well as the medium of film itself) to resonate with and generate physical and emotional processes of memory. Through its multiple reframings of people, things, and stories, moving them in and out of legibility and generating haptic and embodied experiences, the film's makers, subjects, objects, and spectators are provoked to search their own "circuits of sense memory,"[42] bringing forth a range of other powerful memories in the process.

Reconfiguring a collection of discarded objects to stimulate new memories is an act with important ontological implications. By placing things in a new set of relations that are "internal and peculiar to the collection itself,"[43] the collection no longer just recalls the past; it paves the way for alternative formulations of multiple pasts. Returning to Benjamin, the power of objects emerges precisely after they have been removed from circulation, detached from their original contexts and reordered to allow us to make new connections and conclusions.[44] The resulting partial and fragmentary configurations serve as an avenue for piecing together the past not in a chronological, historical way, but in a dialectical fashion. Such dialectical images become legible only at particular moments, with each new reading different from the previous ones.

While the process of making *Memory Objects, Memory Dialogues* involved departures from conventional anthropological research and filming strategies, they were logical responses to the nature of the subject and materials at hand. By handling a collection of forgotten household objects in ways that most ethnographic artifacts are not ordinarily treated, and actively intervening to re-collect and relocate them, Selena and I developed new forms of engagement with the objects, with the medium of film itself and, by extension, with individual and collective memories. Our collaboration shifted the dynamics of fieldwork to allow the artifacts to operate not just as objects of recollection, but also as subjects constituting new memories and associations.[45] "When we arrange the material residues of the past in our impossible inventories," writes Caitlin DeSilvey, "they arrange us in turn."[46] Such reconfigurations might be unsettling as they counter certain expectations about how ethnographic encounters should be translated and understood, but they may also help to steer the discipline of visual anthropology and its practitioners into new and vital methodological and analytical territory.[47]

Notes

1. Laura U. Marks, *The Skin of the Film: Intercultural Cinema, Embodiment, and the Senses* (Durham, NC and London: Duke University Press, 2000), 195.
2. See Anna Grimshaw and Amanda Ravetz, "Introduction: Visualizing Anthropology," in A. Grimshaw and A. Ravetz (eds), *Visualizing Anthropology* (Bristol: Intellect Books, 2005); Anna Grimshaw, "Eyeing the Field: New Horizons for Visual Anthropology," in A. Grimshaw and A. Ravetz (eds), *Visualizing Anthropology*; David MacDougall, *The Corporeal Image: Film, Ethnography, and the Senses* (Princeton, NJ: Princeton University Press, 2006); and Marks, *The Skin of the Film*.
3. Amanda Ravetz, "From Documenting Culture to Experimenting with Cultural Phenomena: Using Fine Art Pedagogies with Visual Anthropology Students," in E. Hallam and T. Ingold (eds), *Creativity and Cultural Improvisation* (Oxford and New York: Berg, 2007), 263.
4. Arnd Schneider, "Expanded Visions: Rethinking Anthropological Research and Representation through Experimental Film," in T. Ingold (ed.), *Redrawing Anthropology: Materials, Movements, Lines* (Burlington, VT: Ashgate, 2011), 186.
5. Arnd Schneider and Chris Wright, "The Challenge of Practice," in A. Schneider and C. Wright (eds), *Contemporary Art and Anthropology* (Oxford and New York: Berg, 2006), 6.

6. A. L. Rees, *A History of Experimental Film and Video: From the Canonical Avant-Garde to Contemporary British Practice* (London: British Film Institute, 1999), 1, 5. See also Arnd Schneider, "Expanded Visions," 178–80.
7. For descriptions of anthropologists and artists "borrowing" from each other's disciplines, see Alex Coles (ed.), *Site-Specificity: The Ethnographic Turn*, vol. 4 (London: Black Dog Publishing, 2000); Caitlin DeSilvey, "Art and Archive: Memory-work on a Montana Homestead," *Journal of Historical Geography*, 33, 2007, 878–900, 881; and Kathryn Ramey, "Productive Dissonance and Sensuous Image-Making: Visual Anthropology and Experimental Film", in M. Banks and J. Ruby (eds), *Made to be Seen: Perspectives on the History of Visual Anthropology* (Chicago, IL: University of Chicago Press, 2011), 256.
8. Barbara A. Misztal, *Theories of Social Remembering* (Maidenhead: Open University Press, 2003), 69.
9. Maurice E. F. Bloch, *How We Think They Think: Anthropological Approaches to Cognition, Memory and Literacy* (Oxford and Colorado, WY: Westview Press, 1998), 24.
10. Edward Casey, *Remembering: A Phenomenological Study* (Indianapolis, IN: Indiana University Press, 1987), 116.
11. Bloch, *How We Think They Think*, 122.
12. *Ibid.*, 123.
13. Casey, *Remembering*, 81 (my emphasis).
14. See Charles Madge and Tom Harrison, *Britain by Mass Observation* (London: Penguin Books, 1939), 10.
15. Angus Calder and Dorothy Sheridan (eds), *Speak for Yourself: A Mass-Observation Anthology, 1937–49* (London: Jonathan Cape, 1984), 4.
16. Casey, *Remembering*, p. 110.
17. Nicolette Makovicky, "Closet and Cabinet: Clutter as Cosmology", *Home Cultures*, 4 (3), 2007, 287–310, 304.
18. Walter Benjamin, *The Arcades Project*, trans. H. Eiland and K. McLaughlin (Cambridge, MA: Harvard University Press, 1999), 205.
19. See Annette Kuhn, "Memory Texts and Memory Work: Performances of Memory in and With Visual Media," in *Memory Studies*, 3 (4), 2010, 298–313, for a discussion on how various forms of "mediated storytelling" can serve both to analyze and perform acts of memory in embodied ways.
20. John Sutton, "Remembering," in P. Robbins and M. Ayede (eds), *The Cambridge Handbook of Situated Cognition* (Cambridge: Cambridge University Press, 2009), 220. See also David Lowenthal, *The Past is a Foreign Country* (Cambridge: Cambridge University Press, 1985), 210.
21. For overviews of theories of memory as a socially, culturally, and politically constructed process, see Misztal, *Theories of Social Remembering*; and Katharine Hodgkin and Susannah Radstone (eds), *Contested Pasts: The Politics of Memory* (London and New York: Routledge, 2003).
22. We have described the details of this collaboration in "The Memory Archive: Filmic Collaborations in Art and Anthropology," *Reconstruction*, 9 (1), 2009, from http://reconstruction.eserver.org/091/grossman&kimball.shtml (accessed December 21, 2013).
23. See Marks, *The Skin of the Film*.
24. Amiria J. M. Henare, Martin Holbraad, and Sari Wastell, "Introduction: Thinking Through Things," in A. Henare, M. Holbraad, and S. Wastell (eds), *Thinking Through Things: Theorising Artefacts Ethnographically* (London: Routledge, 2007), 4.
25. Cf. Daphne Berdahl, "Go, Trabi, Go! Reflections on a Car and its Symbolization Over Time," *Anthropology and Humanism*, 25 (2), 2000, 131–41, 131; Mihaly Csikszentmihalyi and Eugene Rochberg-Halton, *The Meaning of Things: Domestic Symbols and the Self* (Cambridge: Cambridge University Press, 1981), 17.

26. Marks, *The Skin of the Film*, 80.
27. Robert Ascher, "Experimental Archeology," *American Anthropologist, New Series*, 63 (4), 1961, 793–816, 793.
28. Marks, *The Skin of the Film*, 223.
29. Laura U. Marks, *Touch: Sensuous Theory and Multisensory Media* (Minneapolis, MN: University of Minnesota Press, 2002), 10.
30. Marks, *The Skin of the Film*, 163.
31. Marks, *Touch*, 2; see also Jill Bennett, "The Aesthetics of Sense-Memory: Theorising Trauma Through the Visual Arts," in S. Radstone and K. Hodgkin (eds), *Memory Cultures: Memory, Subjectivity and Recognition* (New Brunswick, NJ: Transaction Publishers, 2006), 32.
32. Marks, *The Skin of the Film*, 150. See also Catherine Russell, *Experimental Ethnography: The Work of Film in the Age of Video* (Durham, NC: Duke University Press, 1999), 158.
33. Marks, *The Skin of the Film*, 81.
34. Elizabeth Cowie, "The Spectacle of Actuality," in J. M. Gaines and M. Renov (eds), *Collecting Visible Evidence* (Minneapolis, MN: University of Minnesota Press, 1999), 27–8.
35. Ibid., 25.
36. Ibid., 24–5.
37. David MacDougall, "Films of Memory," *Visual Anthropology Review*, 8 (1), 1992, 29–37, 32.
38. Ibid., 33.
39. See Jacques LeGoff, *History and Memory*, trans. S. Rendall and E. Claman (New York: Columbia University Press, 1992), 89; Lowenthal, *The Past is a Foreign Country*, 243–4.
40. Vincent Crapanzano, *Imaginative Horizons: An Essay in Literary-Philosophical Anthropology* (Chicago, IL: University of Chicago Press, 2004), 163; Adrian Forty, "Introduction," in *The Art of Forgetting* (Oxford: Berg, 1999), 7.
41. Fernando Calzadilla and George Marcus, "Artists in the Field: Between Art and Anthropology," in Schneider and Wright (eds), *Contemporary Art and Anthropology*, 108; Peter Crawford, "Film as Discourse: The Invention of Anthropological Realities," in P. I. Crawford and D. Turton (eds), *Film as Ethnography* (Manchester: Manchester University Press, 1992), 78; Andreas Huyssen, *Present Pasts: Palimpsests and the Politics of Memory* (Stanford, CA: Stanford University Press, 2003), 130; MacDougall, "Films of Memory," 29.
42. Marks, *The Skin of the Film*, 212–13.
43. Henare, Holbraad, and Wastell (eds), "Introduction: Thinking Through Things," 22.
44. Benjamin, *The Arcades Project*, 207.
45. Henare, Holbraad, and Wastell, "Thinking Through Things," 23.
46. DeSilvey, "Art and Archive," 900.
47. Versions of this paper were presented at the workshop "Nouvelles visions: film expérimental et anthropologie," at the Musée du quai Branly, Paris (2011), and at the Critical Heritage Seminar at the University of Gothenburg, Sweden (2012). Many thanks to Arnd Schneider, Caterina Pasqualino, Staffan Appelgren, Anna Bohlin, Katarina Karlsson, and Selena Kimball, for their valuable contributions and comments.

9

BEYOND THE FRAMES OF FILM AND ABORIGINAL FIELDWORK

Barbara Glowczewski

Between 1976 and 1978, I shot several experimental films in Paris which were screened at many art festivals. The following year, while doing anthropological fieldwork in Central Australia, I filmed women's rituals using a frame by frame technique to produce superimpositions, flickering rhythms, and discontinuities, aimed at suggesting the condensation process of dream as an attempt to transpose a cosmological concept central to Warlpiri life: *Jukurrpa*, the Dreaming. It was a mistake. Anthropology and cinema should indeed call on a creative process to give an insight into the heterogeneity of cultural contexts that we analyse in writing or film, but this can only be achieved if the singularity of our subjects' perceptions is taken into account; that is, the way they express their visions, memories, and history, as well as assemblages that include other agents, and all living systems as intertwined with environment and technology.

1970s Experimental Cinema and Anthropology in France

In the 1970s many places in Paris were screening experimental films, from the birth of cinema, with Russian futurists and French Dada, or other avant garde artists such as Man Ray, Len Lye, Germaine Dulac, Luis Bunuel, Jean Cocteau, and Maya Deren, to the 1950s lettrists Isidore Isou, and Maurice Lemaître, or 1960s American figures of underground, non-narrative, or "structural" cinema—Kenneth Anger, Andy Warhol, Michael Snow, Stan Brakhage, Hans Richter, Austrian Peter Kubelka, and Jonas Mekas, who with Adams Sitney founded the Film-Makers Coop in New York (1970).[1] French experimental production was blooming at the time, with oneiric atmospheres like Thierry Garrel's films or experiments from the Paris Film Coop created in 1974 by Claudine Eizykman and other film-makers who promoted an independent cinema of intermittence, searching for "energy-objects" instead of "representing-objects," and advocating for a "maximization of affects," and "psychic connections *branchements*."[2]

After seeing Eizykman's film *VW Vitesse Women* (1974), I enrolled for a cinema degree at the University Paris 8 where she was teaching. The campus, which was then located in the woods of Vincennes, offered radically innovative seminars in different disciplines, including philosophy with Deleuze and Lyotard, who had made a film with Claudine Eizykman, Guy Fihman, and Dominique Avron, *L'autre scène* (1972, 16mm, opt, 6mins), a critique of advertising comparing dream-work and film-work. Eizykman's and Fihman's course on "cinematographic energetics" was based on their films, her book, and Lyotard's notion of "acinema"[3]—providing a theoretical and visual impulse to make non-representational perceptual experimentations of intensities. Even though I had the opportunity to make a video in 1975 and experiment with an image synthesiser, I was more interested in sticking to film materiality in order to experiment such forms of music for the eyes.[4] I made two portraits of female friends: rewinding the same unprocessed 16 mm film strip scene by scene, sometimes only a few frames at a time, I superimposed different camera moves, or in and out zooms, to film each woman sitting, walking, or rolling in opposite directions. There was something magical in waiting for the processing to check the resulting effects: each woman seemed to diverge in reflections of herself, or merge back into one body and multiply again, as in an abyss. To add a new level of texture, I painted the black and white footage with pink and purple *Gros Loup* (1976) and with two shades of green *Fédéfé* as *"feminin désirante feminine"* (1976).

I then co-authored with Martine Zevort two colored silent 16mm films. For *Miradwie* (1976) we filmed in turns, half-frame by half-frame, our own faces reflected in crushed aluminum paper, alternating expressions/looks of fear *notre regard apeuré* or threat *anger au sens où notre regard était agressif*, and sadness or joy: this produced monstrous flickering masks with our eyes, superimposed directly on some frames or through intermittence of successive frames, projecting conflicting moods and emotions. The fast intermittent rhythm created an arbitrary visual perception, the viewer's eye picking randomly this or that frame whose conscious imprint would last longer than the exposure, masking the vision of other frames left to subliminal perception. One would never see exactly the same film twice. The silent contradictory or unconscious visual stimuli provoked a psychic and physical mix of pleasure and uneasiness, and even nausea for some viewers. Whatever the obtained effect, we were enchanted/delighted with this experimental insight into perception. At the time I wrote that *Miradwie* was staging a "conflict between pulsions," "demonstrating an antagonistic emotional process" which "requested from the viewer the perceptive availability to come to terms with the unfolding of the conflict within him/herself": (Figure 9.1) an "exteriorisation of an anthropology of (the) inside." We also refilmed the screen projecting *Miradwie* at different speeds, using filters and a negative stock which was not printed in positive after the edit: the inversed colors transformed the texture of the aluminium paper into an unknown soft skin which created a rather serene effect *Noeuga* (1976).

My next film, *Picturlure* (1977), was based on my "pictures": some 400 small, painted cards of little anthropomorphic figures and numerous abstract shapes

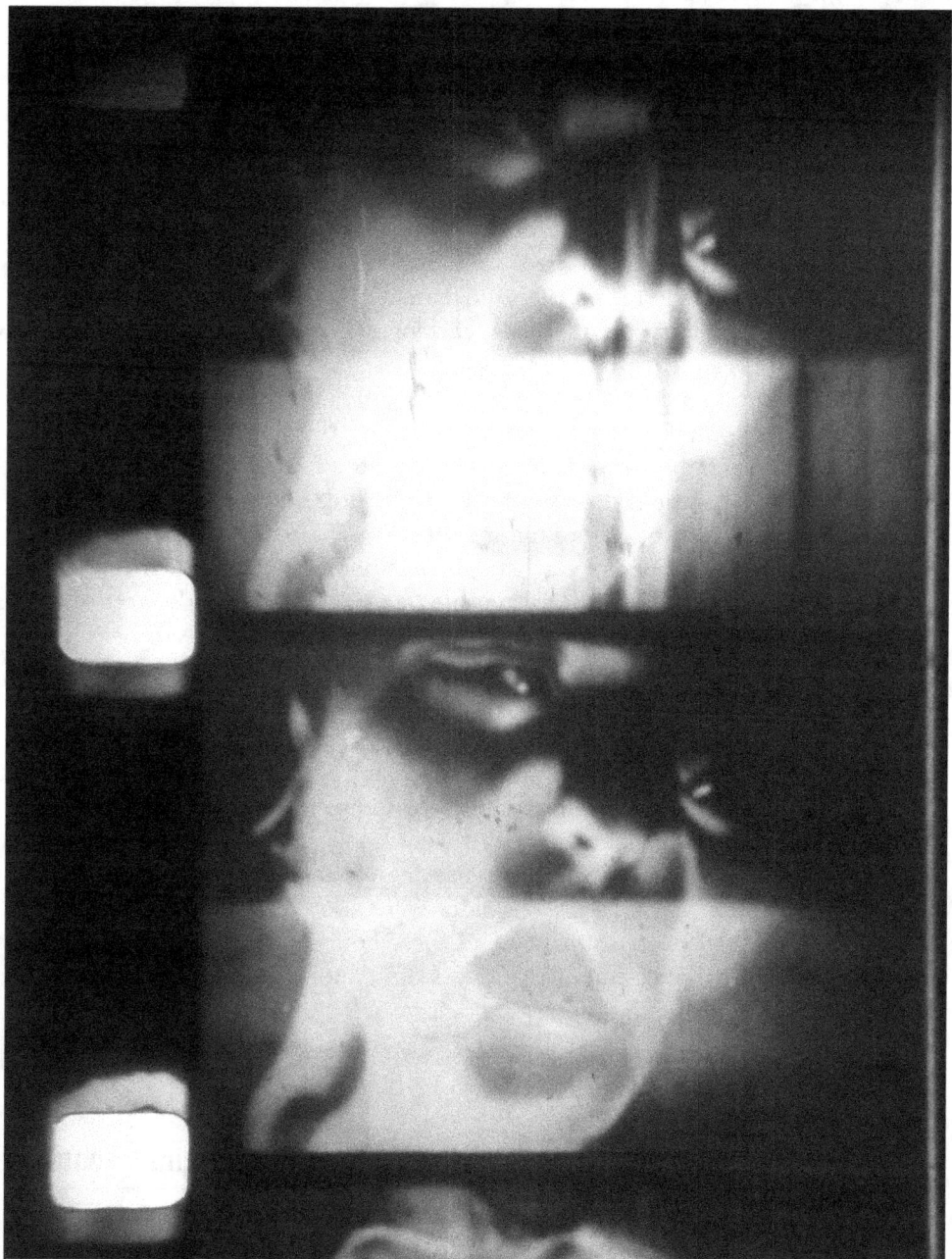

Figure 9.1 Film still, *Miradwie*, 16mm, 1976. Courtesy of Barbara Glowczewski.

made with pencils, gouache, felt pens, and varnish on cellophane or plexiglas. I had built transparent drawers to be able to slide superimposed images as I was filming, and an installation of screens to capture the moving shades of colors projected by transparent mediums hanging on a rope. Starting with grids like partitions to structure different rhythms, I used a tripod while I was painting, but over the weeks the filming became a sort of dance, with the camera turning around the painted images or their projection in the room. During the editing of the 16 mm film stock (Agfacolor, negative and positive Ektachrome), I shortened the shots to just a few frames, but respected the chronological process of the experimentations: the last sequence was the refilming of the printed film running away from the projector. I then experimented with the projection of the film on my body: the projector close enough to fit exactly the size of my chest, my skin providing texture to the projected images that seemed to become solid and which, through my breathing, moved in another direction from their movement on the film. The autonomy they had gained from the frame of the usual rectangular screen was later lost when I improvised an "expanded projection" in a public space, bringing a 1 × 1 meter-board covered with a mosaic of my painted cards, which I used as a backdrop for my naked body, exposed to the projector. The screen of the cinema was so big and high that I had to stand on a stool: I realized too late that, instead of being painted or fused with my paintings, I was simply floodlighted! Nevertheless, the critical analysis of this experience and the filming process validated my degree in cinema.

I also trained in anthropology at the University Paris 7, which, in those days, brought together a group of stimulating thinkers such as Michel de Certeau who supervised my Master's degree on "Anthropology of the 5 Senses." Another lecturer was Jean Monod, the author of a famous survey on Parisian youngsters, who explored drugs and mythical visions with Piroa Indians in Venezuela, making with them a poetic documentary (*Histoire de Wahari*, 1970), before leaving academia to dedicate himself to poetry and art.[5] Jean Arlaud was showing his and others' ethnographic films as well as films produced by indigenous peoples. Robert Jaulin, then famous for his denunciation of the Amazonian ethnocide, was the head of the department which regularly hosted Native Americans so they could speak about the struggle for their rights. Issues of gender were also discussed by the American feminist Judith Friedlander. To validate all these courses, I used my experimental films, the history of optics, and a critique of semiology to try to deconstruct representational interpretation in art and anthropology. Such was my training as I embarked on my doctoral field study in Central Australia.

Conveying Visions: From France to Aboriginal Australia

When I screened *Picturlure* to the Warlpiri people from Lajamanu in 1979, the response was encouraging: some men of ritual authority found it "normal" that I show paintings because they were told that my country, France, was known as a place for painters. They also liked *Généal* (16 mm, silent, 2 mins 30 seconds, 1976), a short montage of 900 family photographs showing my mother as a child in a trendy 1920s Poland, as a teenage Jewish refugee, dressed in school uniform, then as a Zazou, working and playing the piano in an Allied camp established in Algiers during World War II, and later posing with my father during the 1950s in Warsaw, where I was born, before the family moved to France in the 1960s. No photo was filmed for more than a fifth of a second; some were repeated full screen in alternated series, others as windows on a black, pink, or green background (to produce contrasted illusions of inversed colors), creating a quick rhythm, with staccato and superimpositions, especially between the faces of my mother, her mother, and myself. As my Warlpiri audience seemed comfortable with this flickering rhythm, which was new to them (this was before music clips and fast ads on TV), I showed them *Miradwie*. The scary side of the deformed faces did not seem to bother them, many women found my country "good," because it was "full of spirits." Seeing "spirits" beyond physical reality was in a way what we searched for when the flesh of our reflected faces disappeared in the aluminum paper, where our flickering eyes superimposed or alternated contradictory emotions, as if touching directly the organic psychic pulse (Figure 9.2).

The Warlpiri evaluation encouraged me to film the women's rituals using a similar frame-by-frame technique. However, while the refilming of our faces in Paris had only involved my friend and I as voluntary "guinea pigs" of perception, filming Warlpiri women—who were involved in rituals of cosmological significance for the indigenous Australian society and desert culture—confronted me with ethical issues relating to a cognitive process of survival. When watching the silent footage of their *yawulyu* rituals, the Warlpiri women felt that the acceleration of their dancing movements, the superimposition of different dancers, and the upside down filming of the landscape and camp where they performed was making them look "silly." My film effects of dream "condensation" were inappropriate. Women in their *yawulyu* rituals—like the men in theirs—paint their bodies, dance, and sing about the making of the land features and the establishment of social laws by eternal ancestors: their Dreamings. The dancers reenact the Dreamings, each bearing a different animal, plant, or using other totemic names like Rain and Fire. Each of these is called *Jukurrpa* (Dreaming, also translated as the Law). The etymology of *Jukurrpa* refers to *jukurrmanu*: dreams, which are a means to communicate with *Jukurrpa* beings who, during their creative travels, marked the landscape with their *kurruwari* (life forces) living "images," as hills, waterholes, ochre depostis, and other imprints of their passage. The Dreaming beings are said to be present, embodied, and "in becoming" (*palkajarri*) in these sacred features of the Dreaming sites, and also, generation after generation, in the people, animals, plants, water, wind, and other things that share the same Dreaming name and livng image. Through dreams, men and women can receive new Dreaming designs, songs, and dancing patterns attached to particular places to maintain the balance of the land. In this dynamic cosmological understanding, Dreamings redefine totemism as a process of becoming and a production of intensities performed by Warlpiri people.

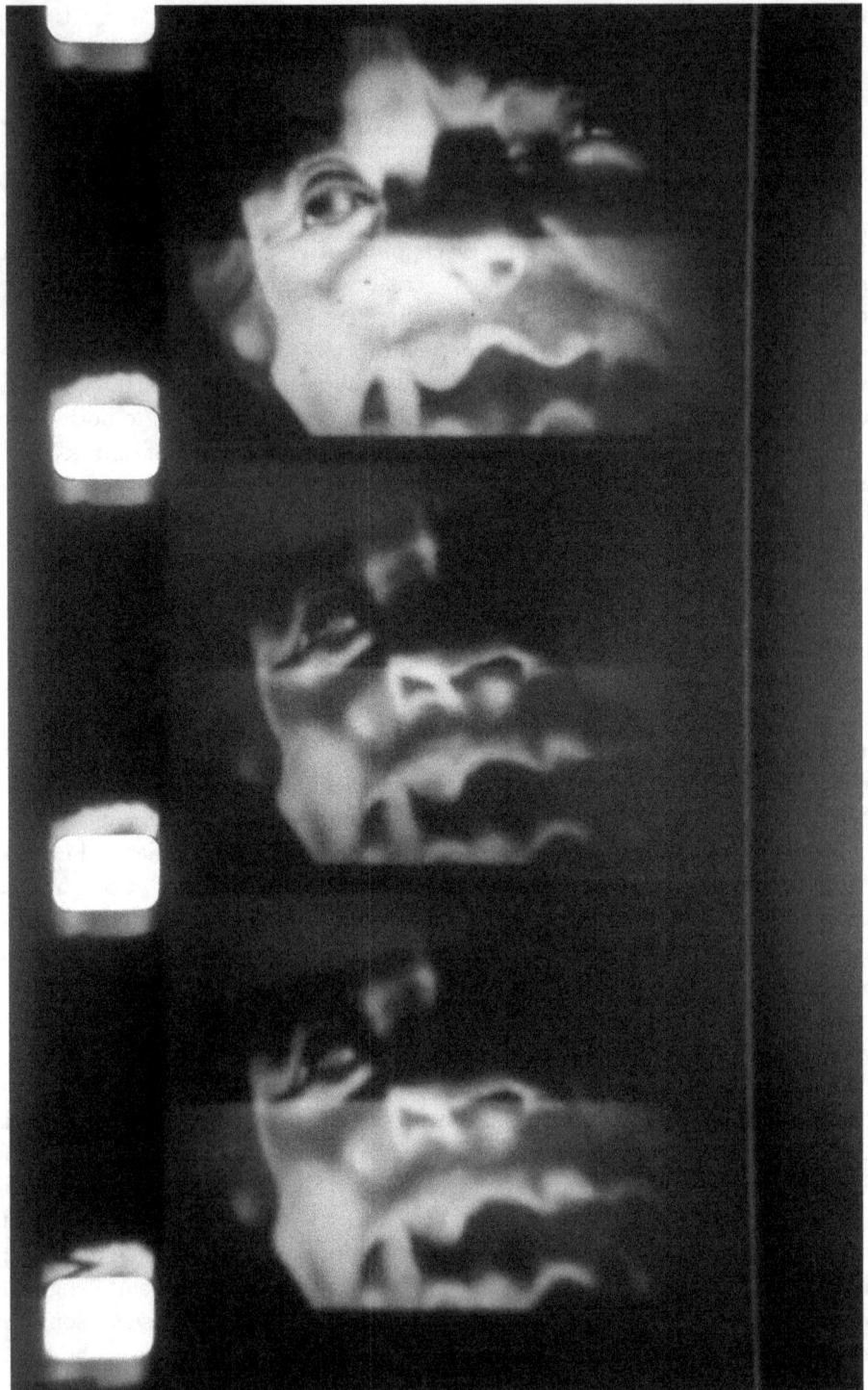

Figure 9.2 Film still, *Miradwie*, 16mm, 1976. Courtesy of Barbara Glowczewski.

For them what was important was the real speed of the performance, of the enactment, of the dance because the speed at which you enact the travelling from one place to another is itself carrying an information. (…) if it's the dry season and there's no water left, for the same distance you have to travel very fast, otherwise you will die. This means you have to dance the ritual fast. Dancing is a way of carrying the message of survival to the people who participate in the dance and who watch the dance. All these meanings are inside the performance itself and it is through rhythm that you can learn these things without it being explicit.[6]

Conception and experience of time and space in the desert are relative, almost in a non-Euclidian way. For example, a pathway linking three waterholes spread over 100 kilometres is relatively longer than another 100 kilometres pathway crossing a country with no waterholes. This relativity comes from the speed at which you need to travel at in order to survive. You need to go fast to reach the next waterhole before being too thirsty, but you can slow down or stop if there is water on the way.[7]

The *businesswomen*, a term used in Warlpiri English for women in charge of rituals dealing with spiritual as well as social "business" (exchange in all forms), asked me to film their dancing "normally": that is, in continuous shots, long enough to respect the rhythm of their movements as being meaningful for them. So I filmed in that way, having to film very selectively over the few months of the continuous ritual activities of the Kajirri cult, as I only had three hours of film stock. My small Pathé Webo camera held three-minutes-long cartridges but shots were constrained to the time allowed by the manual winding of the mechanical motor: that is, 30 seconds. My shots were rarely longer than a few seconds, and I tried to frame the ending of each shot so that it could be spliced with the next one to enable the editing of the painting of bodies, sacred objects, and dancing without cutting out any image shot. Once back in France, I sent the women a copy of the Kajirri cycle spliced in a chronological order/sequence but I was told that they could not watch it because some people I had filmed had since died and their faces could no longer be seen by the mourners: I had to "erase" them like Warlpiri used to do by "blackening" photos. I asked the Australian Institute of Aboriginal Studies in Canberra for the use of their film unit to edit out these images. But during the screening of the edited film in Lajamanu in 1983, there was an uproar of mourning cries when the women saw a group of young men (*malyarra* initiates) coming out of seclusion to be covered by the men with gifts of hair strings and cloth for their mothers. The women had recognized these initiates as being the group from which a young man had just died in a car crash. While the deceased was not on the image, the visual context of this event had become taboo, just like his camp had to be avoided, and neither his name nor the name of any other thing sounding like his name (like France for Francis) could be pronounced. This taboo, which was traditionally applied to names, songs, or visual Dreaming patterns of a deceased person, had been extended to other forms of "re-presentation," such as photographs and films. I was happy to respect these cultural protocols, as it gave me a challenging insight for my own exploration of how to convey anthropological observations: not to "re-present" them but to change perceptions and preconceptions. Because of the invitation to become involved in Warlpiri ritual performances and everyday life—to dance with painted breasts, witness conflicts and resolution, walk hours in the sun to hunt, camp outdoors, etc.—I was given a share of their "spirit": when I woke with strange dreams, the women would connect them to their own dreams, personal events, or elements of their culture and cosmological system of the Dreaming space-time. I would not necessarily "hear" the voice of the spirits that they would hear in the night, but the collective atmosphere often made me "feel" a presence passing by, or crossing through us. I attempted to give an insight into this presence by translating my perception and feelings through writing, audio recordings, and photos of Warlpiri people. However, I stopped filming for ten years.

Women Only and Bodies on the Screen

No matter how we try to transpose our insights, each viewer projects his or her cultural or social presuppositions in relation to the content of films and is also constrained by his or her visual habitus: the familiarity of an image can bring comfort as well as boredom, while strangeness can seduce or destabilize. I experienced this gap when I organized in Paris a screening of the silent rushes of Warlpiri rituals that the desert women had agreed for me to film, provided I would only show these images to women, even in my own country.

> About a hundred came, crowding into a large apartment lent for the occasion. Some were my friends, others simply professional acquaintances, and the rest strangers flocking in as feminists for that women-only event. Personally I did not seek a discourse on liberation, I only hoped to find in the female audience that same complicity I had experienced with the women of the desert. What a mistake!
>
> From the moment the film engaged in the projector I had that sudden feeling of indulging in a lewd act. The image the Warlpiri women presented would be incomplete and risked betraying them. When they appeared on screen, I experienced an unexpected pain as I realised how much I missed their presence. I was torn by a feeling of guilt. I did not know what I was guilty of, but the fault seemed irreparable.
>
> The agony lasted two hours. The silent images of the body paintings and the dances unfolded to the sound of a tape of songs that someone turned systematically every half-hour. I had brought other tapes but I could not move any longer, stuck in a corner, paralysed. Gradually I discovered all the things the images did not tell, that would have had to be told for the spectators simply to *see* them.
>
> I realised clearly that my encounter with the Aboriginal people had, without my knowing, deeply transformed me. That discovery sent me into such a deep feeling of loneliness I was unable to articulate the slightest commentary. The task seemed insurmountable. I wished only to cry out: "No, all you think you're seeing is false!"

I could not bear rediscovering on that screen those corrugated metal shelters or the piles of rubbish that irrevocably reminded all of us of shanty towns. I recalled my dread and repulsion during my first days, then my feeling of detachment towards that environment that I learnt from the Warlpiri people.

Searching for new words to talk about my experience, that sensorial symbiosis with the women of the desert, all I heard in return was hysterical laughter and half-embarrassed, half-mocking exclamations. Why that uneasiness? The absence of a commentary had undoubtedly encouraged all sorts of phantasms.

There was flesh, naked, touched, marked ... too much flesh. Especially breasts, huge and floppy mammaries, hanging down to the waist and bouncing to the rhythm of dances. And all those eyes, impassive, deep, shifty, distant ... so distant, penetrating ... too penetrating. And there were the sacred poles, those smooth sticks, gleaming with ochre, tapered slightly at both ends, rubbed and painted, handed from one to another, raised to the sky, pointed towards the horizon, erected in the ground, unearthed, held at arm's length, slid between legs, thrown, caught again, replanted, bound again with ropes, touched with the hollow of the palm, shaken, massaged with joined hands, in short, manipulated like objects and treated like living beings.

At the end of the projection, the inevitable question, of course, was asked:
"What are those phallic objects?"
"They are the most sacred objects of the women."

Laughter and grins. This time the betrayal of the *businesswomen* was complete. Their rituals seemed to add up to no more than a phallic cult, while my experience with the Walpiri people had consisted in living in a female world autonomous from the male one. However hard I tried to explain that female rituals are a descent into the woman's body, a transformation of the body into earth, a passage to the Dreaming, a universe of metamorphosis where sexual differentiation is no longer a reference because the process of becoming plays with the infinity of terrestrial and cosmic forms, I came up against a question that seemed stupidly reductive:
"Thus the woman is identified with Mother Earth?"

I became agitated, incapable of explaining the relationship of the Aboriginal people to the earth, which is for them, depending on the places, *mother, father, spouse, etc*, that is, as many relatives as there are in the society of relationships differentiated by the Dreamings. In reality, Warlpiri men and women are both on the side of nature and on the side of culture. Being perceived as a succession of trails of the bodies of metamorphosed ancestors, the earth is not just a biological metaphor but also a memory support for the Law which rules society.

I explained the cartography of mythical trails linking the earth to the Dreamings, and I added that women inherited from their father the Dreaming and the vital force with which they became identified. The responses I received were psychoanalytical comments on the Oedipus Complex.

The malaise became heavier and heavier. Some spectators finally admitted they could not bear the constant presence of flesh, that they felt denigrated in their femininity, unable to identify with women so *primitive*. Others did not say anything.

It was true, the body of the Aboriginal women related the power of reproduction. A body damaged by pregnancies and old age, bloated or hollowed by a sedentary life and junk food, shaped by wind, rain and sun, etched by illnesses, ritual wounds or accidents. A body polished by time which reflected a certain image of the mother, undoubtedly universal but from which, often, we protect ourselves. It is the mother who changes into an ogress, mouth that swallows, vagina that consumes, belly that digests, womb that transforms, that mother from which we come and which is virtually there inside us as a destiny, the one we do not want to look like and who haunts us like a fatal repetition, the one from which we would like to detach ourselves but who hurts, pains and aches us.

Some spectators recounted later their emotions on seeing the transfiguration of the painted bodies. They had felt a power that seemed to come from the beginning of time which called them, seduced them, looked familiar. Behind the bodies they had seen the substance carved as a rock, resistant for eternity, full and alive. They had tasted something secret. Whether modesty or an impotence of words, they could not speak, or they did not want to. They had perceived that body which can become all of nature's kingdoms, animal, vegetable or mineral. Perhaps they had felt like me, in the heart of the substance, the earth and the stars, where there is nothing left but the force of fullness which opens onto the void, the force of the inside where all forms are suspended. The dreams of women or the dreams of men.

The essential point of female rituals and, it appears, also of male rituals, is to refer to the Dreaming as a surpassing of dualisms. The Dreaming is the actual experience of the paradoxes, the setting of the inversions, the way to overcome sexual identity and find oneself elsewhere, in the heart of the secret of life, in the heart of the power of metamorphosis.

When I said I had felt a *woman* with the Warlpiri, I was saying that I was on the path that leads right to the edge of human surpassing where sexual identity vanishes. Whether ecstatic or nightmarish, all those impressions and sensations seem then to melt into the collective reality of that female being on its way to dissolution. What happens then I cannot say. I stopped on the path for, not knowing where I was going, I was overwhelmed by terror. The Warlpiri women have the ancestral references of the Dreamings to find their way.[8]

The shared experience with Warlpiri women had in a way shifted my previous questioning of "femininity," especially as expressed in another experimental film I had shot in Greece with Laurence Vale. After discovering a stray hair in most frames, we had decided to mask it by using caches such as incrustations, where we inserted refilmed images different in content, rhythm, and camera movement from the images refilmed in the rest of the screen. The vibrations from the flickering of the original shots were alternated with the slow motion of the refilming which created a very grainy texture and an oneiric atmosphere. Our filmed bodies in the islands of Lindos, Rhodes, and Mytilène became landscapes. *Néroïcal* (1978), commented as "a new representation of the body," "a liberated body,"[9] mixes an atmosphere of joyous play with a sensation of isolation of each woman enclosed in her own universe.

France had no women studies equivalent to the University of Santa Cruz summer course that I had enrolled in just after high school in 1974. Nevertheless, psychoanalytical and political questions about a feminine essence, gender relations, sexual liberation, and desire in general were agitating some public debates, artists, and intellectuals. Such issues were at the heart of Gina Pane and Michel Journiac's teachings at the Department of Arts plastiques (University Paris 1) followed by many young artists and experimental film-makers: for instance Maria Klonaris and Katerina Thomadaki who mixed engaged performance—for example on torture—with film and art installations where they defined themselves as "*actants*" rather then "actors."

> To pass in front of, and behind, the lens—this eye, open to the world—is to destroy the classic dichotomies of subject/object, acting/transcribing, seeing/being seen.
>
> From this flux, from this double stimulation of glances, this interlacing of two bodies and two imaginaries, there emerged the language of the intercorporeal, a language which we have not ceased to explore since.
>
> *Double Labyrinthe* is also the moment in which the unconscious first makes itself tangible.[10]

Dominique Noguez[11] called their work and that of other members of the Collectif Jeune Cinéma "The school of the body" and proposed, as a "multiple posterity to the *Chant d'amour* of Genet," to add other film-makers from the Paris Film Coop, Yann Beauvais and Unglee, who together created in 1981 a third cooperative, Light Cone.[12] Despite this investment in the body, taboos persisted. When I screened *Maladia d'Amour* (1978), a montage of short extracts from 16 mm films found at the death of a grand uncle—1930s pornographic films, 1950s Moscow military parades, and Spanish corridas—part of the audience of a Paris Festival dedicated to women film-makers and eroticism was shocked.

My position was very different from Brakhage's intent, "to elevate the subject of pornography to an art form, an ambition almost totally contrary to that of the Australian film maker, Valie Export, who believes that any representation of sex on the screen is dangerous and an evasion of the central issue, and should be replaced by the direct confrontation with the 'real'."[13]

I had played with *clichés* by fabricating unusual movements and juxtapositions—the Soviet soldiers parading back and forth as in a dance with the toreador's cape beating to the rhythm of their march, and intercourse between women or with men—with the intention that sexual machismo, bullfighting, and the military parades would play each other off as "pornography." Sexual stereotypes and maybe taboos, in relation to the celebrations of the Russian revolution by the Soviet regime, probably prevented some viewers from seizing the derision of my dis-mounting (*dé-montage*) of the obscenity of such reality grounded images.[14]

Negotiating Percepts and Affects

In the 1970s, some alternative or "underground" media, like the French magazine *Actuel*, were promoting a postmodern collusion between indigenous tribes and high tech science fiction. Arriving in Lajamanu in 1979, I was struck with an apocalyptic vision: the entrance of the old Hooker Creek reserve, established on the edge of the Tanami desert hundreds of kilometres from the first petrol station, had piles of old cars, fridges, and other Western waste, spread in the bush as a parody of our consumption society but also like a spare parts shop for the Warlpiri people who would pick up what they needed from there to build shanty camps or repair their cars. I was attracted to this oneiric end of the world landscape, which would later resonate with the "Zone" of *Stalker* (1979) by Tarkovski. The minimalist mental and physical resistance of the "Zone" was a forbidden, "dangerous" place to cross. In a way, during the many months I spent each time in Lajamanu—as well as in other Aboriginal places—I also learned how to maneuver through forbidden spaces of knowledge, embodied in the landscape: zones of information and ritual camps were restricted either to men or women and to different levels/classes/groups of initiates, camping spots and pathways to be avoided because of a death, sacred sites that could not be attended or that needed a ritual protocol of introduction to the spirits. The landscape was full of spirits crossing time in a perpendicular way but leaving traces and symptoms of disease. The language was constantly fragmented with taboo words to be replaced by whispers and gestures evoking the deceased, synonyms, or simply left as holes "without name," a punctuation of memorial vacuums, the space also for virtual reemergence through new dream revelations after the lifting of the mourning period.

The writer and ethnographer Steve Muecke[15] proposes to define as experimental the documentary *Two Laws* (1980) shot in the Northern Territory Aboriginal community of Boroloola at a time of the Indigenous Australians' struggle for land rights. He considers experimental the way the film-makers Alessandro Cavadini and Carolyn Strachan followed visual and meaningful existential priorities as expressed by Aboriginal people after they saw the first footage: for instance they wanted the whole body of Aboriginal narrators to be filmed in the landscape so they would be seen as actors in "co-presence" and not as a simple background: in other words, they wanted the Dreaming ancestors and their marked landscape to be recognized as actors. It is still a challenge to suggest through image—fixed or animated—the presence of the Dreaming involved in the performances of Aboriginal ritual, as well as the content and affects of any dream, spiritual, or mental experiences. Warlpiri and other Aboriginal desert artists have succeeded to do so in their creative way, when transposing onto rectangular canvas with acrylics their own visual tradition of painting with ochres on their bodies, sacred objects, and the ground, as well as drawing stories in the sand.

Women's body painting consists in outlining a basic totemic design with slim lines, alternating white, red, and sometimes also yellow ochre and black charcoal, until the whole body is saturated with lines that seem to absorb the original design. A similar technique has been adapted by men and women to paint with acrylics on canvas: first with the four traditional colors and later with any existing synthetic paint, producing cinetic effects of fusion or inversion of above and underneath, whether the lines are continuous—like in women's body painting,[16] or stippled, made with a series of different sized dots, a technique inspired by men painting their bodies and the sand with wild cotton and bird down. Born in Papunya in 1971, the Aboriginal acrylic movement spread to many desert communities, which over the next decades developed their own styles. Community art centers were established to promote these artists on the contemporary art market, with thousands of highly priced paintings acquired by contemporary art collectors and museums all over the world. Since the early 1980s, many Aboriginal people also turned to video and cinema to stage various aspects of their current life, colonial history, and spirituality. Aboriginal film-makers—like many other indigenous people—have proposed very creative ways to suggest the life of the landscape, expressing their desires and intensities as intertwined with their natural and cultural environment. Some of those films have been awarded prizes in the mainstream but they are also a recombination of Deleuzo-Guattarian minor-cinema, and of what Guattari called ecosophy (binding of mental, social, and environment ecologies) and its aesthetical paradigm, which includes ethics and politics.[17]

I am not a film-maker, but as an anthropologist I started filming again in the 1990s, with a video camera, for the purpose of a multimedia project,[18] and later for the internet, especially with regard to a campaign for social justice, following the arrest of rioters after a death in custody in the Aboriginal community of Palm Island in 2004 (see Figure 9.3).[19]

The growing art production and the claim by people, who were traditionally studied by anthropologists, to control the way they are presented has, over the last 30 years, changed the way we work. Anthropologists have to take into account those claims and the criticism of past and present representations produced by all social sciences, the media, as well as literature. Some anthropologists, both old and young, as well as some film-makers or other artists, believe that their subjective creative approach allows them to do what they want with material collected in the field, in archives, or on the internet. Such a position can deny people's agency and struggle for empowerment to challenge the history of their dispossession. Fieldwork's contextual constraints and rules form a tool to free ourselves from our ethnocentric bias, which is often unconscious. Research implies constant negotiations, as contexts change with time, as do cultural priorities. For instance, some Warlpiri people have changed their relation to images over the years. Restricted knowledge—including some photos and films of secret rituals—is sometimes made public in order to produce art or political statements, while photos of the dead are now framed and exhibited during funerals organized by younger generations. I was allowed to include selected extracts of my 16mm footage of women-only rituals on the *Dream Trackers* CD-ROM I developed in the mid-1990s, and, since 2011,

Figure 9.3 Lex Wotton and his wife Cecilia, Palm Island, 2007: in front of a photo of the debutante ball they won when aged 16. Courtesy of Barbara Glowczewski.

at the request of the Warlpiri, I have transferred all the footage and thousands of photos and hours of ritual songs and Dreaming stories onto a digital open source database which the Warlpiri can annotate online: the access to some files is open, others can only be accessed with a password.[20]

Free knowledge is not knowledge freely transportable on the internet, but knowledge that people can use to free themselves. Such is, for me, the challenge of both cinema and anthropology.[21]

Filmography

L'autre scène, 1972, Jean-François Lyotard, Claudine Eizykman, Guy Fihman, and Dominique Avron, Cinedoc (Paris Film Coop), 16mm, opt, 6mins: http://www.cinedoc.org (accessed December 19, 2013).

Double Labyrinthe, 1975–6, Klonaris/Thomadaki, Super 8 blown in 16mm, 55mins, color, silent: http://www.klonaris-thomadaki.net/16dlfr.htm (accessed December 19, 2013).

Dyonysos, 90', 1984, Jean Rouch, 90mins, color, sound: http://www.youtube.com/watch?v=-grx9C3ymuQ (accessed January 20, 2014).

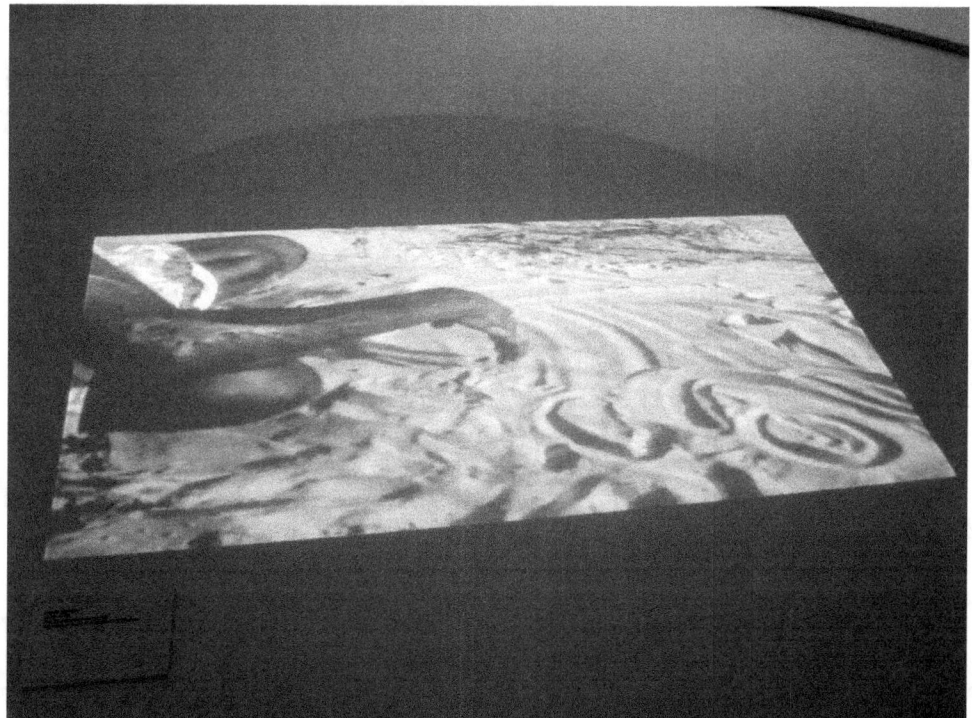

Figure 9.4 *Sand Story* by Barbara Gibson Nakamarra (Glowczewski and Vale, 1994) exhibited at *Mémoires Vives. Une histoire de l'Art aborigène*, Musée d'Aquitaine, 2013. Courtesy of Barbara Glowczewski.

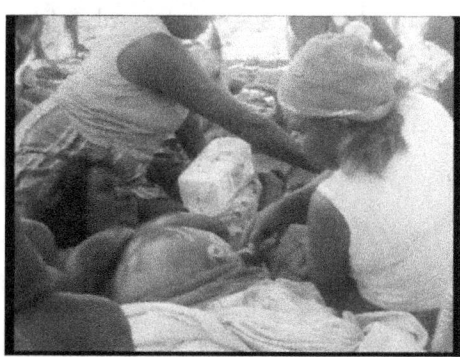

Figure 9.5 Still from *Kajirri Warlpiri Ceremonies Restricted to Women*, Lajamanu, Central Australia, 1979, 16mm: yawulyu healing ritual, the ochre painting on Pampa Napangardi is feeding her body and her spirit. Courtesy of Barbara Glowczewski.

Fédéfé, 1976, Barbara Glowczewska, Cinedoc (Paris Film Coop), France, 16mm, 6 mins, painted b/w, silent.

Gros Loup, 1976, Barbara Glowczewska, Cinedoc (Paris Film Coop), France, 16mm, 8 mins 30 secs, painted b/w, silent.

Histoire de Wahari, 1970, Jean Monod and Vincent Blanchet, self-produced, CNRS Images, France, 16mm, 66 mins, color, sound.

Maladia d'Amour, 1978, Barbara Glowczewski, Cinedoc (Paris Film Coop), France, 16 mm, 10 mins, color, silent.

Miradwie, 1976, Barbara Glowczewska and Martine Zevort, Cinedoc (Paris Film Coop), France, silent.

Néroïcal, 1978, Barbara Glowczewska and Laurence Vale, grant from the GREC, special effects, Magic Studio, 16 mm, silent, 45 mins (*mention spéciale du jury* [special prize] of the Jury Festival of Hyères, 1978).

Noeuga, 1976, Barbara Glowczewska and Martine Zevort, Cinedoc (Paris Film Coop), France, 8 mins 30 secs, silent.

Picturlure, 1977, Barbara Glowczewska, Cinedoc (Paris Film Coop), France, 15 mins, 16 mm, silent (nominated Festival de Hyères, 1977).

Quest in Aboriginal Land, 2000, Barbara Glowczewski and Wayne Jowandi Barker, 2002, interactive DVD, self-produced, Australia and France, 50 mins.

Sand Story *by Barbara Gibson Nakamarra (Ngurlu Jukurrpa – Seed Dreaming)*, 1994, Laurence Vale, Barbara Glowczewski, 20 mins, Betacam video. An expanded screening "Barbara raconte" with B. Glowczewski accompanying the film in French in front of the screen was filmed by Ghislaine Perichet at the Exhibition *Territoires*, Galerie Michel Journiac, Université Paris 4, 2011: http://www.youtube.com/watch?v=NrFxCHeJvvE (accessed January 9, 2014).

Spirit of Anchor, 2002, Wayne Jowandi Barker and Barbara Glowczewski Barker, CNRS Image, France, broadcasted on Arte channel: free viewing on http://videotheque.cnrs.fr/index.php?urlaction=doc&id_doc=980 (accessed December 19, 2013).

Stalker, 1979, Andreï Tarkovski, Soviet Union, 161 mins, color, sound.

Two Laws, 1980, Alessandro Cavadini and Carolyn Strachan, Australia and Italy, 140 mins, color, sound.

VW Vitesse Women, 1974, Claudine Eizykman, Cinedoc (Paris Film Coop), France, 36 mins, 16 mm, silent: http://www.cinedoc.org (accessed December 19, 2013).

Notes

1. Jean Mitry, *Storia del cinema sperimentale* (Milan: Italian Gabriele Mazzota, 1971; trans. in French, *Le cinéma expérimental. Histoires et perspectives*, Cinema 2000/Seghers, 1974; Gregory Battcock (ed.), *The New American Cinema. A Critical Anthology* (New York: Dutton & Co., 1967); Adams P. Sitney (ed.), *Film, Culture Reader* (New York: Praeger, 1970); David Curtis, *Experimental Cinema. A Fifty Year Evolution* (New York: Delta Books, 1971).

2. Jean-Michel Bouhours, Claudine Eizykman, Guy Fihman, Prosper Hillairet, and Christian Lebrat, "parisfilmcoOPTION, parisfilmCOOPTION, parisfilmSCOoPTION, PARISFILMSCOOPtion" (in *La Rochelle, 4e rencontres internationales d'art contemporain*, June 26–July 10, 1976, last page of the Festival catalog, closing the *Cinemarge3* program). Extract of this text on the website of Editions expérimentales, created by Hillairet and Lebrat in 1985: http://www.paris-experimental.asso.fr/index2.php?option=content&task=view&id=93&pop=1&pag (accessed December 18, 2013).

3. Caudine Eizykman, *La Jouissance-cinéma* (Paris: 10/18, 1975); Jean-François Lyotard, "Acinema," in Andrew Benjamin (ed.), *The Lyotard Reader* (Oxford: Blackwell Publishers, 1989).
4. B. Glowczewski, "Collures. Du cinéma experimental à l'anthropologie," *L'unebévue*, 30, 2012, 31–42.
5. Jean Monod, *Les Barjots* (Paris, 10/18, 1970), the word *barjots* is the *verlan* (French popular language game consisting in reversing the syllables of any word) of *jobard*, a slang expression then used by young people claiming to be non-conventional (*déjantés, mabouls*, etc.); Monod also played the main role in Jean Rouch's *Dyonysos* (1984): see filmography.
6. Barbara Glowczewski (interview by Erin Manning and Brian Massumi, November 27, 2008), "Micropolitics in the Desert Politics and the Law in Australian Aboriginal Communities," *Inflexions. A Journal for Research-Creation*, 3, 2009 from http://www.inflexions.org/issues.html#i3 (accessed December 24, 2013).
7. Barbara Glowczewski, "Lines and Criss-crossings: Hyperlinks in Australian Indigenous Narratives," *Media International Australia*, 116, 2005, with a DVD displaying extracts from the interactive film *Quest in Aboriginal Land*, 2002), 27–8.
8. Barbara Glowczewski, *Les Rêveurs du désert* (Paris: Plon, 1989; with new afterword, Actes Sud, 1996), 115–19. Unpublished English translation by Paul Buck; author's copyright.
9. Gérard Courant, "Festival de Nancy: Le corps morcelé," *Cinéma 78*, 1978, 234; and "Festival de Hyères," *Art Presse*, 22, 1978), both from http://www.gerardcourant.com/index.php?t=ecrits&e=t (accessed December 24, 2013). *Néroïcal* received a special mention from the jury in Hyères. A funding from the GREC French film agency allowed the use of a special effects device constructed by Polish film-maker, Julien Pappé, in his Magic Film Studio in Meudon, where Glowczewski worked to fund her 1979 fieldwork in Australia, resynchronizing the French adaptation of *Ubu roi*, a German animation long film by Jan Lenica, a Polish graphic designer.
10. Klonaris and Thomadaki's statement on their website, http://www.klonaris-thomadaki.net/artsite.htm (accessed December 19, 2013).
11. Dominique Noguez, *Trente ans de cinéma experimental en France (1950–1980)* (Catalogue of the retrospective curated by D. Noguez and Catherine Zbinden, Centre Pompidou, Videothèque de Paris, Cinémathèque française, September 28–October 25, 1982, and other cities in France and overseas. Paris: ARCEF, 1982), 27.
12. "Rencontre avec Yann Beauvais: Le cinéma expérimental et sa diffusion sur Internet," 2011, filmed interview, from http://m2jc2010.wordpress.com/2011/03/01/quelle-place-pour-le-cinema-experimental-et-la-video-dart-sur-internet/ (accessed December 19, 2013).
13. Curtis, *Experimental cinema*, 180.
14. Noguez, *Trente ans de cinéma experimental en France*, 29, 36.
15. Stephen Muecke, "Was *Two Laws* Experimental?," from http://www.screeningthepast.com/2011/08/was-two-laws-experimental/ (accessed December 19, 2013). About the film: http://www.reddirtfilms.com/film.html (accessed December 19, 2013).
16. See, for instance, the art of Lorna Fencer, alias Yulyulu, and other artists from Lajamanu, from http://www.warnayaka.com/ (accessed December 19, 2013).
17. Barbara Glowczewski, "Guattari and Anthropology: Existential Territories among Indigenous Australians," in E. Alliez and A. Goffey (eds), *The Guattari Effect* (London: Continuum, 2011). Felix Guattari and Suely Rolnik, *Molecular Revolution in Brazil* (Cambridge, MA: MIT Press, 2007, trans. from *Micropolitica: Cartografias do desejo*, 1986). Félix Guattari, *Chaosophy: Texts and Interviews 1972–1977*, Sylvère Lotringer (ed.) (Los Angeles, CA: Semiotext(e), 2009); *Chaosmosis: An Ethicoaesthetic Paradigm* (Bloomington, IN: Indiana University Press, 1995, trans. from *Chaosmose* by Julian Prefaris and Paul Bains).

18. The author developed, with 50 Warlpiri artists from the Warnayaka Art Center, the CD-ROM *Dream Trackers. Yapa Art and Knowledge of the Australian Desert* (Paris: UNESCO Publishing, 2000). This CD-ROM includes short clips, including a sand story filmed with Laurence Vale and Warlpiri story-teller Barbara Gibson (*Sand Story*, 1994); see comment of the interactivity in Karen O'Rourke, *Walking and Mapping. Artists and Cartographers* (Cambridge, MA: MIT Press, 2013, 119–22). Together with the Aboriginal film-maker Wayne Jowandi Barker, Barbara Glowczewski made an interactive DVD project (*Quest in Aboriginal Land*, 2001) and the documentary *Spirit of Anchor* (2002) shot with the Yolngu people from Bawaka. About this film, see Barbara Glowczewski, *Rêves en colères* (Paris: Plon, 2004, Book 4, 297–364).
19. The photo in Figure 9.3 was taken during the filming of Barbara Glowczewski, *Lex Wotton* (video, 5 mins, edited with Dominique Masson, 2008), from http://semioweb.msh-paris.fr/AAR/FR/_video.asp?id=1635&ress=6071&video=9890&format=68 (accessed December 19, 2013); and *Palm Island Debutante Ball* (video, 10 mins, edited with Ralf Rigsby, JCU, 2005) from http://www.unebevue.org/unebeweb/index.php?option=com_content&view=article&id=103:barbara-glowczewski&catid=12:27&Itemid=159 (accessed December 19, 2013).
20. Barbara Glowczewski, *Kajirri Warlpiri Ceremonies Restricted to Women*, 180 mins, 16 mm, 1979, non-edited rushes deposited at the AIATSIS in Canberra, digitized extracts on *Dream Trackers: Yapa Art and Knowledge of the Australian Desert* (CD-ROM, Paris: UNESCO Publishing, 2000) and in the author's audiovisual collection on http://www.odsas.fr (accessed December 19, 2013).
21. Special thanks to Jessica De Largy Healy for her subtle proofreading of this text.

10

VISUAL MEDIA PRIMITIVISM: TOWARD A POETIC ETHNOGRAPHY

Martino Nicoletti

Truly speaks he who speaks shadows. (Paul Celan)

"Visual Media Primitivism"[1] and the Foundation of Aesthetics of the Aleatory

Over the last years, notwithstanding the increasing monopoly of digital technologies, an important aspect of the most recent experimentation in visual arts has been characterized by the adoption of old analog visual media and practices[2] still partially surviving beside the main and more innovative streams of visual communication.

Far from representing a simple nostalgic and fetishistic desire for "old faded things," this peculiar "primitivism-oriented" trend chiefly focuses on the systematic recovery and revitalization of vanishing non-professional vintage visual media, in order to reintroduce them into the stream of contemporary art as the founding element of a specific aesthetics and a peculiar visual language.[3] In particular, this same wide and non-systematized approach aims at emphasizing the spontaneous expressiveness of the images that characterized the very origins of artistic photography and film-making, in open contrast with widespread manipulative approaches which, conversely, are massively present in most contemporary digital image production and postproduction. Moreover, by subtracting photography and film-making from an obsessive and titanic search for continuous perfectibility of image quality, "visual media primitivism" operates in the direction of a systematic underlining of the naturally limited technical standards of many old-fashioned visual devices. In the primitivism-oriented context, both these elements are actually perceived as potentially powerful expressive tools, capable of giving shape to and profoundly increasing the artist's own creativity and aesthetic potential.

Some of the general reflections about media primitivism thus far expounded have found concrete application in my work in South and Southeast Asia as an "anthropologist-artist." By this—only apparently—hybrid term, in particular I refer to an activity concretely approached over the past ten years after a long-term professional involvement as an ethnographer and visual anthropologist specializing in the Himalayan area, seeking new ways to give voice to the ample, subtle, irrational, and sometimes deeply tragic domain of feelings and occurrences that can hardly be expressed using traditional anthropological language and, notwithstanding, representing in my opinion a fundamental part of any authentic research and any encounter between cultures.[4] In this sense, the way chosen to relate these often vague and naturally elusive aspects hasn't been simply the mechanical overlapping of two different approaches. It has been, rather, an experimental search for new and unpredicted possibilities in both disciplines: above all the construction of a still largely unexploited and *in fieri* innovative language aimed at giving concrete shape to original artworks firmly grounded in solid ethnographic practice. In this sense, in emphasizing the most aesthetic and creative aspects related to—or directly generated by—research, this same language has been conceived as a ductile and multifaceted tool capable of investigating and critically representing contemporary "cultural otherness," its complexity and the infinite reverberations produced by our direct immersion in it.

Partly referring to some aspects of the most recent debate on this delicate and innovative theme,[5] I would probably define this perspective as a sort of "poetic ethnography" or "sensorial anthropology": mere provisional definitions for a better characterization of a field of experimentation where art and anthropology can dialog osmotically. In my own case, this is an authentically shared ground of practice which I have been "pushed" onto by necessity, having experienced a significant crisis in my conventional expressive language as an anthropologist with the related grave risk of a total impasse.[6]

In the overall framework of my recent work this perspective has so far generally been based on the active and practical combination of ethnography with specific art practices, such as creative writing, music, installation, and performances. In the specific field of visual arts it has indeed been systematically based on the adoption of vintage non-professional medium-format analog cameras[7] and Super 8 cine-cameras.[8] These latter devices, despite their inexorable decline brought about by the dissemination of new digital technology[9] and by the consequent drastic reduction in manufacturing of the film destined for them, have been demonstrating considerable resistance, representing one of the most original analog alternatives to digital film-making both in the international artistic context and in independent film production over these past years.[10]

In my work with analog visual media, instead of considering these media as transparent and neutral tools, acting as a—supposedly—impartial eye,[11] I rather feel they are instruments capable of active interaction with the surrounding reality and of deeply modifying its image. Employing them in full accordance with their own technical qualities, objective limits and inherent capabilities, I indeed try to preserve their fundamental expressiveness, their own eloquence; briefly, their own vision of the world. According to this peculiar approach the position of the photographer or film-maker, usually conceived as an active creator, is, on the contrary, seen as being largely subordinate to the autonomous competence of the device itself. This peculiar "self-sufficiency," intrinsically connected to any lens-based device,[12] once applied to the specific context of the non-professional vintage visual appliances, acquires a special meaning. Unlike professional and modern technologies—provided with a wide range of sophisticated functions and settings destined to optimize image quality[13]—these appliances are in fact characterized by demonstrably deficient technical devices to bring about any significant control over the photographic process *strictu sensu*. As a consequence of this circumstance they are thus usually connoted by the radical and intrinsic "randomness" or "unpredictability" of their results. In the case of Super 8 media which, unlike non-professional vintage cameras, has been equipped from its very origin with specific manual controls, this same "unpredictability" is, actually, mainly determined by specific factors related to the low quality of the film standard employed for this kind of cine-camera.

Although in common professional contexts, the "capricious" character of amateur vintage media as well as the randomness so closely related to their use can both be reasonably considered as objective limitations, capable of jeopardizing the quality of results, in the case of "visual media primitivism," they become, on the contrary, the distinctive mark of a well defined language: a language in which "limits" are actively turned into "opportunities" and where apparent "mistakes" are capable of emphasizing the strength of the images, their uniqueness, and their own communicative power.

Through this apparent leap into the dark, produced by intentionally abandoning control over the photographic process, with complete trust in the autonomous capabilities of the camera and cine-camera, image production is being progressively led toward an insecure and highly precarious ground: a ground capable of transforming photographic film into the most propitious and fertile "stage" for the appearance of unexpected and unforeseen results.

It is indeed on the basis of these premises that "visual media primitivism" can entirely express its own peculiar aesthetics, firmly founded on the deliberate assumption of the "aleatory" as a programmatic point of reference and operative tool. Perceived as the natural expression of the spontaneous and self-sufficient character of the visual device employed, this potentially dangerous element is thus deliberately involved in the artist's activity, becoming an integral and structuring element of the creative work itself.

Thanks to the assumption of the "aleatory" as the main generative principle, the images obtained with a vintage still camera or cine-camera no longer represent a simple reflection of the surrounding world. On the contrary, they become concrete evidence of a shared interpretation of reality, obtained by a balanced compromise between the eye of the artist and the mechanical eye; between his impulse and the natural inclination of the tool he employs. In this sense, the artefact produced by virtue of this harmonious cooperation will distinctly bear witness to a simultaneous double presence: the inner feelings of the artist and the spontaneous sensitivity of the device. In what I am saying here there is no difference between still photography and film-making: in my opinion still photographs indeed possess their own inner discursive narratives; filmed images can similarly often be approached through a synoptic perspective.

It should be noted that vintage analog visual media are also connoted by a very specific relationship to the "time" dimension. Unlike such features as "quickness" and "instantaneity," which commonly connote much of contemporary photographic and video digital production, the traditional analog visual media process is actually largely founded on an evident "slowness," on a manifest dilation of time, mainly motivated by the presence of necessarily separate and distinct conceptual, operative, and spatial phases.

In this sense, the act of taking images and consequent processing procedures have commonly had a role of "expanding" and "dichotomizing" the main aspects of the photographic and film-making procedures, as well as of infusing a noteworthy sense of rhythm and progressive approach into our own relationship with visual products.

This intangible diaphragm between the "capturing" act, as such, and the fruition of its outcome, in the contemporary primitivist-oriented perspective, becomes a distinct invitation to recover an authentic sense of distance, capable of stimulating attention and awareness and of keeping our gaze fresh. Indeed, the "liminal" period between taking the images and looking at the photographic print or footage shot enables our vision to "breathe," and, in another sense, to "decant."

Rejecting the bulimic attitude that very often characterizes our common relationship to digital images, this same sense of temporal distance is also—implicitly—a clear admonishment against any overproduction of images, storing, and transferring an immense number of images that would have been simply inconceivable only a few years ago. While the small memory card inserted into a modern digital camera can actually contain several hundred high quality snapshots, a traditional 35 mm analog camera, on the contrary, can host and produce no more than 36 pictures per reel; only 12 in the case of an old 6×6 vintage camera; one, and only one, finally, for a plate camera from the end of the nineteenth century. The same goes for Super 8 which, compared to the length of current digital video-camera storage capacities, employs cartridges the duration of which is only 3 seconds and 20 seconds of continuous filming at 18 frames per second.

In this sense, aiming at a drastic "reduction" of image production, the contemporary revitalization of vintage analog media actually focuses on economizing images, here conceived as a veritable "concentrate" of the artist's creativity and of his own overall visual experience in the field. As is natural, indeed, due to this decisive process of "contraction"—also partially motivated by the not negligible cost of purchasing, processing, and printing the films usually employed in analog photography and film-making—the visual artefacts acquire a specific essential value, each of them being an authentic "artistic distillate," obtained through the slow gestation of a long production process. This same process, owing to current scarcity of structures and laboratories for professional developing and printing, now involves highly fragmented aspects, corresponding in present day terms to a large temporal dilation of post-production procedures.

Beyond its intrinsic aesthetic value, based mainly on the uniqueness deriving from the unpredictable encounter between the artist's sensitivity and the specific "mood" of the device, here, the artistic artefact is consequently enriched by the adjunctive, and non-secondary, seal of "time." This is a dilated time, directly reflecting an expanded, slow and, above all, discreet approach to reality.[14]

"Visual Media Primitivism" Applied: Visiting the Zoo of the "Giraffe Women"

Most of the theoretical aspects so far presented in relation to media primitivism have recently found a specific synthesis in the form of an experimental multimedia artwork that I produced thanks to a direct combination of creative and ethnographic writing, analog photography, film-making, and sound composition.[15]

A pivotal element of this same artwork, devoted to ethnic tourism among the Kayan minority in Thailand and recently published in the form of a book with attached DVD,[16] is represented by a black-and-white Super 8 short, with all the typical features of a cine-poem,[17] entitled *I Must not Look you in the Eyes: The Zoo of the Giraffe Women*.[18]

Known worldwide for the traditional female custom of wearing a long coiled brass necklace causing a considerable extension of the neck, the Kayan are a Tibeto-Burman ethnic group originally from Burma. Due to the prolonged bloody civil war in their own homeland, a large number of Kayan, during the 1980s and 1990s, fled from Burma to take refuge in neighboring Thailand. Here, over the past years, in response to the "incisive" tourism policy systematically promoted by the Thai government in the northern areas of the country, some families, abandoning the refugee camps where they were hosted, have been resettled in several new, artificially created, villages, open to tourists on payment of a modest entrance fee. Here the Kayan, their culture and daily life, extending an ancient elitist fashion of remote origins, have been transformed into an authentic tourist attraction for Thai and Western visitors traveling in the mountainous regions of Thailand[19] (Figure 10.1).

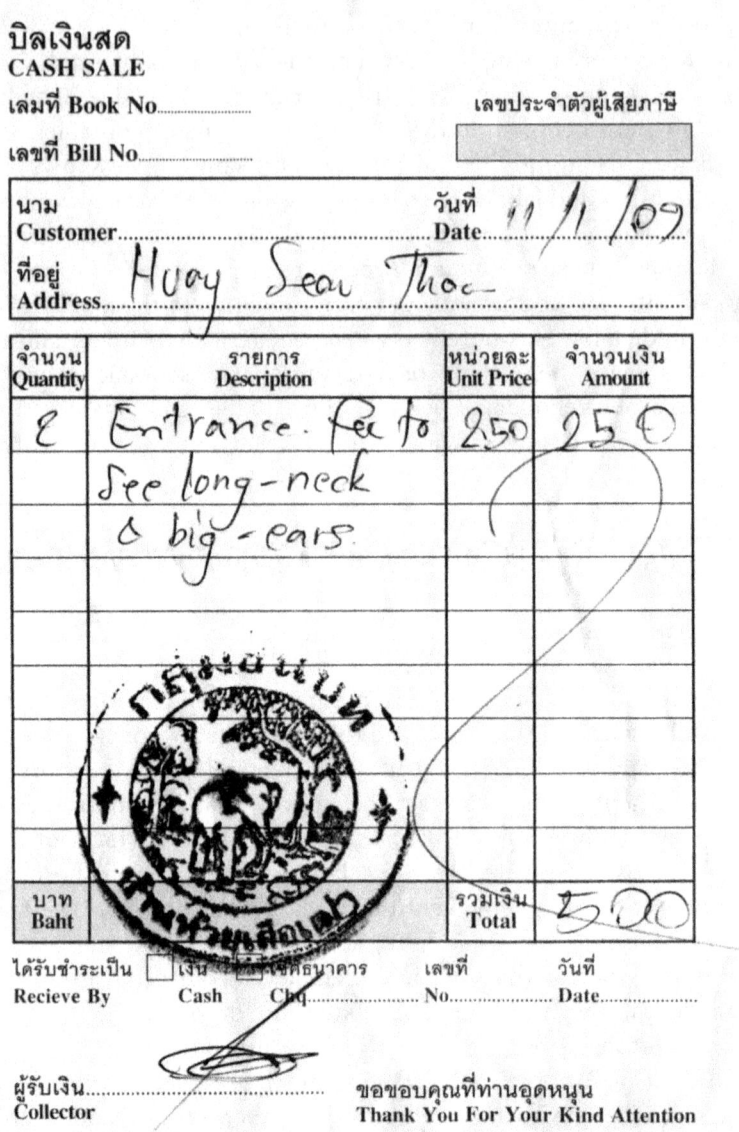

Figure 10.1 Huai Suea Tao village: "Entrance fee to see long-neck & big-ears." Nothing more, nothing less.

With 10,000 tourists a year paying visits to Kayan "villages," Kayan ethnic tourism fits perfectly into an overwhelming, massive circuit, usually presented as one of the most outstanding "musts" recommended by international guidebooks, specialist magazines, and tourist agencies for any tourist visiting the "Land of

Smiles." Like other ethnic minorities of Thailand such as the Akha, Lisu, or Lahu, the goods sold to the visitor, besides the morbid voyeuristic opportunity of getting closer to the "culturally altered" living bodies of the "giraffe women," includes the temporary privilege of gaining access to a supposedly intact and primeval ethnic dimension. This is a privilege nevertheless founded on a systematically concealed paradoxical condition: that of people who originally settled in Thailand as refugees from Burma, but who are now officially and publicly presented and displayed "as if" they were one of the numerous autochthonous ethnic groups of the region.

In this sense, thanks to skilful manipulation of cultural identity and its conversion into a desirable market product, the Kayan represent one of the most significant contemporary examples of mass exploitation of "ethnicity," and, it is worth noting, of violence to women, who are the most exposed component in this destructive deculturation process (Figure 10.2).

Indeed, the short film, shot during several sojourns in Kayan settlements in 2009 and 2010, focuses on this last aspect, critically presenting the highly anaerobic and profoundly miserable condition of Kayan women's lives nowadays.

Taking a radical distance from systematic exposition and coherent narrative form, the film mostly bears witness to a specific "synecdochal"[20] approach, in which each single visual fragment acts as a "hint," allusively referring to a voluntarily unexpressed

Figure 10.2 A civilization converted into a desirable market product (frame from the short).

totality, a "disclosure" that does not claim to be exhaustive. In this sense, every frame, just like every part of the poetic text that accompanies the short as a voice off, thus simply invites the spectator to reconstruct inferentially what is not directly or tangibly presented. From this perspective, the work, absorbing conceptual assumptions specifically related to the aesthetics of visual primitivism, aims primarily at stimulating interest rather than systematically providing information from an exclusive angle.

In order to emphasize the specific situation experienced by the contemporary Kayan, the images and text of the short also provide a vivid contrast between direct references to the mythical accounts recalling the Edenic condition of their tribal ancestors, offspring of a divine long-necked dragoness, and the current reality of Kayan women: derelict "giraffe ladies" permanently confined in their narrow zoos; human beings daily exposed to the camera flashes of hundreds and hundreds of "stainless," unemotional tourists (Figures 10.3 and 10.4).

Figure 10.3 An intense contrast between mythical accounts recalling the divine origin of the group ...:

My grandmother was a dragon.
She was the "lady of the mountains".
She had gorgeous clothes and a long, long neck.
I saw that.
I am like her.
I was like her.

(Frame from the short and excerpt from the text of the soundtrack.)

Figure 10.4 ... and current reality of the Kayan women:

> My daughter is now a mannequin: every day from 10 AM to 5 PM.
> I am as you want me to be.
> If you follow me, I flee.
> Then, as soon as you reach me, docile, I let you capture me.
> I do not offer any resistance.
> I give way.
> I surrender.
> I leave you to it.
>
> (Frame from the short and excerpt from the text of the soundtrack.)

In my experience, during my sojourn among the Kayan, this same unemotional attitude was specifically echoed by the constantly detached mood of the "giraffe women" while shooting the short. Such a disposition unmistakably bears witness to their complete addiction to the presence of visual appliances: a dependence derived from their systematic and prolonged daily exposition to them which, conversely, presents a marked contrast to the authentic curiosity and interest shown by the Kayan—outside the shooting sessions—in my "odd" old-fashioned analog devices and even their operational aspects.

Throughout the narration, an essential role is played by the specific quality of Super 8 images. Concretely expressing most of the artistic and epistemological assumptions typical of my primitivist approach, they are actually uneven, dirty, faded, blurred images; images apparently belonging to another age. Far from any outright melancholic sentimentalism, the apparent deficiency of information so typical of Super 8 is here expressly employed for the purpose of creating a deep sense of "distance" between the images and the observer. This is a very peculiar kind of "conceptual distance," which can be expressed as the particular sense of remoteness felt by the observer, whenever he/she approaches a visual artistic artefact, created thanks to vanishing archaic media but, in actual fact, produced now and strictly relating to our contemporary world.

Looking at the crowded district of the contemporary City of London through the crystalline eye of a black-and-white Super 8 cine-camera from the 1970s, or the modern Bangkok skyline thanks to the coarse lenses of a Kodak box camera of the mid-1920s, are both experiences that indeed impose a spontaneous distance on the observer as well as his/her active participation. Such images cannot be approached and understood in the same way and with the same attitude usually reserved for the uninterrupted visual flow to which one is accustomed. Indeed, before one's eyes are pictures that seem to belong to the past, but which, in actual fact, clearly refer to the observer's own world. A subtle, imperceptible and indefinable veil covers these images. One feels as though an eye belonging to the past were scrutinizing our present, or, more precisely, as if the past itself were mixed with the present. Although perfectly aware that this is not so, one is nevertheless caught by an unusual feeling of disorientation and estrangement. One recognizes and fails to recognize at the same time. In the same photograph, or film, proximity and remoteness are in fact inexplicably merged.

The better to "understand" what is before his/her eyes, the observer is consequently forced to take a step backward. He/she attempts to find the right distance, look again, trying to re-focus. Despite repeated efforts, the observer distinctly perceives that the images cannot be easily "grasped": they hide "something" irreducible that prevents him/her from approaching them as he/she wishes. Silently, within them lies a sort of impalpable intangibility, and, from this same intangibility, a sharp power of attraction spontaneously spreads.

It is precisely due to the strong tension produced by this same fundamental indefinability that primitivist visual artefacts have here, in my opinion, the authentic potential of re-acquiring their own distinctive uniqueness and—as Walter Benjamin would probably have said—their own "aura";[21] of winning moreover a place apart from other visual artefacts, so as to be progressively subtracted from mass production and mass consumption circuits. Paradoxically, this unusual outcome—right in the opposite direction of Benjamin's aesthetic theory first elaborated in relation to traditional artworks, not produced using mechanical reproduction techniques—is here obtained by employing mechanical visual devices originally destined to give shape to an image of reality, susceptible to conversion into a serial and indefinite number of copies.

The nature and meaning of this peculiar temporal warp, that so profoundly connotes the very nature of the primitivist visual approach, can furthermore be decisively clarified by reference to Roland Barthes's well-known aesthetic thought relating to the notion of *"punctum,"* which—in contrast with *"studium,"* representing a largely rational, shared, and taste-oriented approach to the photograph's multiple meanings—is chiefly conceived as arising from an often involuntary and unpredictable manifestation of the very personal feelings and biography of the observer.[22]

Resulting from a totally subjective, private, and instinctive relationship to the images, the *"punctum"* has indeed that rare power of reaching our innermost intimate self and causing it to emerge: a territory usually formed of indistinct memories, hazy perceptions, and pale images. As an effect of this unforeseeable and sharpened geography of the *"punctum,"* the observer is peremptorily invited to question the very meaning of the image he or she is looking at, whose innermost character, according to Barthes, is indeed represented by its inescapable non-dialectical nature.[23] This specific quality, in producing an abrupt halt to the observer's interpretation, has in fact as a consequence the recognition of the unequivocal evidence that: "… however hard I look, I discover nothing … the turn of the screw had produced nothing."[24]

The sense of "distance", perceived in Benjamin's thought as the necessary precondition for the existence of the "aura" here—meaning in Barthes's theory—is felt as the only possible means of transcending a limited rational understanding of images in order to access their private meanings, the only way capable of resonating authentically with our own subjectivity and feelings. Once applied to the context of visual primitivism, this same conceptual distance, induced in the observer by the virtual deformation of temporal coordinates typical of vintage media, inserts the images in a sort of authentic projective circuit. This is a play of reciprocal reflections between visual artefact and spectator aimed at stimulating the latter's creative attitude in his/her appreciation of the images and in exploring their own multiple meanings. Such a circumstance, indeed, could not take place in presenting an image that, due to its absolute chronological proximity, "displays all," or that, owing to its wide temporal gap, "hides all."

Conceptual distance has here moreover an effective, non-secondary, elicitor in the natural lack of visual information that is as a rule characteristic of amateur vintage media, as compared to professional analog visual media or current consumer and professional digital photography and video, all generally characterized by high quality images. In this respect, the vague and sometimes elusive status of these same primitive images, their fundamentally ambiguous nature, indeed, simultaneously confers on them the double status of "artefacts" and "mirrors" to a considerable extent. In this sense, instead of faithfully representing a given reality, on the contrary, they become a propitious occasion for fathoming and revealing unknown landscapes that lightly take shape in the precarious and suspended space existing between the images and ourselves. They are largely submerged landscapes, their contours probably shaped like a light-pencil drawing, rather than those of a paintbrush's bold stroke; landscapes that could never have emerged on the surface of our consciousness without the stimulus and the build-up of this oblique and intangible ground of vision.

At a different level, directly related to the mere context of visual perception, this same natural "remoteness" elicited by the "uneven" black and white images of the short also aims in fact at creating a deep "fracture" in our daily attitude toward images, capable of refreshing our own gaze and abruptly overcoming our common addiction to color pictures or films. The vacuum created by this same "crack," instead of being a neutral and empty region, is on the contrary a productive space that induces an incessant cognitive inferential process, stimulating not only our personal interpretation of the images presented but also promoting a personal reconstruction of a wide set of elements not directly presented by the short. In this sense, the lack of information and definition characteristic of Super 8 media, far from representing a deficiency, paradoxically has the capacity of turning into a specific "visual reagent," an active "device" aimed at increasing the effective role of the observer and his/her own creativity.[25]

Directly focusing on a recovery of the communicative power inherent in vintage visual media, the Super 8 short devoted to the Kayan operates in this direction also thanks to the special kind of images selected in editing the film.

With a direct reference to Susan Sontag's ideas in relation to the meaning and role of photography in representing tragedy and pain,[26] the images—instead of presenting a direct report or straight comment on the contradictions and violence in which Kayan ethnic tourism is steeped—deliberately show little (Figure 10.5). In my opinion, it being absolutely true that "the image as shock and the image as cliché are two aspects of the same presence,"[27] in order to transcend this same evidence and the related risk of any manipulative use of the footage selected, the latter lie at an expressly intermediate level between these two possible extremes. Appearing as "plane" images, they reveal themselves and their authentic meaning only after attentive observation.

This circumstance, beside its merely aesthetic implications, is motivated by the specific desire to neutralize systematically any preconceived approach, stereotyped reactions, judgment, or expectations of the observer.

Since, in some respects, the purpose of my work is to raise the observer's awareness of a little known story of a forgotten people, I have cautiously avoided encouraging it through shocking and direct frontal images. Apart from its ethical evidence, this choice responds to the communicative need both to overcome potential defenses and to avoid possible addiction. As Susan Sontag admirably notes, indeed "shock can become familiar. Shock can wear off ... People have means to defend themselves against what is upsetting ... As one becomes habituated to horror in real life, one can become habituated to the horror of certain images."[28]

Due to this real risk, in my work understanding is, on the contrary, assumed to emerge as the result of a silent and slow approach to the suffused eloquence of apparently anonymous and anodyne images.

In this same respect, the dedicated soundtrack accompanying the cine-poem, composed by me thanks to a fusion of sounds recorded in the field with electronic music,[29] as well as the poetic text associated with the images, has the similar

Figure 10.5 *They aren't smiles.*

They actually are smiles with a woman behind.
Smiles to put on when someone comes from outside.
Smiles to take off, removing the rubber band, when he leaves again.
Smiles to slip on and slip off.
To lay down, to put back, and to take again when necessary.
(Frame from the short and excerpt from the text of the soundtrack.)

principal aim of diverting the observer's expectations; other devices aim at promoting a non-preconfigured relationship to the images and their meaning.

Beyond any single aspect, the primitivist visual approach and the short here presented, representing a direct expression of its most essential premises, are both inspired by the deep desire to create artworks that are not easy to place: artworks not easy to place, therefore, but perhaps, potentially effective in their aspiration to say something meaningful, in their humble attempt to bring contents, feelings, and awareness from one locality to another.

The way chosen to make this possibility concrete is that of a drastic reduction and rarefaction of any form of expressive language, so as to approach and cross a sort of point zero: the only real ground, in my opinion, from which new paths open to the possibility of experiencing and, consequently, of "saying"; also saying how a private life and personal drama can be transformed into the enjoyment and the entertainment of others:

"Giraffe women.
People for the zoo.
Bodies tampered with.
Beauty in the stocks".[30]

Notes

1. The notion of "visual media primitivism," here only briefly presented, has been the subject of a systematic exposition in my practice-based Ph.D. thesis in multimedia arts and creative writing: Martino Nicoletti, *Submerged Landscapes: Aesthetics of Visual Primitivism* (Ph.D. thesis; School of Creative and Cultural Industries—University of the West of Scotland, 2012).

    As will be explained in detail in this work, the term "primitivism" is here employed to define a specific approach in which the recovery of vintage analog visual media, beyond its mere technological aspect, presents a manifestly "ideological" component, mainly represented by a deliberate reaction to prevailing contemporary digital photography and film-making and to their specific aesthetics and conventions, as well as by a programmatic rejection of the massive "hypertrophic" image production commonly related to their employment.

    In this sense, its expression—preferable to other, more neutral, similar terms—to a certain extent entails a reference to primitivism, which historically arises as a polymorphic and multifaceted movement in the field of arts at the end of the nineteenth and beginning of the twentieth centuries and to the same criticism toward the aesthetic canons and formal rules typical of academic fine arts at that time. It is widely known that this criticism arose mainly from a systematic assimilation and subsequent re-elaboration of artistic motifs, themes, and techniques originally thought of as belonging to "primitive" indigenous cultures, or, in specific cases, to definite archaic civilizations. In my case, my similar perspective is directly obtained thanks to the experimental employment of old-fashioned non-professional visual analog technologies and to the peculiarity of their visual language.

2. Here I refer in particular not only to the recent revival of Super 8 media, pinhole photography, or Polaroid instant photography, but also to the revitalization of the very archaic technique of wet-plate collodion photography, as well as the recent innovative approach to photography known as Lomography, mainly based on the use of vintage low-cost analog cameras.

3. In the field of mere photography I instinctively think of the work of contemporary international photographers such as Abelardo Morell, Ian Paterson, Marja Pirilä, the Italian Roberto Aita, Paolo Gioli and Vincenzo Marzocchini, mainly focusing on pinhole photography; to the activity of Manuel Alvarez Bravo, Barbara Crane and Patrizio Esposito aimed at instant photography, or, finally, the production of photographers like Quinn Jacobson, Roman Kravchenko, Sally Mann, Stefan Sappert, or the pioneer artist in Asia, Ho Man Kei, in relation to wet-plate collodion photography.

4. The results of this peculiar approach—chiefly discussed in Nicoletti, *Submerged Landscapes*—have so far mainly taken the shape of multimedia books, travel accounts, and artist's books, Super 8 shorts and cine-poems as well as of multimedia solo and collective artistic exhibitions in Europe, Asia, and the US.

    On this subject see: Martino Nicoletti, *Chaturman Rai, Fotografo contadino dell'Himalaya* (Rome: Exòrma, 2010); Martino Nicoletti, *Interregnum* (Bangkok: Parbpim, 2010); Martino Nicoletti, *Submerged Landscapes: A Pinhole Photographic Tale* (Bangkok: Parbpim, 2010); Martino Nicoletti, *Kathmandu. Lezioni di Tenebre* (Rome: CasadeiLibri Edizioni, 2012); Martino Nicoletti, *The Nomadic Sacrifice: the Chöd Pilgrimage among the Bönpo of Dolpo* (Western

Nepal) (Kathmandu: Vajra Publication, 2013); Martino Nicoletti, *Anime di sabbia (Souls of Sand)* (forthcoming novel).

In the context of shorts and cine-poem production: *Chöd, Offering the Self* (2008), Dir. M. Nicoletti. UK. Stenopeica. 6 mins; *Kulunge Super 8* (2010), Dir. M. Nicoletti, UK, Stenopeica, 6 mins.

5. I here refer in particular, not only to the recent debate on anthropological epistemology and language promoted by James Clifford, James Faubion, Michael Fisher, George Marcus, and Fred Myers, but also and overall to the highly stimulating theoretical contributions on new frontiers between art and anthropology presented in the works curated by Arnd Schneider and Christopher Wright, especially in relation to the idea of a "sensory turn" in anthropology as limpidly exposed by John Wynne, in Arnd Schneider and Christopher Wright (eds), *Between Art and Anthropology: Contemporary Ethnographic Practice* (Oxford and New York: Berg, 2010), 50. On this same theme, see also Huber Fichte, *Xango. Die afroamerikanischen Religionen II. Bahia. Haiti. Trinidad* (Frankfurt: Fischer Verlag, 1976); Huber Fichte, *Petersilie. Die afroamerikanischen Religionen IV. Santo Domingo. Venezuela. Miami. Grenada* (Frankfurt: Fischer Verlag, 1980); on Fichte see also Arnd Schneider's chapter in this volume, pp. 29–34. Arnd Schneider and Christopher Wright (eds), *Contemporary Art and Anthropology* (Oxford and New York: Berg, 2006); Sarah Pink, *Doing Sensory Ethnography* (London: Sage, 2009); Chiara Ruffinengo, *Les chemins qui mènent vers la réalité : Une lecture anthropologique de l'œuvre de Natalia Ginzburg* (Ph.D. thesis; Université Sorbonne Nouvelle—Paris 3, 2008), as well as the interview with the German anthropologist Michael Oppitz presented in Martino Nicoletti, *L'uomo che dialogava con il coyote: una breve incursione sul tema Joseph Beuys e sciamanesimo* (Rome: Exòrma, 2011).

6. On the autobiographical elements connected to this approach: Martino Nicoletti, *Shamanic Solitudes: Ecstasy, Madness and Spirit Possession in the Nepal Himalayas* (Kathmandu: Vajra Publications, 2006) and Martino Nicoletti, *Submerged Landscapes*.

7. They include, in particular, old-fashioned Kodak box cameras dating back to the second half of the 1920s and some medium format metal or plastic Agfa cameras from the beginning of the 1960s.

8. In this case, some Super 8 Canon silent cine-cameras from the beginning of the 1970s.

9. Super 8 mm, introduced in 1965 by Eastman Kodak as a revolutionary home movie format, became widespread in amateur and professional film-making between the 1960s and 1970s. It came to an abrupt stop with the introduction of magnetic tape-based systems of video recording, whose emblem was the home movie VHS system introduced to the market in the late 1970s. On this subject, see: Lenny Lipton, *The Super 8 Book* (San Francisco, CA: Straight Arrow Books, 1975); Don Diego Ramirez, *A Super 8 Filmmaker's Journal: A Guide to Super 8 Filmmaking in the Age of the Internet* (Charleston, SC: Create Space, 2010).

10. Such, for instance, is the case of the avant garde Austrian film-maker Peter Tscherkassky, or the independent German film-makers Christiane Heuwinkel, Matthias Müller, and Maja-Lene Rettig, founders of the *Alte Kinder Film Collective*. In this same context we can also mention the Canadian visual artist Kara Blake, the British independent film director Andy Marsh, as well as the Dutch film-maker Jaap Pieters.

11. This is, for instance, the case of my professional use of digital professional photography and film-making in the framework of ethnographic documentation or photojournalistic reportages.

12. This peculiar concept has been magistrally expounded by the photographer Franco Vaccari through the notion of *inconscio tecnologico* ("technological unconscious"), according to which any picture, at the very moment of its creation, is already a codified reality, being indeed the product of the technological unconscious of the specific media employed. On this subject see:

Ugo Mulas, *La fotografia* (Turin: Einaudi, 1973); Roberto Signorini, *Arte del fotografico: i confini della fotografia e la riflessione teorica degli ultimi vent'anni* (Pistoia: C.R.T., 2001); Franco Vaccari, *Fotografia e inconscio tecnologico* (Turin: Agorà, 1994).

13. These elements usually include focus regulation, diaphragm aperture, shutter speed, light metering, as well as, secondarily, the possibility of determining the focal angle by using the zoom or interchangeable lenses.
14. On this same theme, see also Vincenzo Marzocchini, *La fotografia stenopeica: Storia, tecnica, estetica delle riprese stenopeiche* (Brescia: Agora35, 2004); Vincenzo Marzocchini, *Camera oscura: la lentezza dell'istantanea* (Palermo: Lanterna Magica, 2011).
15. The artwork represented in particular the practical-artistic section of my second Ph.D. thesis: Martino Nicoletti, *Submerged Landscapes*.
16. Martino Nicoletti, *The Zoo of the Giraffe Women: A Journey among the Kayan of Northern Thailand* (Kathmandu: Vajra Publications, 2013). Original edition: Martino Nicoletti: *Lo zoo delle donne giraffa: un viaggio tra i Kayan nella Tailandia del nord* (Rome: Exòrma, 2011).
17. Although this term basically refers to a wide range of visual artistic artefacts created thanks to the convergence of images and poetic texts, currently the expression is used for any film based on a poem, as well as any film generated according to the form, the rhythm, and aesthetics of poetry.

    On this theme, see Robert Scott Speranza, *Verses in the Celluloid: Poetry in Film from 1910–2002, with Special Attention to the Development of the Film-poem* (Ph.D. thesis; University of Sheffield, 2002); Christophe Wall-Romana, *French Cinepoetry: Imaginary Cinemas in French Poetry* (New York: Fordham University Press, 2013); William C. Wees, *Light Moving in Time: Studies in the Visual Aesthetics of Avant-Garde Film* (Berkeley, CA: University of California Press, 1992).
18. Directed by Martino Nicoletti. UK-Italy. Stenopeica, 2011, 6mins.
19. On Kayan ethnic tourism, see Erik Cohen, *Thai Tourism: Hill Tribes, Islands and Open-ended Prostitution* (Bangkok: White Lotus, 2001); Prasit Leepreecha, *The Politics of Ethnic Tourism in Northern Thailand*, from http://www.akha.org/content/tourismecotourism/ethnictourism.pdf, (accessed March 25, 2013), 2010; Edith T. Mirante, "Breaking out the Tourist Trap—Part I," *Cultural Survival Quarterly*, 14 (1), from http://www.culturalsurvival.org/ourpublications/csq/article/hostages-tourism (accessed April 8, 2011), 1990; Edith T. Mirante, *Burmese Looking Glass: A Human Rights Adventure and a Jungle Revolution* (New York: Atlantic Monthly Press, 1994); Edith T. Mirante, *The Dragon Mothers Polish their Metal Coils*, 2006, from http://www.guernicamag.com/features/229/the_dragon_mothers/ (accessed March 25, 2013).
20. Here in the sense proposed by James Clifford, *The Predicament of Culture: Twentieth-Century Ethnography, Literature, and Art* (Cambridge, MA: Harvard University Press, 1988).
21. For Benjamin, "aura" precisely represents: "... a unique manifestation of a remoteness, however close it may be." As an expression of the profound ritual connotation traditionally attributed to ancient artworks and of their fundamental status as intangible cult objects, this same notion represents a direct reflection of the archaic conceptual separation existing between the spheres of "sacred" and "profane." Walter Benjamin, *The Work of Art in the Age of Mechanical Reproduction* (London: Penguin, 2008), 9. On this subject, see also: Martino Nicoletti, *Submerged Landscapes*.
22. Roland Barthes, *Camera Lucida: Reflections on Photography* (London: Vintage, 2000).
23. Ibid., 90, 106–7.
24. Ibid., 100.
25. On this same concept, see also: Martino Nicoletti, *Vintage Visual Anthropology: A Himalayan Pilgrimage Narrated through 16 Black and White Photographs, 34 Pages of Field-work Journal*

and 6 Minutes of Super 8 Film, 2011, from http://www.anthropology-photo-film-symposium-edu.org/index.php/en/speakers-3/nicolleti (accessed March 25, 2013).
26. Susan Sontag, *Regarding the Pain of Others* (London: Penguin, 2004).
27. Ibid., 20.
28. Ibid., 73.
29. The original soundtrack of the Italian edition of the short was, on the contrary, created by the composer Roberto Passuti—co-founder with me of the independent multimedia production label *Stenopeica*—and interpreted by the voice of the Italian singer Giovanni Lindo Ferretti.
30. Excerpt from the text of the short's soundtrack.

11

FROM THE GRAIN TO THE PIXEL, AESTHETIC AND POLITICAL CHOICES

Nadine Wanono

By considering the evolution of some technical aspects of film culture and industry, the idea was on the one hand to concentrate on the role and place of mechanical aspects in our discipline, and on the other hand to demonstrate how technical choices could help us to resolve the challenging question of the representation of time in a documentary narrative manner. I will examine how fieldwork, feedback, and analysis of a few specific rituals organized in the Dogon country forced me to reconsider the treatment of the representation of time and space in my ethnographic documentaries. After realizing how deeply these contradictions forced me to reconsider my methodology and my technical choices, I chose to concentrate on digital programming as a possible language to address this challenging topic and to offer possibilities to propose new forms of representations.

In the event, by considering the role and place of digital programming, I realized how techniques had been isolated from the social and cultural context they emerged from.

By comparing the notion of grain that came from the analog film industry to the one of pixels which came out of the digital era, the purpose was to underline the aesthetic and political choices embedded in this technical criterion and how the spectators, whatever their age, could create or recreate their time perception according to the resonance of the grain or the pixel, from the viewpoint of a personal and social imaginary construction.

Dogon Fieldwork and Feedback

Trained as a visual anthropologist, I spent long periods of time in Dogon country, sharing the daily life activities of the women and filming their ongoing actions. One of the films I made on my own as a camera person and film-maker dealt with the rituals following the birth of a baby. When I decided to concentrate on this specific aspect of women's life, I had already spent almost ten years traveling back and forth between Sanga and Paris. During this time, I had also become a mother. When I went back to Dogon country in 1989, with my one-year-old baby boy, my girlfriends told me they finally perceived me as a woman, since before that I was perceived as an asexual person; leaving my family, my parents, living on my own for several months seemed to them more masculine than feminine. My status, until then, had always been unclear.

This situation explained the feeling and the challenge you are faced with when you spend several months in the middle of a Dogon village. Surprisingly enough, it was quite difficult for me to render all these emotions in the final editing of the film. To obtain a scientific label the academic system in France requires you to follow implicit and very specific rules and to adapt consequently your own creativity and interpretation. You inevitably have to thoroughly erase all the emotional aspects, the personal dimension, and any subjective accounts.

In order to analyse the birth ritual, I filmed for a month. It took me quite a long time to understand the structure, the different steps, and especially the specific moment when the ritual started. I conducted several surveys in order to complete as precisely as I could the unfolding process. In short, I eventually could say that the whole process starts at the birth of the future mother and after families have decided to marry their sons and daughters to each other. From that specific moment, numerous exchanges of gifts, sacrifices, and rituals could be done in favor of the future wife's family. To understand the naming process celebrated after three weeks of reclusion of the mother and her baby, it was necessary to perceive that the ongoing process started almost 18 or 19 years earlier.

I could offer the same analysis regarding our perception of space in a filmic narrative and the way Dogon people consider their space, the crucial separation between the bush and the village, the space occupied by the wilderness and the space somehow structured by men.

When I clearly realized the gap existing between my filmic narrative, which introduced a linear perspective of time, and the time period at stake understanding the relationship between the families and the place of the newborn in the village, I was quite disappointed and realized how much the film represented our own perception of a society, through our own codes, rules, and technics; it was like a two-way mirror.

From the Anthropology Department to the Media Art and Technology Program

From this obvious and painful acknowledgment of failure and obsessed with the question of space and time representation in my documentary, I decided to follow new paths by leaving the anthropological "structure" for a transdisciplinary program held in the Media Art and Technology edifice at University of California, Santa Barbara (UCSB).

I decided to concentrate on more experimental ways to represent these essential cultural aspects. I produced two experimental pieces during a workshop organized by Marcos Novak. From these experiments I started to consider programming as a language with creative power.

During this interdisciplinary workshop led by Marcos Novak, the professionally recognized artist who created the concepts of virtual and liquid architecture, I have been introduced to a new trajectory into his work which deals with the epistemological changes that digital technology has provoked. Transvergence is one of the concepts around which Novak structured our workshop. He opposes transvergence to convergence and divergence. Whereas the last two notions are "simple linear extrapolations that proceed by strategies of alignment, transvergence advances translinearly by tactics of derailment. … While convergence and divergence contain the hidden assumption that the true, in either a cultural or an objective sense, is a continuous landmass, transvergence recognizes true statements to be islands in an alien archipelago, sometimes only accessible by leaps, flights, and voyages on vessels of artifice."[1] As Novak explains: "transvergence, in a pedagogical and research context, refers to the study and applications of concepts and methods by which convergence of disciplines, media and technologies is seen not as a goal in itself, not as the focal point of a predictable origin for divergences but as an opportunity to speculate and propose novel transdisciplinary epistemological and creative formations. Using willful strategies of derailment, it seeks to promote the mergence of previously unattainable but presently potentially viable species of efforts: future genres, future fields of inquiry, future arts, media and sciences."[2]

We reconsidered, for example, the notion of "duende," beauty, subjectivity, and the difference between invention, discovery, and creation. In parallel I discovered notions such as Autopoiesis, a process whereby an organization produces itself and constitutes itself in space, e.g. biological cell, living organism, and some extend to a corporation or a society; Alloselves, for the concept of putting together two antithetic notions: the alien as the other belonging to another order entirely and the self or the reflexive. As author of this alien, the alloself is derived from our own understanding of what self and consciousness may involve. Transmodernity is characterized, for Novak, by the extensive and deliberate production of an extreme form of the other; Accretion, an agglomerate of material or cells, and the Entanglement, a concept which comes from Quantum Mechanics, refers to the state of separate particles, which are mutually interdependent even if they exist at great distance from each other. We discovered the structures of the infinitely small, the nature of new species, and the survival attitudes of parasites in order to transmit the diversity and the complexity of structures that already exist. This intense experience was not just another instance of the usual repetitive process that academic teaching is based on. We were in a creative process, experiencing somehow the apodictic aesthetic, which was at times provocative, making us experience a "necessary discomfort". As the main goal of Novak's workshop was to produce objects, shapes, and a network as a kind of embodiment of our research, I did some detailed research into the questions of translation.

If the visual anthropologist, facing the task of translating audiovisual data into words, tries to translate her material with a software other than Word, what will be the gain? Can we imagine a new open space, next to the books, the articles, and the bibliography where students and anthropologists could produce queer objects?

I quickly understood this apprehension of computing language also with Lisa Jevbratt and Geogres Legady who, each of them at different levels, gave me the opportunity to collaborate with digital artists to conceive and create specific prototypes.

With a very simple algorithm conceived by a colleague from the Media Art and Technology department, one sequence of my film on the baby naming ritual was integrated into a software algorithm and the deformation of the pictures introduced the spectator to a complete abstract reality. Simultaneously, the sound was amplified and reproduced through software and the spectators could play around with the sound intensity by waving their hands near the loudspeakers. By placing their hands nearer and nearer the loudspeaker the pictures became more and more abstract, reaching at some point a new sense of space, like the bush. The pictures indeed looked like particles of sand. It left the description process to enter in a creation process where the texture, the colors, the rhythm, the dynamic could change and the spectators could interact with all these elements.

These successive translations of my material were an attempt to shape and visualize them in accordance with their, so called, irrational dimension (see Figure 11.1).

Probably the obvious transformation and the distance between the original and the reproduction could provoke some uneasiness in some of us. Personally it is this friction between different levels of realities, which could give a new dimension to my work.

Even if this experiment was more than modest and aesthetically very basic, I realized how programming could be a language in itself for social scientists, and it became obvious that we needed to be trained to program ourselves or at least to have academic structures where the collaboration with programmers or digital artists could be promoted.

This intensive experimentation over a period of six months on the specific role and power of the techniques in our discipline convinced me of the embarrassment of social sciences regarding the technical apparatus of our research. Ideas, concepts, and analysis seemed free from all kinds of technical constraints and remained completely outside our field of interest.

Trained by Jean Rouch, I remembered well the close links he established between the technical apparatus and the specific narrative he decided to unfold. We could

Figure 11.1 Interactive Composition conceived by Andi Sojamo from *Ibani or the Blue Scarf*, a film of Nadine Wanono, © N. Wanono.

quote, for example, the importance of the lens used by Michel Brault during filming of *Chronicles of a Summer*, or the way Rouch related the times spent rewinding his small Bell & Howell camera as a necessary time gap to conceive his next shots. I should add the distaste and frontal opposition he sometimes manifested towards video, which was closely linked to the fact he couldn't have any further kind of control on the microprocessor behind each element of the camera or the sound equipment. Also, he was closely linked to the aesthetics of grain and its political dimension. Ritually Rouch sat in the second row either at la Cinémathèque française or at the Musée de l'Homme in order to be "in" the screen, to perceive the grainy aspect of the high speed black and white stock and the texture of the projector screen.

Concepts of Approach Techniques

These different experiences, developed over time, have led me to consider the links uniting the cinematic and technical act with the knowledge-production device. Indeed, the camera as a technical apparatus allows the production of theories and diverging interpretations concerning its possibilities as highlighted by Schneider and Wright (2006).[3]

The History of Technology as presented by Singer, Hall, and Holmyard (1954),[4] or more recently by Bertrand Gille (1978),[5] alludes clearly to the fact that objects are divided and classified in accordance with their technical characteristics which make up coherent wholes of compatible structures. While looking in depth at the fabrication process, these analyses completely forget about the objects' relation to the cultural, economic, and sociological worlds. As shown by Feenberg (1995) in *The Politics of Knowledge*,[6] Technique is a medium fully integrated in the everyday life of modern societies: important technical changes thus have a direct impact on economy, politics, religion, and culture.

The merging of the Science of Technique with the Humanities was not an obvious step and occurred only in a late phase of their development; as Philippe Bruneau notes in his article "Histoire des techniques, ergologie, archéologie," "Technique is a distinct and independent branch of Reason and thus is no more foreign to humankind than logic, ethnicity or ethics."[7] In fact, Bruneau makes the point that some areas are neglected by the history of techniques, like, for example, "architecture, image, writing, music in favor of the production of Raw materials and foodstuffs ..."[8]

For Gille,[9] one needs to analyse the technical and economic systems because the adoption of a technical construction necessarily leads to the adoption of a social system corresponding to it in order for coherence to be maintained. This line of thought is the one that Bruno Bachimont[10] and Georges Simondon[11] largely build upon.

If one accepts that Technique and Device are linked to the socio-economic reality that surrounds them, one is able to approach the idea of "machinic layout" coined by Felix Guattari.[12] He calls for the need to save and enhance the processes of transversal singularization which should be able to escape mercantile standardization in order to better communicate political, social, or economic questions as well as techno-scientific transformations and artistic creation.

The video camera or programming codes illustrate perfectly this layout that all the subjective or ideological powers have given room for the "machine fictionnante" as Bruno Bachimont calls it: "Technique becomes fictionnante (or "fictionning") not only when it allows for the materialisation of an idea but when it becomes a machine or a device with the possibility to create fiction in itself. What symbolic nature shows us is the boundless creativity of inscribing techniques."[13] Subjectivity is thus always a process that is elaborated between social systems of differing sizes and that is lived and experienced by individuals in their singular existences. Each one can allow himself to be influenced passively by the modes of subjectivity that are offered him, or claim for himself the building blocks of subjectivity in order to put together a creative process of singularization.

With the notion of layout, Guattari expresses the way in which an object, individual or collective is "produced," in part, by technical devices that are themselves made up of diverse types of machines: "technical machines, economic writing machines but also conceptual machines, religious machines, aesthetic machines, perceptive machines, desiring machines ..."[14]

Digital code is, in fact, both a physical input into a system and a symbolic expression needing interpretation. It leads to deep changes in the basis of our thought and action devices and mechanisms. Lev Manovich, in *The Language of New Media*,[15] affirms that to understand the logic of new media one should investigate the field of computer science for the "new terms, categories, and operations that characterise media and that become programmable."[16] This is a call for software as *logos*. It attempts to solidify theory by giving it a specific direction—the logic and objects of software.

Chun proposes the acceptance of code as a resource, a perspective that "enables us to think in terms of the gap between source and execution."[17] This gap seemingly includes, or perhaps is, the "borderland" that in Hayles signifies materiality, "the connective tissue joining the physical and mental, the artifact and the user."[18] When Chun identifies the "code as re-source" perspective, positioning an "interface as a process rather than as a stable thing," it resonates with Simondon and the transduction concept: it is a physical, biological, mental, or social operation, by which an activity propagates itself from one element to the next, within a given domain, and bases this propagation through structuring the domain, something that moves from one place to another; each area of the constituted structure serves as the principle and the model for the next area, as a primer for its constitution, to the extent that the modification expands progressively at the same time as the structuring operation.[19]

Aware of what is at stake on the epistemological level and of the consequences they can have on the social and political spheres, I have centered my research on the values and beliefs imparted to the technologies of the mind or to the cultural technologies in the way Stiegler[20] uses the term, meaning the convergence of the audiovisual, telecommunications, and information technologies.

To tackle this cross-disciplinary approach I organized my research project around the links between certain technologies of knowledge (video camera, microscope, telescope, programming codes) and the concepts they engender, the impact of historical, political, and economic conditions on their use and on their positions in popular imagination. I will be focusing in particular on the aesthetic and technical notion of grain, commonly used during the analog era, and the pixel as a notion which has already undermined several layers of sensibility, ways of life, style, and film dynamics.

By going from analog technologies to digital ones, the concepts offered to define them and our modes of relating to these knowledge mediums will be revisited and looked at transversally. Achieving this will then allow us to underline the break lines, continuities, and structures of the hopes, aspirations, and fears that these technologies awaken in us.

The Grain: Aesthetic and Political Choices

Shiny or grainy? Probably for the young generation the shiny aesthetics of the digital flat screen and of the digital technologies at large couldn't help them to understand the political and aesthetic battle around the choice of grain.

From the type of stock, the quality of the light and right to the choice of equipment, every single option in the *mise en scène* was a meaningful step for the film-makers involved in documentary and more specifically in ethnographic film. Michel Brault, Ricky Leacock, and John Marshall, as camera persons for their own documentaries, chose the freedom to move, the freedom to be as close as possible to their subjects by refusing supposedly sophisticated equipment: they affirmed very vigorously their position.

We can quote Richard Leacock:

> The next step in my de-professionalization came a few weeks later, when Roger Tilton came to me with what seemed at that time to be a wild idea. He wanted to make a short film about an evening at a dance hall in New York's East Village: A wild evening of Dixieland Jazz. He had spoken to several cameramen and they had all told him that the only way to do it was with the big studio cameras, the microphone boom, the clap sticks, setting up and shooting each individual shot—the same old routine. Roger refused to agree to this. A kindred spirit! So I agreed to try making this film the way we had filmed combat ... We shot wild! No tripod! Move! Shoot! I was all over the place, having the time of my life, jumping, dancing, shooting right in the midst of everything. We spent a fabulous evening shooting to our hearts' content ... Tilton tells me that he was invited out to Hollywood by the biggies, but when he told them that they couldn't do this sort of thing with their clumsy equipment they told him to get lost and didn't even pay his fare back![21] (Also see Figure 11.2)

This short story represents clearly the political situation in Hollywood, in the film industry, and in major companies. We experienced the same problem as numerous young film-makers who decided to use the Super 8 mm format to produce documentary: the rules promulgated by the television system and the festivals encouraged films made with much more expensive and specific equipment, thus preventing film-makers from outside the business system distributing their films, which were able to challenge not only the power of the film industry but also the rules established by the unions.

This event took place in 1954, and if we move further in time we could refer to *Blow Up* (1966), the Antonioni film, which deals with the relationship between the perceiving subject and the perceived object. Without describing the whole film, the story is about a still photographer who, during a photo session in the

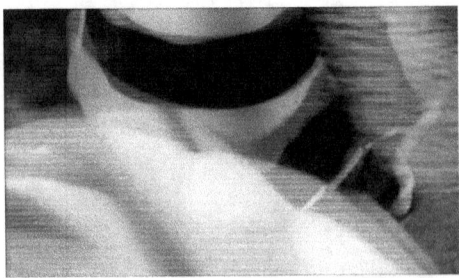

Figure 11.2 Rhythm. From the film *Jazz Dance*, © Canarybananafilms.

middle of a London park, unconsciously witnesses a crime. He slowly realizes what happened during this photo session and decides to blow up the photo in order to see properly what is behind the apparent reality. By playing around with the notion of perception and the embedded meaning in the grain resolution of the photo, Antonioni as a film-maker is offering a challenge to the spectators who are watching two stories unfolding at the same time. The narrative is structured on the perception and their possible interpretations but also on the space notion blown up into a time relationship. In 1966, Michelangelo Antonioni said about *Blow Up*, "I think this is another way of making cinéma vérité—to endow a person with a story, that is, with the story which corresponds to their appearance, to their position, their weight, the volume they occupy in a particular space."[22] As Colin Gardner explains,[23] "In fact, the brute reality must first be textualized through the storyboarding of the photographs before it can offer up meaning. The meaning of the whole situation is thereby inextricably constructed as a clear interpretation of the real, as well as an embodied memory." Seymour Chatman,[24] for example, argues that there is a direct parallel between Thomas's (photographer) and Antonioni's enunciative practice as the film's ostensible author. Both activities involve the creation/production of filmic interpretation. Thus Chatman describes the photographs, saying: "Indeed, much of the film can be seen as an account of the artist's effort to textualize a puzzling experience … Narration is both the readiest and the most dramatic way of explaining an otherwise incomprehensible group of events."

The sequence also affords Antonioni the opportunity to comment on the hermeneutic nature of the apparatus's memory. This is what we could call the central perceptual studium of the film. Thus, in one instance, Thomas enlarges a detail of one photo against his enlargement screen, projecting the light of his enlarger onto the carefully positioned emulsion paper. This acts as a static parallel to the actual movement of the film we are watching projected, as light, onto the cinema screen, the site of our viewed vision. Thomas stands in relation to us as the spectator of a viewed vision, just as the enlargement stands in relation to *Blow Up* itself.

This intersection of viewing and viewed visions within the all-encompassing field of the apparatus is a profound one, because it reiterates the visible/invisible chasm that we have already discussed. We and Thomas can see the apparatus from which he creates his enlargement, but only we are aware of another (invisible) apparatus that makes Thomas's image possible at all: the cinema projector and screen.

Within these examples the grain from a political to an aesthetic affirmation gains its autonomy as part of an active and powerful element of the *mise en scène*.

The Pixel

As the grain is almost the smallest part of the film stock, the pixel can be perceived as the smallest visible element of the code language.[25] In order to explain my position and the comparison I established between both these structures belonging to the world of technique, I have to refer to the artwork of two digital artists, Lisa Jevbratt and Hee Won Lee.

The former established in an article the clear difference between writing and programming. The writing process of words and sentences could produce literacy and poetry, but coding, she added, created reality. "It is similar to the act of making a sculpture or designing and sewing clothes—to start with a material and feel how it folds and falls and cutting out two dimensional surfaces, that turn into three dimensional shapes by sewing them together in a specific way." She pursued her thought process by creating a word, the *infome*, "to denote this all-encompassing network environment/organism that consists of all computers and code language." "The term is derived from the word 'information' and the suffix 'ome,' which is used in biology and genetics to mean the totality of something as in chromosome. Within the Infome, artist programmers are more landscape-artists than writers, software is more like earthworks than narratives. The 'soil' we move, displace and map is not the soil created by geological processes. It is made up of language, communication protocols and written agreements."[26] The pixel could have some kind of autonomy and Lisa Jevbratt illustrated it perfectly when she worked on the data visualization as an indexical trace of the reality, an imprint.

She conceived "Mapping the Web Infome" (see Figure 11.3) project which consisted of software that she made in 2001 with some help of students and friends, and the "crawler" could visualize several types of information activities on the internet. You could search by name, by webpage, or by acronym and have some indexical information resulting from this search engine. She collaborated with ten artists, one of whom was Lev Manovich, who decided to aestheticize the software activity in itself, and to interpret the visualization of the mapping as paintings created by information space in the software. When you clicked on each pixel, the IP address appeared as well as the country where the information came from. The person using this crawler could decide which colors, which shape, which formal representation could be used to represent this reality. For Jevbratt[27] these lines, dots, bits, pixels were not representations of a reality: they were reality. We could see them as objects for interpretation but not interpretations. They stuck to the real ... On a more basic level it allows the image to teach us something about the data, it allows us to use our vision to think (see Figure 11.4). On another level it makes the visualizations function as art in more interesting ways, connecting them in various ways to artistic traditions from pre-modern art such as cave paintings, to abstract expressionism, color-filled minimalism, to post-structuralist deconstructions of power structures embedded in data. The visual appearance that follows is very "plain." It is strict and "limited" in order not to impose its structure on its possible interpretations and meanings. "The visualizations avoid looking like something we have seen before or they playfully allude to some recognizable form yet slip away from it. Viewed from outside the *Infome*, from where we stand, they are abstract— abstract realism."[28]

Figure 11.3 *The Crawler,* © Mapping the Web Infome by Lisa Jevbratt.

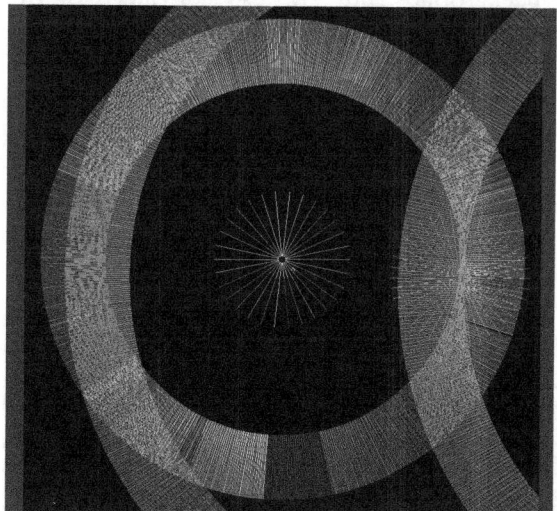

Figure 11.4 *Data Beautiful* by Lev Manovich, © Mapping the Web Infome by Lisa Jevbratt.

A few years later, during an encounter called Singular Narrativities organized at Le Cube,[29] we presented *Phone Tapping* made by Hee Won Lee.

The film is constructed from that single, imperceptible instant which signals the shift from day to night, a fleeting moment in which what was is no more, where things might acquire fresh significance. Voices guide us through the city while the camera seems to be searching for a specific plot of land, for the coincidence between narrative and image. The topography of the site continues to advance, while in parallel there emerges a second topography—mental this time—until, perhaps, they meet, somewhere here, in a new psychical space. Using the city of

Seoul, and using personal stories that are being told, the spectator's role is to follow it and select a locus of interpretation: truth, urban folktale. With *Phone Tapping*, we are faced with our own fantasy interacting with a reality that keeps evaporating and being reconstructed ... we are dissolved while simultaneously constructing ourselves and propelling our desires beyond what the image shows us.

The pixels were not just independent elements with an autonomous power of constructing or deconstructing your perception of the reality (see Figure 11.5). They also gave you the possibility to engage with your own insight of time and space. At the personal level, this film was a concrete shift in terms of sensibility: the shiny aesthetic closely integrated with the globalized digital devices could give rise to a singular approach of your own perception of the real. It was promising from an aesthetical point of view but also from a "New Wave" point of view. Just as in 1960, the emergence of the "French New Wave" in cinema was linked to a new kind of equipment but also to the necessity of deconstructing reality as shown by the mainstream film industry. Now, from 2012, many digital artists are engaged in this challenging reconstruction of the real. They are inspired by different aesthetic languages, political analysis, social backgrounds, but are also convinced of the necessity to introduce queer objects into the field, to challenge its boundaries and limitations.

In this specific case, the programming language introduced us to the pixel as a particular identity but also as an autonomous character. Grain or pixel could be equally perceived as narrative choice. In *The Names of Love*, a Michel Leclerc film, there are three different types of film used: first, the fake Super 8 archive images which were intended to match the real Super 8 archive of the Algerian War. Then,

Figure 11.5 Urban folktale in Pixels. *Phone Tapping*, © Hee Won Lee and Le Fresnoy—Studio national.

the wedding of Bahia's parents, which was designed to also look like Super 8 family footage.[30] Finally, there are the subjective visions of the characters, which are distinguished from the other fictional images via the change in texture of the image. It is this textural change, the appearance of the grain, and the colorimetric modifications that precisely represent this subjectivity in the images. The film-maker tried to recreate the grainy aspect of the analog stock with a digital device and admitted it was not successful. To obtain the grain aspect and its metaphoric dimension, he decided to use a real Super 8 mm camera.

From another perspective, it is very interesting to underline how critics can present and analyse specific characters in fiction film. I would like to refer for example to *Collateral* (2004), a film by Michael Mann. From the analysis of this film, one could say that in his mind, Vincent, one of the characters, is representative of the digital age: his binary, trenchant side (yes or no, dead or alive, target or attacker), the fact that he has a very modern mindset (the post-yuppie sociopath out of a novel by Brett Easton Ellis, as Vincent Malausa described it) and all the computer equipment he uses. Max, another character, with his "cool," more traditional personality, would be the representative of the analog world. In the same spirit, we could quote the book *In the Beginning ... Was the Command Line* by Neal Stephenson, which illustrates and reveals in a hilarious and provocative way how an operating system tyrannizes and downloads popular revelations. The author, by making the comparison between car brand reputation and operating systems, portrayed characters who behave like a Mac OS operating system or a Microsoft operating system. For Stephenson, "ever since the Mac came out, our operating systems have been based on metaphors, and anything with metaphors in it is fair game as far as I'm concerned ..."

> In retrospect, this was telling me two things about peoples' relationships to technology. One was that romance and image go a long way towards shaping their opinions. If you doubt it (and if you have a lot of spare time on your hands) just ask anyone who owns a Macintosh and who, on those grounds, imagines himself or herself to be a member of an oppressed minority group. The other, somewhat subtler point, was that interface is very important. Imagine a crossroads where four competing auto dealerships are situated. One of them (Microsoft) is much, much bigger than the others. It started out years ago selling three-speed bicycles (MS-DOS); these were not perfect, but they worked, and when they broke you could easily fix them. There was a competing bicycle dealership next door (Apple) that one day began selling motorized vehicles—expensive but attractively styled cars with their innards hermetically sealed, so that how they worked was something of a mystery.[31]

These different examples illustrate the close relationship between our perception of the real through technical objects or devices and how we could identify ourselves with it.

I'm not sure we could affirm that the hand-held camera and the grainy pictures were politically more engaged than the shiny digital pictures being produced today, but the relationship between the film-maker and his or her equipment, the political surrounding and the economic dimension, clearly influenced our perception of what could be seen as political engagement. Without going back to the history of specific equipment such as the Super 8, for example, we should remind ourselves that this amateur hand-held camera was released for a family purpose and deeply rooted within the middle-class American family. It was intentionally diverted from its original utilization by independent film-makers to give credit not only to a political discourse but also to a very specific movement with Super 8 film festivals all over the world.

By concentrating on this comparison between pixel and grain, my goal was to underline the crucial importance of taking into account on the one hand the technical aspects of the apparatus surrounding our work, and on the other hand discourses surrounding their capacities. As we are in our academic system in a permanent interface with techniques, it is time to consider it as part of our values, our ways of thinking and our way of imagining and dreaming. As we are dealing permanently with a very difficult and challenging task in order to translate from one culture to another the significance, the relationship people entertain within the real, we should therefore be aware of the close intricacy between technical and scientific discourses and their respective power to guide and/or overwhelm our own imagination.

Filmography

Blow Up, 1966, Michelangelo Antonioni, Italy/UK, 110 mins.
Collateral, 2004, Michael Mann, Paramount Pictures and DreamWorks SKG, 120 mm.
Ibani or the Blue Scarf, naming ritual of a Dogon baby, 1991, Nadine Wanono, CNRSIMages, Mali/France, 51 mins, 16 mm, DVCAM, English and French subtitles.
In the Shadow of the Sun, Arou Hogon's funeral and enthronement ritual, 1997, Nadine Wanono and Philippe Lourdou, La Sept-Arte, CNRSImages, Mali/France, 83 mins, 16 mm, video, English and French subtitles.
Jazz Dance, 1954, Roger Tilton, USA, 20 mins, 35 mm.
Phone Tapping, 2009, Hee Won Lee, Studio Le Fresnoy, Corée du Sud, 9 mins 30 seconds, experimental video.
The Names of Love, 2010, Michel Leclerc, France, Delante Films, Karé Productions, 100 mins.

Notes

1. M. Novak, Speciation, Transvergence, Allogenesis, Notes on the Production of the Alien, 2004, from http://www.mat.ucsb.edu/~marcos/transvergence.pdf (accessed December 13, 2013).

2. *Idem.*
3. A. Schneider and C. Wright, "The Challenge of Practice," in Arnd Schneider and Christopher Wright (eds), *Contemporary Art and Anthropology* (Oxford: Berg, 2006).
4. C. Singer, A. R. Hall, and E. J. Holmyard, *History of Technology* (Oxford and New York: Oxford University Press, 1954).
5. B. Gille, *Histoire des Techniques* (Paris: Gallimard Coll La pleiade, 1978).
6. A. Feenberg and A. Hannay, *Technology and the Politics of Knowledge* (Bloomington, IN: Indiana University Press, 1995).
7. P. Bruneau, "Histoire des techniques, ergologie, archéologie," in Jean-Pierre Brun and Philippe Hockey (eds), *Techniques et Sociétés en Méditerranée* (Aix-en-Provence: Maison méditerranéenne des sciences de l'homme, 2011), 35.
8. *Ibid.* 31.
9. Gille, *Histoire des Techniques*, 31.
10. Bruno Bachimont, *Le sens de la technique: Le numérique et le calcul*, Encre marine (Paris: Editions les Belles Lettres, 2010).
11. Georges Simondon, *L'individuation psychique et collective* (Paris: Aubier, 1989).
12. Felix Guattari, *L'inconscient machinique, Essai de Schizon-analyse* (Paris: Editions Recherches, 1979).
13. Bruno Bachimont, *Connaissance, activité, organisation* (Paris: La Découverte, 2004).
14. Guattari, *L'inconscient machinique*, 183.
15. L. Manovich, *The Language of New Media* (Cambridge, MA: MIT Press, 2001).
16. Manovich, *The Language of New Media*, 48.
17. W. H. K. Chun, "On 'Sourcery,' or Code as Fetish," *Configurations*, 16 (3), 2008, 299–324.
18. N. K. Hayles, *Nanoculture: Implications of the New Technoscience* (Bristol: Intellect Books, 2004), 72.
19. G. Simondon, *The Position of the Problem of Ontogenesis*, trans. Gregor Flanders, parrhesiajournal. org, 7, 2009, 11, from http://parrhesiajournal.org/parrhesia07/parrhesia07_simondon1.pdf (accessed December 31, 2013).
20. B. Stiegler, *Technics and Time, 1—The Fault of Epimetheus*, trans. Richard Beardsworth and George Collins (Stanford, CA: Stanford University Press, 1998).
21. http://www.richardleacock.com/Jazz-Dance (accessed December 31, 2013).
22. Michelangelo Antonioni, "Reality and Cinema-Verite," in *Blow-Up* (London: Lorrimer, 1971), 13.
23. C. Gardner, Antonioni's Blow Up and the Chiasmus of Memory, from http://www.artbrain.org/antonionis-blow-up-and-the-chiasmus-of-memory (accessed December 31, 2013).
24. Seymour Chatman, *Antonioni or The Surface of the World* (Berkeley and Los Angeles, CA: University of California Press, 1985), 149.
25. From Webopedia: Short for *Picture Element,* a pixel is a single point in a graphic image. Graphics monitors display pictures by dividing the display screen into thousands (or millions) of pixels, arranged in rows and columns. The pixels are so close together that they appear connected.
26. L. Jevbratt, "Coding the Infome: Writing Abstract Reality," *Dichtung Digital*, 2003, from http://www.dichtung-digital.de/2003/3-jevbratt.htm (accessed December 31, 2013).
27. *Ibid.*
28. *Ibid.*
29. This event took place during the Thirtieth Bilan du Film Ethnographique. Jacques Lombard, President of the Film Committee du Film Ethnographique and myself as General Secretary both conceived and organized this event, in order to encourage new forms of structure in ethnographic film.

30. I took these examples from a master course by François Belin at Ecole Louis Lumière and entitled Image argentique/image numérique: hybridations esthétiques, mélange des moyens de captation au sein d'un film.
31. Neal Stephenson, *In the Beginning was the Command Line* (New York: Avon, 1999).

INDEX OF NAMES

Abouda, Djouhra 63
Adachi, Masao 76
Adair, John 2, 19, 97, 99
Afonso, Ana Isabel 94n. 12
Aita, Roberto 178
Allen, Kevin T. 2, 43n. 26, 113, 129nn. 20, 21, 25, 30nn. 26, 29, 34
Alliez, E. 163n. 17
Amanatidis, Agapi 43n. 24
Anger, Kenneth 147
Antonioni, Michelangelo 190–1, 197n. 22
Apollonio, Umbro 110n. 11
Appelgren, Staffan 145n. 47
Arlaud, Jean 150
Arnheim, Rudolf 41n. 9
Aróstegui, Natalia Bolivar 59–60n. 4
Artaud, Antonin 8, 12, 21n. 32, 22nn. 33, 40, 77n. 3
Asch, Timothy 36, 43n. 22, 84, 86
Ascher, Marcia 98, 109n. 2
Ascher, Robert 2, 14, 27, 97–108, 109nn. 1–3, 5, 110nn. 8, 9, 14, 111nn. 17–20, 22, 26, 30, 31, 35, 138, 145n. 27
Averea, Peter 89
Avron, Dominique 148
Ayede, M. 144n. 20

Bachimont, Bruno 188, 197n. 10
Bains, Paul 163n. 17
Balzac, Honoré de 102
Banks, Marcus 20n. 18, 26, 41n. 2, 110n. 8, 111n. 28, 144n. 7
Barker, Wayne Jowandi 164n. 18
Barthes, Roland 13, 23n. 45, 55–6, 61n. 21, 175, 180n. 22
Basso, Keith 128n. 4
Bastide, Roger 45, 59n. 1

Bateson, Gregory 2
Battcock, Gregory 162n. 1
Baudrillard, Jean 61n. 30
Baume, Nicholas 94n. 8
Beardsworth, Richard 197n. 20
Beauvaos, Yann 157, 163n. 12
Becker, Judith 21n. 26
Behrend, Heike 21n. 25
Benitez, Lucas 130n. 33
Benjamin, Walter 61n. 30, 74, 89, 95, 135, 143, 144n. 18, 145n. 44, 174–5, 180n. 21
Bennett, Jill 144n. 31
Benning, James 67
Berdahl, Daphne 144n. 25
Bergum, Clintum 2
Biella, Peter di 22n. 36, 42–3n. 21
Bing, Wang 67
Birdwhistell, Ray 1
Blake, Kara 179n. 10
Blanke, Olaf 22n. 39, 60n. 10
Blau, Dick 38, 40, 43n. 24
Bloch, Maurice E. F. 133, 144n. 9
Blundell, David 19–20n. 7
Boly, M . 60n. 14
Bohlin, Anna 145n. 47
Bokanowski, Thierry 95n. 30
Boltanski, Christian 65
Bonnamy, Alain 63
Bosch, Hieronymus 51
Bouhours, Jean-Michel 53, 60n. 15, 162n. 2
Boveroux, P. 60n. 14
Bradley, John 111n. 37
Brakhage, Stan 7, 53–4, 58, 65, 60nn. 15–18, 61n. 29, 147, 157
Brault, Michel 186, 190
Bravo, Manuel Alvarez 178n. 3

Brecht, Bertolt 9
Brenez, Nicole 6, 63
Brenneis, Donald 115, 129n. 13
Brigard, Emilie De 19n. 4
Brown, Marion 68
Brun, Jean-Pierre 197n. 7
Bruneau, Philippe 188, 197n. 7
Bruno, M. A. 60n. 14
Buck, Paul 163n. 8
Bünning, Silvia 22n. 39, 60n. 10
Bunuel, Luis 147
Burckhardt, Rudy 65, 76
Butler, Brad 5, 18, 20n. 19

Cabrera, Lydia 59–60n. 4
Calzadilla, Fernando 145n. 41
Calder, Angus 144n. 15
Calle, Sophie 30
Camper, Fred 60n. 16
Carasco, Raymonde 8, 22n. 33
Cardiff, Janet 10
Caro, Bruno 99
Casey, Edward 144n. 10
Castaing-Taylor, Lucien 95, 129n. 16
Cavadini, Alessandro 158
Cavalcanti, Alberto 63
Celan, Paul 165
Chagnon, Napoleon A. 42–3n. 21, 84
Chalfen, Richard 97
Chambers, Iain 22n. 35
Chandler, Tom 111n. 37
Charbonier, Jean-Jaques 60n. 8
Chatman, Seymour 191, 197n. 24
Chion, Michel 43n. 26, 129n. 10
Chnakers, C. S. 60n. 14
Chun, W. H. K. 189, 197n. 17
Claman, E. 145n. 39
Clémenti, Pierre 63, 76
Clifford, James 20n. 8, 179n. 5, 80n. 20
Clottes, Jean 60n. 11
Cocteau, Jean 147
Cohen, Erik 180n. 19
Cokes, Tony 68
Coles, Alex 144n. 7
Collins, George 197n. 20
Coover, Roderick 42–3n. 21

Corbin, Alan 109n. 4
Cornrich, Ian 110n. 12
Cortázar, Julio 28
Courant, Gérard 163n. 9
Cowie, Elizabeth 141, 145n. 34
Crane, Barbara 178n. 3
Crapanzano, Vincent 145n. 40
Crawford, Peter 110n. 10, 145n. 41
Csikszentmihalyi, Mihaly 144n. 25
Curtis, David 20n. 16, 162n. 1, 1633n. 13

Debord, Guy 14, 23n. 49, 65
Deleuze, Gilles 84, 90, 92–3, 94nn. 9, 16,
    95nn. 28, 33, 39, 148
Delgueldre, C. Phillips 61n. 27
Deliss, Clémentine 42n. 13
Delpeut, Peter 13, 23n. 46
Demenÿ, Georges 75
Demeuldre, Michel 23–3n. 44
Deren, Maya 5–7, 20nn. 13, 18, 21n. 24,
    55, 61n. 22, 147
Descola, Philippe 43n. 31
DeSilvey, Caitlin 143, 144n. 7, 145n. 45
Dewavrin, P. 52, 60n. 12
Dobson, Terence 110n. 13
Dorksy, Nathaniel 120
Downey, Juan 2
Dreschke, Anja 21n. 25
Dulac, Germaine 147

Eagleton, Terry 94n. 10
Eiland, H. 144n. 18
Eisenstein, Sergei 5, 28, 79, 94nn. 1–3
Eizykman, Claudine 147–8, 162n. 2,
    163n. 3
Elhaik, Tarek 22n. 35
Ellis, Brett Easton 195
Epstein, Jean 64–5
Esposito, Patrizio 178n. 3
Export, Valie 157

Fairbanks, Charles 109n. 3
Farocki, Harum 65
Faubion, James 179n. 5
Fausing, Bent 87, 95n. 23
Faymonville E. L. 61n. 27

Feenberg, A. 187, 197n. 6
Feld, Steven 38–9, 43n. 24, 115, 128n. 4, 129n. 13
Fencer, Lorna 163n. 16
Fenz, Robert 6, 63–8, 73–6, 77n. 6
Ferretti, Giovanni Lindo 181n. 29
Fessendon, Mary 111n. 35
Fichte, Hubert 29–30 32, 34, 40, 42nn. 13–15, 20, 179n. 5
Fihman, Guy 148, 162n. 2
Filser, Barbara 27, 41n. 6, 43n. 27
Fiore, C. 61n. 27
Fiorini, Leticia Glocer 95n. 30
Fisher, Michael 179n. 5
Flanders, Gregor 197n. 19
Forty, Adrian 145n. 40
Foucault, Michel 12, 22n. 38
Fragner, Denise 42n. 12
Franke, Anselm 43n. 31
Franklin, Ursula 114, 129n. 8
Frederickson, Don 99
Freud, Sigmund 90, 95n. 30
Friedlander, Judith 150
Frost, Mark 95n. 22
Furniss, Maureen 108

Gaines, J. M. 145n. 34
Gallopp, Jane 43n. 24
Gardner, Colin 191, 197n. 23
Gardner, Robert 1, 65, 74
Garrel, Thierry 147
Gehr, Ernie 75
Gell, Alfred 14, 23n. 47, 58, 61n. 28
Genet, Jean 157
Gérard, Stéphane 22n. 37
Gianvito, John 67
Gille, Bertrand 187–8, 197n. 5
Gioli, Paolo 178
Gitlin, Michael 129n. 25
Gladys, Gonzales Bueno 59–60n. 4
Glowczewski, Barbara 2, 5, 147, 163nn. 4, 6–9, 17, 164nn. 18–20
Goffey, A. 163n. 17
Goldman, Emanuel 63
Gorbman, Claudia 129n. 10
Gordon, Douglas 57

Graham, Dan 9–10
Greco, Michael A. 95n. 37
Grimshaw, Anna 143n. 2
Gröning, Philip 90, 95n. 29
Grossman, Alyssa 14, 131, 144n. 22
Grotowski, Jerzy 8, 21n. 32
Guattari, Félix 159, 163n. 17, 188, 197n. 12
Guillain, Alix 77
Gumbrecht, Hans Ulrich 129n. 18

Habib, André 13, 23n. 46
Hadj–Moussa, Ratiba 60n. 6
Hall, A. R. 187, 197n. 4
Hallam, E. 143n. 3
Hallock–Greenwalt, Mary 99
Hallward, Peter 95n. 39
Hamayon, Roberte 7, 21n. 27
Hamlyn, Nicky 4, 15, 20n. 12, 23n. 50, 42n. 11
Hamon, Philippe 77n. 1
Hámos, Gusztáv 41nn, 7, 10, 42n. 16
Hannay, A. 197n. 6
Hanoun, Marcel 65
Harrison, Tom 144n. 14
Harrocks, Roger 41n. 5, 100
Haviland, John 34–6, 40
Hayles, N. K. 189, 197n. 18
Healy, Jessica De Largy 164n. 21
Hébraud, Régis 22n. 33
Hell, Bertrand 58, 59n. 2, 60n. 6, 61n. 26
Henare, Amiria J. M. 22–3n. 43, 137, 144n. 25, 145nn. 43, 45
Henley, Paul 7, 19n. 5, 21n. 29, 92, 94nn. 12, 15, 95n. 36
Heusch, Luc de 58, 61n. 25
Heuson, Jennifer 2, 43n. 26, 113, 129n. 15, 130n. 29
Heuwinkel, Christiane 179n. 10
Heydenreich, Ludwig H. 22n. 42
Hillairet, Prosper 162n. 2
Hitchcock, Alfred 57
Hobart, Angela 20n. 15
Hockey, Philippe 197n. 7
Hodgkin, Katharine 144n. 21, 145n. 31
Holbraad, Martin 22–3n. 44, 137, 144n. 24, 145nn. 43, 45

Holmyard, E. J. 187, 197n. 4
Howes, David 127, 129nn, 12, 16, 130n. 43
Hsiang, Jieh 19–20n. 7
Huillet, Danièle 76
Hutton, Peter 65, 67, 74–5
Huyssen, Andreas 145n. 41

Idemitsu, Mako 76
Ingold, Tim 20n. 10, 42n. 11, 95n. 10, 143nn. 3, 4
Isou, Isidore 147
Ito, Teiji 5
Iversen, Gunnar 38, 43n. 26

Jackson, Michael 109n. 4
Jacobs, Ken 65, 75
Jacobson, Quinn 178n. 3
James, Figarola Joel 59–60n. 4
Jaulin, Robert 150
Jevbratt, Lisa 186, 192, 197n. 26
Journiac, Michel 157
Jung, Carl 113, 128n. 3

Kajimura, Masayo 22n. 37
Kapferer, Bruce 20n. 15, 90, 95n. 31
Karl, Brian 17, 23n. 55
Karlsson, Katarina 145n. 47
Kearney, Amanda 111n. 37
Kei, Ho Man 178n. 3
Keil, Charles 43n. 24
Keuken, Johan, Van der 65
Khan, Albert 74
Kiener, Wilma 95n. 19
Kildea, Gary 87, 95n. 25
Kimball, Selena 132, 136, 145n. 47
Klonaris, Maria 157, 163n. 10
Kosarik, Mark 75
Kowalski, Lech 67
Kravchenko, Roman 178n. 3
Kubelka, Peter 147
Kuhn, Annette 144n. 19
Kunuk, Zacharias 95n. 20
Kürti, László 94n. 12

Lamy, M. 61n. 27
Lancker, Laurent van 5, 20–1n. 19

Latour, Bruno 14, 23n. 47
Lattas, Andrew 89
Laureys, Steven 22n. 39, 60n. 14, 61n. 27
Leacock, Richard 190
Lebrat, Christian 162n. 2
Leccia, Ange 76
Leclerc, Michel 194
Lee, Hee Wong 192–3
Leepreecha, Prasit 180n. 19
Lefrant, Emmanuel 15, 23n. 52
Legady, Georgres 186
LeGoff, Jacques 145n. 39
Leiris, Michel 6, 21nn. 25, 26, 45, 59n. 1
Lemaître, Maurice 147
Lenica, Jan 163n. 9
Lévinas, Emmanuel 83, 93, 94n. 14
Lévi-Strauss, Claude 42n. 13, 57–8, 61n. 24
Lewis-Williams, David 60n. 11
Lewkowics, Sergio 95n. 30
Liebling, Jerome 37
Lingis, Alphonso 94n. 14
Lipton, Lenny 179n. 9
Livingston, Jason 111n. 35
Lockhart, Sharon 2
Loisy, Lean de 60n. 6
Loizos, Peter 19n. 1
Lombard, Jacques 197n. 29
Lotringer, Sylvère 163n. 17
Lowenthal, David 145n. 39
Luxen, A. 61n. 27
Lye, Len 27, 41n. 5, 99–100, 110n. 12, 147
Lynch, David 87, 95n. 22
Lyotard, Jean-François 148, 163n. 3

MacDougall, David 1, 83, 142, 143n. 2, 145n. 37
MacDougall, Judith 83
Madge, Charles 144n. 14
Makovicky, Nicolette 134, 144n. 17
Malinowski, Bronislaw 102
Mann, Michael 195
Mann, Sally 178n. 3
Manovich, Lev 188, 192, 197n. 15
Maquet, P. 61n. 27

Masson, Dominique 164n. 19
Mau, Leonore 29, 30, 32, 34, 40, 42nn. 15, 20
Mauss, Marcel 13, 22n. 43, 64, 77n. 2
Marcie, Florent 67
Marcus, George E. 20n. 8, 95n. 19, 145n. 41, 179n. 5
Marey, Etienne-Jules 28, 66, 75
Marker, Chris 28, 72
Marks, Laura 15, 23n. 51, 138, 140, 143n. 23, 145nn. 26, 28, 29, 31–3, 42
Marsh, Andy 179n. 10
Marshall, Barbara 110n. 14
Marshall, John 190
Martinez, Wilton 110n. 10
Marzocchini, Vincenzo 178n. 3, 180n. 14
Massumi, Erin 163n. 6
Mayadas, Frank 128n. 7
McKee, Brent 111n. 37
McLaren, Norman 99–101, 110n. 14
McLaughlin K. 144n. 18
McMahon, Philip 22n. 42
Mead, Margaret 2
Meintjes, Louise 129n. 12
Mekas, Jonas 14, 23n. 48, 64, 147
Merleau-Ponty, Maurice 60n. 15, 77n. 4
Métraux, Alfred 45, 59n. 1
Mesguisch, Félix 75
Metz, Christian 102
Michelson, Annette 21n. 20, 94n. 7
Miller, George Bures 10
Minh, Ho Chi 116, 117, 119, 129n. 20
Minh-ha, Trinh T. 2, 7, 105, 111n. 25
Mirante, Edith T. 180n. 19
Mirza, Karen 5, 18, 20n. 20
Misztal, Barbara A. 144n. 8
Mitry, Jean 162n. 1
Monod, Jean 150, 163n. 5
Moody, Raymond 51, 60n. 9
Morell, Abelardo 178n. 15
Muecke, Stephen 158, 163n. 12
Mulas, Ugo 179n. 10
Müller, Matthias 179n. 10
Murray, Stuart 110n. 12
Muybridge, Eadweard 28
Myers, Chris J. 128n. 6

Myers, Fred 107, 111n. 32, 179n. 5

Neimann, Catrina 20n. 18
Niblock, Phill 66
Nicoletti, Martino 17, 23n. 57, 165, 178nn. 1, 4, 179nn. 5, 6, 180nn. 15, 16, 18, 21, 25
Nijhawan, Michael 60n. 6
Noguez, Dominique 20n. 16, 157, 163nn. 11, 14
Novak, Marcos 1 85–6, 196n. 1

Ochoa, Ana Maria 129n. 12
Ochoa, Todd Ramon 59–60n. 4, 129n. 12
Oppitz, Michael 179n. 5
O'Rourke, Karen 164n. 18
Ortiz, Fernando 59–60n. 4
Ortiz, Rafael Montañez 65

Paiva, Margarida 12, 22n. 41
Pandian, Karthik 15
Pane, Gina 157
Panopoulos, Panayotis 43n. 24
Pappé, Julien 163n. 9
Paravel, Véréna 129n. 16
Pasqualino, Caterina 1, 7, 10, 13, 20n. 15, 22nn. 36, 37, 44, 27, 45, 60nn. 6, 7, 19, 145n. 47
Passos, John Dos 32
Passuti, Roberto 181n. 29
Paterson, Ian 178n. 3
Pelechian, Artavazd 74
Perez, Gilberto 80, 94n. 5
Peterson, Oscar 100
Piault, Colette 22n. 36
Picasso, Pablo 53
Pieters, Jaap 179n. 10
Pink, Sarah 94n. 12, 179n. 5
Pirilä, Marja 178n. 3
Porcello, Thomas 129n. 12
Prada, Triny 56, 61n. 23
Pratschke, Katja 41n. 8, 10, 42n. 16
Prefaris, Julian 163n. 17
Promio, Alexandre 75

Radstone, Susannah 144n. 21, 145n. 31

Rabinow, Paul 42n. 20
Rai, Chaturman 178–9n. 4.
Ramey, Kathryn 2, 14, 17, 23n. 49, 27, 97, 111nn. 28, 34, 144n. 7
Ramirez, Don Diego 179n. 9
Rancière, Jacques 17, 23n. 54, 114, 123, 128nn. 2, 5, 129n. 11, 130n. 28
Rasmussen, Knud 86, 93, 95n. 21
Ravetz, Amanda 143n. 2
Ray, Man 147
Rees, A. L. 19n. 2, 20n. 16, 21n. 63, 42n. 11, 144n. 6
Regnault, Felix–Louis 28
Rendall, S. 145n. 39
Renov, M. 145n. 34
Resnais, Alain 28, 37
Rettig, Maja–Lene 179n. 10
Richter, Hans 147
Rimbaud, Arthur 63
Ring, Kenneth 52, 60n. 13
Robbins, P. 144n. 19
Rochberg–Halton, Eugene 144n. 25
Rockhill, Gabriel 128n. 2
Roediger, G. D. 61n. 27
Rollwagen, Jack 19–20n. 7, 97, 110n. 9, 111n. 19
Rolnik, Suely 163n. 17
Roscher, Gerd 30, 42n. 16
Rouch, Jean 1, 6–7, 22n. 36, 92, 95n. 34, 107, 116, 129n. 17, 163n. 5, 186–7
Rouget, Gilbert 21n. 26, 59n. 3
Roussopoulos, Carole 67
Rubel, Sasha 90, 92, 95n. 32
Ruby, Jay 20n. 18, 42n. 21, 94n. 18, 107, 110n. 8, 111n. 28, 144n. 7
Ruffinengo, Chiara 179n. 5
Rundstrom, Donald 2, 19–20n. 7
Rundstrom, Ronald 2, 19–20n. 7
Russell, Ben 7, 21n. 30
Russell, Catherine 5–6, 19–21n., 83, 94n. 11, 95n. 37, 145n. 31
Russett, Robert 110n. 13

Salloum, Jayce 68
Samuels, David W. 129n. 12, 130n. 42
Sappert, Stefan 178n. 3

Schechner, Richard 8, 21n. 31
Scheeler, Charles 65
Scheugl, Hans 20n. 16
Schmickl, Silke 22n. 36
Schmidt, Ernst 20n. 16
Schneider, Arnd 1–2, 13, 20nn. 9, 10, 13, 18, 19, 22n. 36, 23n. 49, 58,, 25, 41n. 7, 42n. 19, 95n., 128, 130n. 44, 131–2, 143nn. 4, 5, 144n. 6, 145nn. 45, 49, 179n. 5, 187, 197n. 3
Seaman, G. 42–3n. 21
Seeler, Uwe 30
Serematakis, C. Nadia 127
Serin, Özge 17
Sharits, Paul 7, 75
Sheridan, Dorothy 144n. 15
Signorini, Roberto 179–80n. 12
Simmel, Georg 74, 77n. 5
Simon, Andrea 87, 95n. 25
Simondon, Georges 188–9, 197n. 11
Simonsen, Jan Ketil 43n. 4
Singer, C. 187, 197n.
Siodmak, Robert 28
Sitney, P. Adams 20n. 16, 23n. 48, 147, 162n. 1
Smith, Daniel W. 95n. 38
Smith, Wadada Leo 66, 74, 77nn. 6, 7
Snow, Michael 147
Sontag, Susan 28, 41n. 9, 176, 181n. 26
Soukaz, Lionel 67
Speranza, Robert Scott 180n. 17
Starr, Cecille 107, 110n. 13, 111n. 29
Stephenson, Neal 195, 198n. 31
Stewart, Kathleen C. 124, 128n.4, 130n. 27
Stiegler, B. 189, 197n. 20
Stoller, Paul 107, 109n. 4, 111n. 31, 128n. 1
Strachan, Carolyn 158
Strand, Chick 76
Straub, Jean–Marie 76
Sudre, Alan Alcide 21n. 24
Suhr, Christian 1, 5, 21n. 2179, 94n. 11, 95nn. 19, 31
Sullivan, Moira 20n. 18
Swiderski, Richard 40, 43n. 30

Tarkovski, Andreï 158
Taussig, Michael 7, 21n. 28, 92, 95nn. 35, 37
Taylor, Anne Christine 20n. 15, 22–3n. 44, 60n. 19
Taylor, Charles 93
Thng, Victric 22n. 37
Thomadaki, Katerina 157, 163n. 10
Thonnard, M. 60n. 14
Tilton, Roger 190
Tode, Thomas 28, 41nn. 8, 10, 42n. 16
Tristan, Flora 68
Tscherkassky, Peter 179n. 10
Turton, David 110n. 10, 145n. 41

Vaccari, Franco 179–80n. 12
Vale, Laurence 156, 164n. 18
Vanhaudenhuyse, A. 60n. 14
Varda, Agnès 28
Vertov, Dziga 5, 7, 21n. 7, 28, 74, 80–4, 92
Veyre, Gabriel 75
Vigo, Jean 65
Villegas, Carmen Gonzalez Diaz de 59–60n. 4
Vinci, Leonardo da 13, 22n. 42
Viola, Bill 6, 57

Walker, William 14, 23n. 49

Wall-Romana, Christophe 180n. 17
Wanono, Nadine 18, 183
Warhol, Andy 147
Wastell, Sari 22–3n. 43, 137, 144n. 24, 145nn. 43, 45
Wees, William C. 180n. 17
Wiedemann, Dawn 43n. 29
Wilkerson, Travis 67
Willerslev, Rane 1, 5, 21n. 21, 79, 94n. 11, 95nn. 19, 31
Williams, Patrick 22–3n. 44
Winadzi, James 108
Wood, Rulon Matley 42–3n. 21
Worth, Sol 2, 19n., 97, 99
Wotton, Lex 164n. 19
Wright, Christopher 20n. 19, 22n. 36, 23nn. 49, 58, 41n. 7, 130n. 44, 143n. 5, 145n. 41, 179n. 5, 187, 197n. 3
Wynne, John 179n. 5

Yue, Geneviève 7, 21n. 30

Zaatari, Akram 67
Zbinden, Catherine 163n. 11
Zevort, Martine 148
Zillinger, Martin 21n. 25
Zryd, Michael 111n. 34

For Product Safety Concerns and Information please contact our EU
representative GPSR@taylorandfrancis.com
Taylor & Francis Verlag GmbH, Kaufingerstraße 24, 80331 München, Germany

www.ingramcontent.com/pod-product-compliance
Lightning Source LLC
Chambersburg PA
CBHW070606300426
44113CB00010B/1425